until 1988. ∼ In 1837, Ebenezer Adams bought the [a...] [...] been built several years before by his future father-in-law, Thomas F. Davies, minister of the Greens Farms Congregational Church. Adams operated it until 1867, when he was forced to retire due to an injury that left him severely restricted. Adams Academy served as a private high school for the community and out-of-towners. Adams added the north wing to his house, about 1848, to serve as quarters for some of his students. Ebenezer's grandson, Joseph, was born in the house in 1876, and lived there most of his life. He served as judge of the town court from 1923 until 1931 and was tax assessor for more than fifty years. Near the end of his tenure as tax assessor, Judge Adams compiled a street-by-street narrative of all the pre-1945 houses in Westport. It is one of the most important local history documents in the county, an invaluable source of information about people as well as the buildings in Westport. Judge Adams's sister, Dorothy Ripley Adams, also lived in the house from 1879 until 1966. She continued the family devotion to education, serving as a Westport schoolteacher and, from 1919 until 1947, as principal of the Saugatuck Elementary School. After their deaths, the house passed to Joseph's daughter, Ruth, who was head reference librarian at the Westport Library. The house is being restored by Martha Stewart for a book she is writing on renovation.

MARTHA STEWART'S NEW OLD HOUSE

MARTHA STEWART'S
NEW OLD HOUSE

RESTORATION

RENOVATION

DECORATION

LANDSCAPING

PHOTOGRAPHS BY
MATHIEU ROBERTS

ILLUSTRATIONS BY
RODICA PRATO

CLARKSON POTTER/
PUBLISHERS
NEW YORK

I dedicate this book to my brother George Kostyra Christiansen.
With his wonderful skills, and hardworking, talented crew, he
transformed this house into a beautiful home.

Published by Clarkson N. Potter, Inc., 201 East 50th Street, New York, New York 10022.
Member of the Crown Publishing Group.

Clarkson N. Potter, Potter, and colophon are trademarks of Clarkson N. Potter, Inc.

Manufactured in Japan

Design by Doug Turshen and Howard Klein

Library of Congress Cataloging-in-Publication Data

Stewart, Martha

Martha Stewart's new old house / by Martha Stewart.

1. Architecture—Conservation and restoration. 2. Interior architecture—Conservation and restoration.
3. Interior decoration—Themes, motives. I. Title. II. Title: New old house.

NA7125.S74 1992
728' .372' 0288—dc20
92-15900
ISBN 0-517-57701-1
10 9 8 7 6 5 4 3 2 1

First Edition

ACKNOWLEDGMENTS

Mathieu Roberts, a young filmmaker and photographer, took the photographs for this book. He was energetic and enthusiastic during the entire project, which lasted almost two years, and his beautiful and evocative photos help tell the story of the old house.

Thanks to Doug Turshen for the bold design of this book; to Rodica Prato for her beautiful, clapboard-by-clapboard architectural renderings; and to the indefatigable Carol Southern, Editorial Director of Clarkson Potter, for her intense hard work pulling loose ends together.

Every building project requires the attention, skills, and talents of myriad people. The old house was no exception, and I have many wonderful craftsmen, artists, artisans, businesses, and volunteers to whom I wish to offer my sincerest thanks:

General contractor, George Christiansen, and his crew: Thomas Ball, Ross Bedard, Brad Leamer, Larry McDonough, Anthony Metty, John Minnock, Terry Walley; Dennis Rowan and his painters; Cornell McNeill, Sr., and his associate, Eric Logan; Pat Saltarelli, plasterer; and excavator Victor F. Perkowski. Bert Dumas, copper gutters and flashing; Larry Weiss of LHW Design; Harry Hulse, heating; Ralph and Ricky Renzulli, plumbers; Bill Kopta of Coastal Woodworking; the Tatko family of Tatko Slate Products; Leo Leonard, surveyors; Honiker and Son, floor sanders; Emilio's Power Sanding; Manny Ferreira, stone mason; Dave Towner, stone mason; D&J Masonry Construction; Charlie Perelli and Son; Connecticut Stone, marble; Maselli Marble; Harry and Steve of H&S Electric; Steve Davidson, electrician; Waterworks, bathroom fixtures; Stan, of Gilbert's Paints; Dave Itoro and Rocky

Lasaro of Aitoro Appliances, who recommended Elkay Manufacturing for kitchen sinks, the Gaggenau grill and deep fryer, the Garland kitchen range, the Sub-Zero refrigerator/freezer, the Maytag dishwasher, and the Vent-a-Hood.

Special thanks to all of the wonderful designers: Rose Adams, Pamela Barnett, Justin Baxter, Barbara Brooks of *Family Circle* magazine, Rosemary Casey, Susan Colley, Maggie Daly, Roger de Cabrol, Joel Clark Gevis, Mary Gilliatt, Holly Gillin, Ann Hagerty, Deirdre and Nora Humphrey, Endie Jaynes, Miranda Kettlewell, Lisa Krieger, Robert K. Lewis, Mark Lupo, Suzanne Miller, Melissa Neufeld, John C. Newcomer, Paul & Betty Phillips, Virginia Pierrepont, Nora Bohan Potter, Karen Tarshis, Melanie Taylor, and Jeroen Vcenema.

And to the artisans: Pam Asanovic, Steven Bielitz, David Bishop, Lisa Breznak, Linn Cassetta, Virginia Cooper, Jane Crawford, John Curry, Mark Hart Devins, Mary Engelbreit, Mary Ann Freeman, Tom Geusz, Greg Giesey, Thomas Giordano, Bob Gross, Bob Harrison, Pamela Hatfield, John Heath, Bob Hoven, Judy Krammer, Walter Jaykus, Eva Llanos, G. W. Moffett, Jr., Marlowe Monfort, Caitlin Nammack, Sandra Peterson-Bruno, Fiona Prichard, Kim Proctor, Frank Reijnen, Joseph Ribot, Sherry A. Ringler, Richard Rudich, Raphael Serrano, Wendy Stone, Diane Voyentzie, Marla Weinhoff, and Elizabeth Wolnick.

Thanks to Tom Balsley, who opened up a whole new world of landscape architecture to me, and Charlie Hyatt of Evergreen Enterprises; the landscape designers Jim Bleuer and Casa Verde Gardens, Laura Coen, Sal Gilbertie, Carol Jessup, Candace Newton, Mary Norton, Susan Robinson, Peter E. Stephens, Priscilla

Galpin Twombly, and Kenneth T. Twombly.

And thanks to all the wonderful staff and volunteers who worked so selflessly to make this benefit for the Hole In The Wall Gang Camp a resounding success, including Karen Tarshis, Rita Christiansen, Mariana Pasternak, Laura Herbert, Carolyn Kelly, Karen Farrell, Brie Garrison, Lisa Wagner, Tanis Bond, Courtenay Hardy, Judith Johnston, Penny Lyons, Jean Mason, Georgia Munsell, Jackie Richardson, Norma Schuyler, Linda Sullivan, Charlotte Werner, and Helen Leudke and all the fabulous volunteers from the Westport area. To Ursula Hotchner and Paul Newman of Newman's Own and The Hole In The Wall Gang Camp Fund, and all their staff and volunteers.

And, of course, thanks to my mother, Martha Kostyra who helped me keep the daily diary of everything that went on in the house so that I could write this book.

To all my friends at Clarkson Potter who worked so hard on producing and publishing this book: Howard Klein, Art Director; my publicist, Susan Magrino; the brilliant production team Teresa Nicholas and Ed Otto; and the ever-vigilant Mark McCauslin and Laurie Stark; Bo Niles; Bill Nave; Jennifer Altemus; Maggie Hinders; Eliza Scott; Kristina Stewart; and to Crown's Publisher and President, Michelle Sidrane; and Random House's President, Chairman & Chief Executive Officer, Alberto Vitale.

Thanks to the research consultants John Ingersoll, Jim Kemp, Deborah Smith, Denise Martin, Christine Douglas, and Merv Kaufman.

And thanks also to my regular household staff, Renato Abreu, Renaldo Abreu, and Necy Fernandes.

CONTENTS

DECORATING THE ROOMS

LANDSCAPING THE PROPERTY

Additional Information

INTRODUCTION

Old houses have always been intriguing to me. For as long as I can remember, I have loved their inherent beauty, their architectural diversity and details, their unique positioning on their plots of land, and most of all their history. The house in which I grew up was an ordinary frame house on a crowded street. One of hundreds built in the thirties, it differed from its neighbors

only in minor stylistic differences imposed on a very basic design. Purchased by my parents in the 1940s for $8,000, our house was a three-bedroom construction on Elm Place in Nutley, New Jersey. It was situated on a small lot and had a front yard with a sidewalk, a very narrow driveway wide enough for exactly one car, and a long, rather narrow backyard

that Dad had beautifully terraced. ■ The three bedrooms were really not large enough for our family of eight, but space never seemed to be a problem. In addition to the basic rooms, there was a small dark "sunroom," a very small "sewing room" on the second floor, and an unfinished attic, which Kathy and I used for dressing up. Most important of all, we had a full and really very good basement where we cooked (there was a second kitchen), laundered,

did small carpentry projects and worked on hobbies. ■ As I was growing up, I learned about different kinds of houses from my travels to historic sites, to local restorations, and from my forays into the world's great literature.

ABOVE: The 86 Elm Place house was modest but friendly, originally covered in a wide, crinkled asbestos-type siding. The steep front brick stoop was the place where we congregated en masse with our friends and neighbors as soon as the weather was warm enough to sit outdoors. The lot, with the Maus' on one side and the Allegris' on the other, was just one-fifth of an acre. Aside from the postage-stamp front lawn, every square inch was planted with vegetables and flowers.

BELOW: By 1960, the family income was larger, and there was some money to spare to do renovating. The asbestos siding and the storm windows were replaced, and a railing was built for the front stairs. With a coat of new paint, a new roof, and new leaders and gutters, the house looked wonderful to all of us. Many of the old, overgrown shrubs were taken out and replaced with very plain, simple landscaping.

Hawthorne's *House of the Seven Gables*, Edith Wharton's *Ethan Frome*, Tolstoy's *Anna Karenina*, and Jane Austen's *Sense and Sensibility* were just a few of the novels that transported me into different worlds and different times. During college, I turned this fascination with architecture and lifestyle into my course of study: history, art, and architectural history. ■ The first property my husband and I purchased was a tiny one-room schoolhouse built in 1850 in the tiny Massachusetts village of Middlefield (population 100). It was so exciting for us to have a house of our own, even if only for weekends and summers. For $5,000 we got a cottage with no running water, no plumbing, and no heat—and fifty glorious Berkshire acres on a deserted road on the outskirts of town. We were in ecstasy over our find! We lugged water from the stream hundreds of feet from the house, we happily used the "out potty," we began constructing, digging ditches and trenches, planting gardens, roofing, doing carpentry, painting, and bricklaying. It was a wonderful training ground, for we really did everything from scratch, learning about the construction trades by doing everything we could ourselves, by experimenting, and by reading and talking to the local experts about our problems. I remember whole weekends spent discussing the water supply, whole days spent looking for the correct stovepipe for the wood-burning range that we had bought at an auction for ten dollars. ■ When my husband, small daughter, and I were ready for our first real house, we jumped at the chance to buy a

ABOVE: **My husband and I bought Middlefield in 1965, shortly after Alexis was born, from an antiques dealer. This property had been a one-room schoolhouse, haphazardly enlarged to include two little bedrooms, a kitchen-dining area, and a shed; it was devoid of plumbing and heating and had only a modicum of electricity. The gardens were my modest attempt to create a little "Williamsburg" in front of the open porch.**

BELOW: **The rear portion of the Turkey Hill house needed vast improvement, and we built our first serious addition here, abutting the kitchen of the main house. It incorporates a back hall, where we still enter the house, a full bathroom, and an office-storeroom for me.**

rundown but very beautiful Federal farmhouse in Westport, Connecticut. Enamored of the view of Long Island Sound, the charming southern exposure, and the intact features (original mantels, flooring, woodwork) amid the chaos of neglect, we tackled this much larger project with gusto. Plastering, painting, woodworking and refinishing, window glazing, stenciling, insulating, and roofing: none of these techniques was, or could be, avoided. We studied each process of restoration and renovation, and we remade every inch of that house. ■ While we worked on these projects, we haphazardly photographed some of the progress,

but most of the work remained unrecorded. Often I wished that I had kept a diary or a photograph album so that the many, many hours spent tearing out and rebuilding, removing the unsightly, and replacing it with the beautiful would be saved for our reflection. ■ When I embarked on the new old house I immediately began keeping a photographic record. Only after we had taken many rolls of film did I realize that this was going to be a really fascinating undertaking and that it had the makings of an unusual step-by-step how-to book. ■ What follows is the story of the restoration, the renovation, the decoration, and the initial landscaping of the new old house. Each project

like this is really a work in progress, an ever-changing environment that is altered by time, by weather, by whim, and by necessity. One learns, one experiments, one is frustrated, and one enjoys the extraordinary variety of problems and solutions posed by such a commitment. The thrill of near completion keeps one going.

—M.S.

ABOVE: After Middlefield, we felt like such grown-ups at Turkey Hill. We found the 1805 Federal farmhouse large, elegant, and, we thought, easily transformed into a beautiful home. Our approach toward its restoration grew directly out of our prior efforts in Massachusetts, and because we tried to do everything ourselves, we lived amid a mess for three years. Here is a view of the renovated house, ready for the Christmas holidays.

BELOW: I found I really loved constructing stone walls and built the entire entrance to our basement, an entrance not dissimilar to that of the Adams house.

FINDING T

HE HOUSE

I had lived and worked in Westport, Connecticut, for almost fifteen years when I heard through a friend that the Adams homestead was to be put up for sale. I knew at that moment that I would buy it and restore it. Though it is not an especially fine example of Connecticut farmhouse Federal architecture, I had revered this house ever since I first saw it. What drew me to it was its proximity to my own home up the hill and the fact that many of its features seemed to have been executed by the same hands. It also had a rather mysterious provenance as a "haunted house," one of several that I adored in the vicinity of Greens Farms. This transitional Federal-style farmhouse is prominently placed on a very well traveled corner. It is seen by virtually thousands of people every day, by commuters on their way to the highway or railroad and children on their way to and from school. Many stories, part fable, part truth, circulated about this "down

at the heels" house that sat amid tangled masses of bittersweet, poison ivy, sumac, and ash. ■ The house had been built in 1838 for Ebenezer Adams, a well-known local educator who ran a preparatory academy for boys. While he occupied the house, he built a large wing on the back to accommodate his schoolboy boarders. This wing was uninsulated and unheated, with no plumbing or running water. After the Reverend Adams retired, other family members moved in and out. When I first noticed the house, it was lived in by his last remaining great-granddaughter, Ruth Adams, a retired reference librarian. Miss Adams had little inter-

LEFT: **The rear portion of the house was constructed at different times. The original 1838 house was left intact, while less well made additions were built later. They were poorly constructed but in keeping with the architecture of the main house.**

est in the house other than as a roof over her head. Clearly a frugal spirit, she had no plans to restore the house, and she lived there until she could no longer cope with the maintenance and upkeep of the place. The house was in dire need of attention, and since no other family members wanted to assume the responsibility, Miss Adams reluctantly decided to sell her family home. I wanted very much to save the Adams house, to put it to rights, to return its history to it, to make it liveable once again.

Being incorrigibly romantic and optimistic by nature, and not wanting to chance losing the house to a higher bidder, I began negotiations with the listing broker immediately after one viewing, making an offer with no contingencies. I knew the house was a wreck and that it needed serious rebuilding. I had basically figured the costs in my head. What spurred me on was envisioning the final result, the gracious home that this house would become.

I did not worry about all the usual things a new homeowner is cautioned to worry about. I knew I had my brother George as contractor and that the architectural features of the house were sound and aesthetically pleasing and that they could be enhanced to make the project viable. Initially I regarded the rebuilding as a pure restoration/renovation, as an investment, and as a very pleasant opportunity to spend time doing something that I knew would be rewarding and enjoyable. At that early date I did not know that I would write a book about the place or that I would have such a wonderful time finding and working with such a fine group of artisans and craftsmen.

SCRUTINIZING THE INTERIOR

Buying an old house is an emotional decision for most people, as it was for me. When you find a house you love, it is often necessary to make a leap of faith and plunge in. But regardless of your passion for the house you've found, a careful inspection needs to be made, preferably before you sign the contract. There are instances when you may decide that, no matter how much you love the house, the necessary repairs are

ABOVE: **An old photograph of some of the early inhabitants of the Adams house.**

RIGHT: **In a first-floor bedroom we discovered a tremendous collection of periodicals: years' and years' accumulations of** *National Geographic, Ladies' Home Journal, House & Garden,* **and** *Saturday Evening Post.* **In one box I found the front pages of dozens of national newspapers from the day Roosevelt died. Nothing was in any order, yet nothing was rotten because no moisture had ever accumulated to cause disintegration of the materials. A special "paper" auction was held to dispose of the family collection of letters, magazines, and periodicals.**

far too extensive for you to undertake.

Take a general walk-through to get an overall impression, followed by a close inspection. Allow the agent to present the house to you; the agent—and owner, if present—will mention the good points of the house, some of which may not be obvious, and they may even point out the problems. Take notes on your positive and negative impressions; it can be hard to remember the details.

The arrangement of rooms in many old houses was dictated by the number and placement of chimneys and staircases, the size of the entry hall, a preference for symmetry and square rooms or for rooms of varied size and shape—all elements that helped define the architectural styles of 18th- and 19th-century America. Very early Connecticut houses usually had one central chimney, with a small hall in front, a parlor on one side, a bedroom on the other, and the kitchen in the back.

The two-chimney Adams house floorplan is actually more typical of an 18th-century plan than a 19th-century design. It has a center hall extending only halfway back, flanked by two front parlors. Behind these was a small office to the left, a large dining room in the center, and a library to the right.

When you are considering whether the layout of the house will meet your needs, remember that you can make many changes as we did in the Adams house. But it's important to keep the character and the history of the house; after all, that's what gives old homes their appeal.

Like many old houses, the Adams house had wonderful extras, such as a butler's pantry and a library, rooms that can provide storage for books and glassware as well as additional space for reading and cooking.

As you go through, make a sketch of the layout. Consider whether there are enough bedrooms to accommodate your family and guests. If you want a master suite and this house, like most older ones, does not have one, look to see if a bedroom can be renovated to include an adjoining bath. If you want your master bedroom isolated from the others for privacy—either on a different floor or separated from the other bedrooms—consider how difficult it would be to achieve.

Cupboards and chests provided much of the storage space in old houses, so you may need to create closets. Compare the storage space you have in your current house with what's available in this one. Count closets; note sizes.

Follow up your casual tour with a thorough examination.

WALLS: In an old house, the walls are undoubtedly out of plumb, which usually does not indicate problems. However, they should not bow out significantly. Note the condition of the plaster. If it is crumbling, water may be leaking behind the wall. If the plaster has become dry and powdery, it may need to be replaced.

CEILINGS: Water stains could indicate a roof leak. Large cracks in the ceilings and walls may mean the house has been settling unevenly. Open doors to check their swing; doors tend to scrape the floor if the house has settled unevenly.

FLOORS: As you walk across the floor of each room, look and listen. Notice whether floors are uneven or buckling, if they squeak or if any are rotten. Repairs range from replacing individual boards to installing an all-new floor. If the floor is covered with carpeting or linoleum, ask what type of flooring is underneath or loosen a corner of the covering and see for yourself.

BATHROOMS: Bathrooms and the kitchen are usually the rooms most in need of renovation when buying an old house. Often changes to the plumbing, electrical wiring, fixtures, or cabinetry are necessary. Inspect fixtures for signs of age and disrepair, but remember that antique fixtures may work perfectly well and are often charming. If the owner is not sure about the age of the fixtures, you may find a stamp with the year of manufacture inside the tank of the toilet. (In many cases, this one clue will date the entire house.)

Look for telltale stains that can indicate water leaks around the bottom of the toilet and tub. Check the walls for damage from moisture. Inspect the condition of the tile.

KITCHEN: If you plan to renovate this room extensively, its present state may not be crucial to you. Otherwise, it is very important. In the 19th century, people didn't regard the kitchen as a gathering place; it was a workplace—and often not a very efficient one. Imagine you are cooking a meal and consider how convenient it is to move from one appliance to another.

Ask the real estate agent if the appliances are included in the purchase. If they are, see if any need replacing; ask if any are still under warranty and request

that the owner bring the warranty papers to the closing.

ATTIC: This space will tell you how energy efficient the house may be. Notice whether or not there is insulation and, if so, what kind of shape it's in.

BASEMENT: The condition of the basement is a clue to the structural soundness of the entire house. Look for straight walls and an even ceiling. Look, too, for a dry floor; a wet basement signals a faulty foundation.

MECHANICAL SYSTEMS: Ask about the electrical service to the house to see if it will meet your needs. Also ask about the water source and the condition of the hot water heater. See if there are any stains that may indicate leaks in the water pipes. Check every faucet for drips or leaks. Also ask about the heating system. Will it have to be replaced? In each room, count the number of electrical outlets; this is especially important in the kitchen if you have a number of small appliances and in the bathroom, too, which may have none.

Armed with your notes and rough sketch, you can then decide if this is the house for you—and begin to think about what changes you'll make.

ABOVE: **Probably the most fascinating part of the Adams house to me was its attic. I wanted so much to study each object I found there and to learn its history. It was a habit of the Adamses never to throw anything away that might be of future use or interest. When a chair broke, all the pieces were bundled and tied together with a rag and placed in the attic. The accumulation was overwhelming and varied: antique clothing, ancestor portraits, sleighs, sleds, and baby carriages—all part of a family's heritage.**

ABOVE: Most of the windows in the house were darkened by inexpensive shades and shabby curtains. Because I bought the house and not the contents, everything in the house, including the hoard in the attic—frames, boxes, chairs, and tables, everything that "might be useful some-day"—was auctioned off. Despite decades of accumulation of dirt and dust, several objects fetched amazing prices.

The attic floor was wide-board pine, and the walls were hog-hair-reinforced plaster applied to fir sheathing. As we undid the house, we discovered that extraordinary materials and techniques had been used throughout, indicative of 19th-century ingenuity and Yankee inventiveness.

1. Gnawed by mice and soiled by errant birds, many of the contents of the attic were ruined. These straw bonnets were dry and intact, having been stored for many years in a wooden trunk.

2. Old frames, boxes, and chairs were placed or tossed amid the clutter of a true "Grandma's Attic."

3. Because Miss Adams kept a good roof on the house, the attic beams, rough-sawn 5-by-5-inch pine rafters and 1-by-10-inch sheathing boards, were in fine shape, even after 150 years. The spiders had a good time in the peaks, weaving their gossamer webs.

4. A collection of umbrellas and canes, decayed and soiled, a reminder of the family's habit of saving everything. The wicker chair was meant to be pulled on large iron wheels, like a wagon.

5. Two prize antique miniature globes were in a tiny room at the top of the stairs. The family's rare books—Connecticut histories, treatises on education, old atlases, and other esoterica—were also stored in this room.

6. Other than a light fixture on the first floor, the only object in the house I coveted was a 19th-century orrery, a pre-Neptune model of the solar system with its then-known six planets. There are very few of these instructional toys left in existence; most of them are in museum collections. This one was purchased by a Connecticut museum for $2,600. Miss Adams's best books had been stored in the glass-fronted Gothic-style bookcase.

7. Thousands of postcards from family members were kept in old suitcases, testimony to their love of travel and writing.

8. The Reverend Adams's leather-bound volumes included biographies, histories, and scientific works.

9. In Miss Adams's parlor, atop a side table, stood a photograph of the home-stead as it had looked many years ago. Two of the three large trees in front are gone. Only the gigantic tulip tree, reputedly the largest in Connecticut, is still in place. Gilt frames adorn an old engraving and an early family photograph.

LEFT: Ruth Adams's bedroom was one of only four rooms of eighteen that was habitable. It had never been painted and was sparsely appointed with a ladderback chair and one-drawer stand. The rugs were hideous: always brown or brownish and very worn. A cross-stitch "Home Sweet Home" sampler and a hand-crocheted tablecover added two homey touches to an otherwise cold and cluttered space.

RIGHT: In the front hall hung an 1840 oil lamp with a hand-blown and etched shade and "smoke bell" (to keep the ceiling from being blackened). I wanted very much to keep it, but because it was not electrified and therefore not technically considered a "fixture" (that is, something permanently connected to the house), it went to auction. I tried to buy it—but passed as the price soared to $2,500.

FAR RIGHT: Miss Adams's desk in the room she used most frequently, the west parlor. It was a very dark and uncozy room, with a threadbare carpet, piles of correspondence, much of it dating back many years, and myriad books, Miss Adams's passion.

BELOW RIGHT: A parchment lampshade, hand-painted by an Adams aunt, depicts in paint and cutouts the Adams house. Lighted, the shade evokes a livelier day when all eighteen of its rooms were occupied, inhabited by the Reverend Adams's family and his schoolboy charges, who were preparing for admission to Yale.

EXAMINING THE EXTERIOR

You will also need to make a thorough inspection of the exterior to determine the extent of necessary repairs. Take a camera and a pencil, notebook, and tape measure with you when you investigate. We photographed the Adams house from every angle. Whether you restore the exterior completely or simply undertake a few repairs, your photos will be invaluable to whoever designs and handles the renovation—especially if you must conform to local historic house restrictions. Later, the photos will become an integral part of the history of the house—and of your family, too.

As you look over the house and grounds, jot down notes and take measurements, if necessary, of anything you will want to replace or replicate.

GROUNDS: Assess the state of the overall landscaping. Is it unsightly? Does it conceal a treasure such as a once-beautiful

LEFT: **The front portico, adorned with just a simple Doric-columned porch, was in total disrepair. During Miss Adams's occupancy the shuttered storm doors were seldom opened, and the narrow side shutters were nailed in place.**

ABOVE RIGHT: **The glass in the many windows was in good condition, as were the frames, but the glazing was gone in many places. The shutters were in relatively good, usable condition, but they required a good power washing to clean them of peeling and thickly caked paint before being spray painted Hunt Club Teal.**

garden or stone wall? Are the grounds worth restoring to an original design? Inspect the driveway for large cracks, missing sections, and low areas where rainwater can pool. Measure its width to insure it can accommodate a modern car; many old driveways are not wide enough.

GENERAL APPEARANCE: Check to see if all the walls meet at crisp right angles. If not, the foundation could be severely damaged. Check the foundation, too, for stains and cracks to ascertain if it can be repaired—or if it must be replaced. Are additions, if any, structurally sound?

PORCH: Because it receives the most traffic, more wear and tear occurs on the porch than almost any other area of the house. If the porch is in danger of caving in, it will have to be repaired right away so that workers can enter the house

safely. If columns support the porch or the roof, are they solid and straight? The columns on our small porch, our portico, were not expensive to replace; often those supporting an overhanging roof have to be custom-made making them more costly.

SIDING: Most old houses are clad with clapboard wood siding. Look at individual boards for obvious signs of water staining and softness or rotting. Are the boards straight? The bottom edge of each board should overlap the top of the one below, sealing the wall from penetration by wind and rain. Finally, check to see if the exterior is due for repainting.

WINDOWS: Windows are one of the most distinctive features of an old house. From the inside, open them to see how they operate. Are windowpanes and muntins loose or broken? If muntins are salvageable, they must be stripped and repainted. Because of damage from exposure and use, old windows often have to be replaced altogether. This can be costly, because windows did not conform to an industry standard as they do today. Finally, have sills deteriorated? Replacing a rotted sill is not too expensive, but it is complicated.

DECORATIVE TRIM: Inspect all trimwork, including shutters, to see if it can be repaired or must be replaced. Trim replacement may require extensive handwork if the facade of your house is protected by a local historic commission.

DRAINSPOUTS AND GUTTERS: On an old house, these may have to be replaced. If not, they will probably require cleaning.

ROOF: Most old roofs are made of wood shingles. Are any missing—or damaged?

INSPECTIONS

Although you may have examined all the elements of the house, from chimney and roof to basement supports, in the case of an old house, you will need professional inspections to determine how much renovation will be necessary. Inspections are often done after the contract for the sale has been signed. However, if the house you are buying has serious problems, it is worth arranging inspections before commitment to the sale.

You, as the buyer, are responsible for arranging and paying for inspections by a licensed engineer, plumber, and electrician. The easiest way to get names is to ask for a referral from the real estate agent handling the sale. Most agents are impartial in making referrals; they want to get the inspections conducted quickly and fairly so the sale can go through without problems. Some may make the necessary arrangements for you.

THE ENGINEER: The foundation is the single most important element of a house because it supports the entire structure. It should be inspected by a state-licensed engineer who can distinguish deterioration caused by water and uneven settling from damage due to less serious causes. A high water table and uneven settling may create problems that make repairs impossible, requiring a new foundation. Small cracks, on the other hand, are to be expected and should not cause alarm.

Water damage is revealed by stains on the outside wall of the foundation and dampness inside. The cause can be a clogged drain or an ungraded lawn that allows water to collect around the house. The engineer will evaluate the damage and suggest remedies. Clogged drains and spouts may require only a thorough cleaning, but pooling of water will probably require regrading around the house .

The engineer will inspect chimneys and fireplaces, looking for cracks and loose mortar caused by uneven settling. He will check to be sure the chimney has a secure footing, and that it is not supported by the timber structure of the house, which constitutes a fire hazard.

He will also inspect the roof, looking first for stains caused by leaks. He will see if the roof sags along the ridgelines, check the rafters for adequate spacing of timbers, and examine the shingles or other roofing material for cracking and deterioration. He also inspects all metal flashing—the metal "seam" that connects the roof to the walls and to the chimney—as well as the gutters and downspouts for corrosion. Corroded metal needs to be replaced.

LEFT: The timber frame of the house was constructed in the post-and-beam style typical of early New England houses. The 8-by-8-inch beams were sturdy, hand-hewn, and carefully mortised and tenoned, a process similar to creating a plug to fit a receptacle. Where post and beam are joined, a hole is drilled and a peg is inserted to lock them in place. Luckily, we found the frame to be basically sound; it needed only to be tightened up a bit. Some sections had to be replaced; others, straightened. And bracing was installed where we needed to strengthen the structure.

Your engineer will also conduct a termite inspection, looking for telltale tunnels the insects have built on the surface of the foundation leading right up into the wood framing. Termites do not actually eat wood, but they burrow through it, causing dust, holes, and weakness. Black carpenter ants *do* eat wood, causing massive structural damage. The presence of one or two ants anywhere in your house tells an inspector that a whole colony exists. Powderpost beetles are another pest that eats wood; their telltale mark is little piles of sawdust in the house. Either pest must be exterminated and damage will need to be repaired.

THE PLUMBER: A state-licensed plumber will examine all aspects of the plumbing, from pipes to valves to fixtures. He looks for leaks indicated by dampness and rust; he reviews the service line from the water supply to the house to ensure that it is large enough to handle your demands; and he checks the plumbing lines for signs of decay. He also determines if the pipe joints are soldered with lead, which can leach into the water supply. Today, more and more building codes require the use of lead-free solder joints to connect potable-water lines. Since redoing the solder is impractical, the old pipes should be replaced—by copper or PVC lines, whatever the local building code allows.

Next the inspector checks to be sure that the pressure tank, which ensures an even flow of water throughout the house, reads between 40 and 50 pounds of pressure. All shutoff valves are inspected to determine if they work properly. If they have not been used in a long time or are corroded, they should be replaced.

Finally, he will inspect the water heater to determine its age, condition, and capacity. If you plan to upgrade appliances or add bathrooms, the water heater may have to be replaced.

THE ELECTRICIAN: Many old houses have inadequate electrical service. Your electrician will determine if the system meets local code and if the amount of electricity coming into the house is satisfactory. In addition, he inspects the wiring, which is often exposed in the attic and basement. If it is decayed, or if you expect to install appliances and other equipment, such as air-conditioning units, which require extra power, the wiring should be replaced.

SEPTIC AND WATER WELL: Strict standards apply to both of these. A septic engineer will check the water well for water quality and test the septic system.

TOWN AND SEWER: The only pipes to which an inspector has access would be in your basement or crawl space. There he will check the integrity of the system, verifying that the connections are made according to your area's building-code specifications.

LEFT: The foot traffic must have been quite heavy to wear the pine saddle down so severely. These are the features of an old house that evoke questions and suggestions about the people who once lived there.

RIGHT: The basement was perhaps the most depressing portion of the entire house. When I first saw it, it was filled from dirt floor to cobwebbed ceiling with old farm equipment, scraps of wood and metal, and other debris. Walls had been fabricated over the years from leftover beams and odd bits of sheathing, creating a rabbit warren of dim little rooms, some heaped with canning jars, others with paints and brushes, and tools and boxes.

One was crammed with all sorts of jars and bottles and wine jugs filled with a clear liquid, each carefully wrapped and tied in brown paper. I couldn't imagine what these jars held or why they were there until Miss Adams told me that in the forties, during a severe drought, her family had hoarded water. The drought had passed, but the bottles had remained.

The best basement discovery was the smokehouse, used to cure meats. It still funtioned, and since it could be used, we left it in its original state.

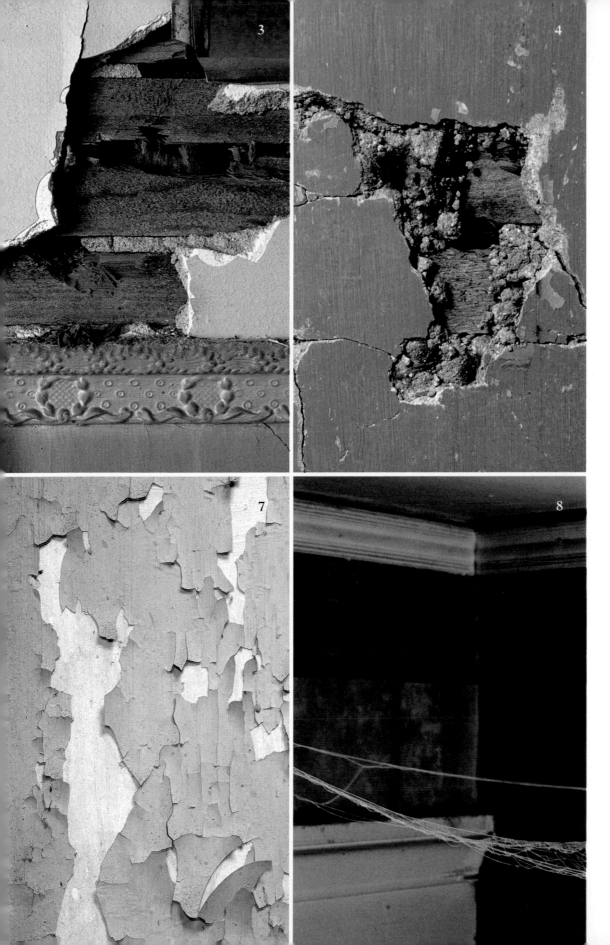

1. Throughout the house, spiders had spun beautiful webs. Because of Miss Adams's less than avid housekeeping, some of the huge webs were probably years old.

2. Most of the mortar between chimney bricks and around the beams was powdery and soft and had to be picked out. The chimney was repointed with a new, harder mixture of sand and cement, which strengthened the brickwork.

3–4. Cracked, broken, and loose plaster was removed from the lath in most rooms. The plaster had been reinforced with tufts of hair probably curried from the backs of hogs or horses. The hair helped hold the plaster to the irregularities in the boards. Today, strands of plastic or fiberglass are used for the same purpose.

5. Most of the pine woodwork was of a very simple design, built with rough handmade nails. The walls' cracks were opened up for replastering. A sample of the old green paint was saved and later matched as one of the kitchen cupboard colors.

6. The Adams family appeared to have been very frugal in their living habits. Old stove pipe holes, generally sealed up when not in use, were covered with tin plates with moveable vents allowing hot air from the chimney to be released into the rooms.

7. Whatever paint had been applied over the years had cracked, peeled, or fallen away. If only the plaster had been in good shape, it would have been a blessing, but in most instances it was not.

8. Overall, the decoration in the house was dismal and dark. Even minor decorative attempts, like this wallpaper border, were drab. Ceiling moldings, were basic but useful for hanging pictures.

WORKING WITH AN ARCHITECT

Many people who undertake restoration and renovation, especially when their projects are small, choose not to use an architect. For these instances, the right contractor, an interior designer with some architectural background, or even a carpenter can do the job. In many states, however, an architect's services are required to obtain a building permit for a large-scale project, and some communities will not issue any permits unless the plans have an architect's seal attesting that they meet local building codes. Connecticut does not have this requirement, but because the Adams house was a fairly complex project, I very much wanted an architect or architectural historian to help me enlarge some of the spaces without destroying the architectural integrity of the house.

An architect brings a wealth of skill and experience to renovation: five years of schooling and at least three years as an apprentice, followed in most cases by a state exam. To become registered, an architect must understand the mechanics of construction, acoustics, and lighting, have a thorough knowledge of building materials, and be conversant with local building codes. And, of course, most important is design expertise and talent.

An architect creates a vision of the finished project based on an in-depth consultation with you. The design process begins with preliminary drawings, which are then refined through a dialogue between you and your architect. Once you have approved the scheme, the

architect drafts the final plans or working drawings, specifies and lists all building materials, draws up a budget based on what you tell him you can afford to spend, and schedules the work.

Most architects prefer to hire and supervise the contractor, but if you wish, you can negotiate for plans only, as I did, so that you can work with your own

contractor. For a fee, the architect may continue to offer design advice and, if invited, visit the site on an informal basis to check on progress.

FINDING AN ARCHITECT: The tried-and-true method, personal referrals, come ideally from friends and neighbors who have collaborated with an architect on a specific project. Friends will be candid about an architect's creative input, work habits, and adherence to schedule and budget, and you can *see* the final result.

Keeping a clip file of newspaper and magazine articles about renovations you admire will give you a catalog of architect's names—as well as a record of your personal style, which is useful to have during your preliminary consultation with an architect.

The American Institute of Architects, the national professional group to which many registered architects belong, maintains a membership list that you can receive upon request. Check the phone book for the local AIA chapter in your neighborhood.

Professionals who deal regularly with architects—your real estate broker, banker or loan officer, or a tradesman, such as an electrician who has served you in the past—may have suggestions. It is also a good idea to check with suppliers, such as your lumber yard.

Once you have gathered your list of candidates, winnow it down to three, preferably three who concentrate on

LEFT: **One of the first things I had to do after buying the house was obtain a permit for the reconstruction. For this, I had to submit a detailed floor plan to the community zoning board and the building department, so I called on architectural historian and draftsman Larry Weiss to draw up my plans. He helped me come up with a solution to our stair problem. We eliminated an awkward and dangerous turn in the main staircase to create a large, open landing.**

home restoration. Interview each one in your home so he or she can observe how you live and get a sense of your personal style. Describe your project. Note whether or not the architect seems genuinely interested in your project, your needs, and your aesthetic ideas.

Ask how long the architect has been in practice, how many projects similar to yours he has undertaken recently, and note whether or not he seems to be up to date on regulations. Consider whether the practice is large or small. A one- or two-man office may offer plenty of personal attention, and a newer practice may be eager to take on your project. But some small offices fall down on scheduling, clerical details, and the like. A large, well-established office, on the other hand, offers the economy of scale and departments staffed by experts in specific phases of the job, but a potential drawback is lack of personal attention.

Find out exactly with whom you'll be dealing. In a small practice, you'll probably work directly with the architect; in a larger office, you may be assigned to an associate.

During the interview, ask to see photographs of the architect's recent projects that are similar to yours. Request the owners' names and visit them; ask them if the architect came in on budget and on time. Remember, though, that most projects come in at least ten percent over budget and exceed the schedule by days or even weeks.

Take a critical look at any houses you visit; they provide a real-life view of how the renovation has stood the test of time. See how well the materials and traffic

patterns have worn and whether there seem to be enough electrical outlets and storage spaces.

Bear in mind that many homeowners do their own decorating or hire an interior designer who is not affiliated with the architect. So, don't judge the architect by the decoration of the house.

FEES: If your renovation is big enough to require a building permit, you will need, at minimum, detailed floor plans indicating placement of structural elements like windows, doors, and built-ins, as well as plans of the mechanical systems and a cross section of the house from foundation to roof. If the remodeling includes changes to the outside of the house, you should get a drawing, or rendering, of the exterior. The architect should also produce a complete list of building materials and working drawings that show the contractor how to build every element included in the job. Architects bill in one of three ways: a flat fee, an hourly rate, or 20 percent of the construction cost. However it's calculated, the fee is usually divided into a series of payments, with no charge for the initial consultation. Ask the architect when he will bill you and if there are billable "extras"—the cost of inspections, making copies of the plans, telephone calls, travel expenses, and so on. The architect you select will ask you to sign a contract, usually one of the standard AIA forms.

If you must have a registered architect sign off on plans prepared by someone else, he will usually charge a fee. Besides the standard floor plans, an architect may propose additional drawings to clarify specific aspects of the work: plans for

electrical and communication systems (including alarm and security setups and intercom connections), wall elevations, and, especially when an addition is requested, site plans. I asked for suggested elevations of my kitchen so I could see how cabinets would fit into the scheme. You may want to request plans of the house as it exists so that the architect and/or the contractor—and you—can see if the structural changes you desire involve moving walls, relocating doors, or shifting electrical or plumbing lines.

READING A FLOOR PLAN: A floor plan is essentially a visual aid, a map to guide the contractor and workmen through the renovation. Plans, one for each floor from basement to attic, are usually drawn to a one-quarter scale, where one-quarter inch equals one foot ($\frac{1}{4}$" = 1').

To help you relate a plan to its elevations—four walls of any room—you will find small circles, labeled E for elevation, divided into quarters like a gun-sight; each quadrant matches up with one wall.

The floor plan is tagged with appropriate abbreviations for each room, such as MBR for master bedroom, plus the following elements:

OPENINGS: Location and size of door-ways, windows, archways, and the like. Openings are indicated by symbols that are explained on the legend on the floor plan; standard doors are indicated with arcs that represent their swing.

STAIRWAYS: A series of parallel lines slashed partway on an angle is superimposed with arrows—to indicate direction of stairs—and labeled with the words "up" or "down."

SOME SPECIFICS: Closets (labeled CL), fireplaces (WBF), skylights (dotted rectangles), and any built-ins such as bookcases, kitchen cabinets, and bathroom vanities (also "dotted" in place). Bath fixtures are drawn in with templates.

KITCHEN APPLIANCES: Cooktops and ranges are marked by four circles representing burners. A refrigerator is simply tagged REF. The positions of under-counter appliances are noted with dotted lines; each appliance is identified by its initials, such as DW for dishwasher. Sometimes the exact dimensions of the appliances are written in.

MECHANICAL SYSTEMS: Electrical outlets are represented by various symbols; the most common, a 110-volt outlet, is indicated by a circle pierced with two parallel lines. A switchplate is tagged with the letter S, a ceiling light fixture by a circle, a gas line by a series of dashes and G's.

FLOORING: The material, such as tile, brick, or slate, is specified.

CEILINGS: A sloped ceiling is indicated by an arrow pointing upward, and beams are marked by parallel broken lines.

When your floor plans are complete, photocopy them (reducing them to a manageable size) so you can experiment with furniture arrangements.

LEFT: The plans Larry Weiss drew up showed me how we could eliminate walls in the old kitchen area to create a whole new space that could be perfectly zoned around the existing back-to-back fireplaces for cooking and entertaining. One area could be devoted to food preparation, while the other could be entirely for dining and storage.

Cellar Doors

Kitchen

Pantry

Ice Pit

Pantry

UP

Toilet

Porch

Bedroom

Office

Hall

UP DN

Office

Dining Room

Bedroom

UP

Southwest Parlor

UP

Southeast Parlor

Front Hall

UP

ORIGINAL FIRST FLOOR

The first floor is an unusual variation on the typical center hall design for a two-chimney house. The center hall is truncated (it does not run straight through the house from front to back) and the center-rear portion is occupied by a large dining room area. Usually a house like this would conform to a standard four-over-four room plan. I found that the Adams house plan had a great deal of charm and a much better traffic-flow pattern than the traditional plan. The rear of the house was altered much more than the front. A full bath was installed off the laundry room.

The dining room was opened up to light by means of skylights and French doors that provided access to a new sunroom. The new kitchen was a result of eliminating many walls, small pantries, and closets to create one large space with two fireplaces and two distinct areas—a work area and an eating space. A very large and useful terrace was built behind the sunroom. A mudroom eliminated the necessity of entering the kitchen directly from the outside and also provided a convenient place to leave coats and shoes.

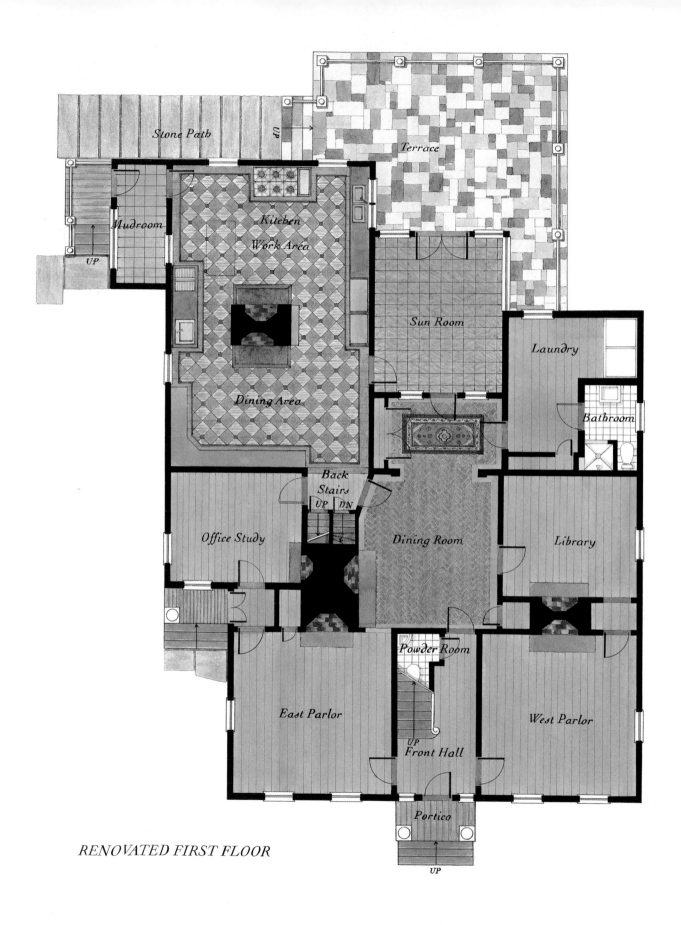

Stone Path

Terrace

Mudroom

Kitchen
Work Area

Sun Room

Laundry

Bathroom

Dining Area

Back
Stairs
UP   DN

Office Study

Dining Room

Library

Powder Room

East Parlor

West Parlor

UP
Front Hall

Portico

UP

RENOVATED FIRST FLOOR

37

Bedroom

Bedroom

Bedroom

Hall

Flat Roof

Bath

UP DN

Hall

Bedroom

Bedroom

Hall

Master Bedroom

Little Library

DN

DN

DN

Bedroom

ORIGINAL SECOND FLOOR

The boys' dorm setup on the second floor and the stairway leading up to it created many problems. The stairway rising straight from the first-floor center hall split two ways at the top; to the right (east) it led into a narrow hall, and to the left (west) into the master bedroom via dangerous triangular stair treads. There was no landing, and most of the bedrooms were too cramped and dark for modern living. Most problematic was the absence of sufficient bathrooms: one antiquated bathroom served the eight bedrooms.

A bright, sunny, spacious hall was created at the top of the stairs by making a landing two-thirds up the stairs and turning the staircase at a right angle to the east. The wall at the top of the stairs was eliminated, allowing light and air to enter the stairwell, and a balustrade installed at the top. The little library between the front two bedrooms was transformed into the master bath. Three bedrooms were converted into one large bedroom off the landing.

The original bathroom was rebuilt; the long hallway then opened into another full bathroom and two bedrooms at the rear of the house.

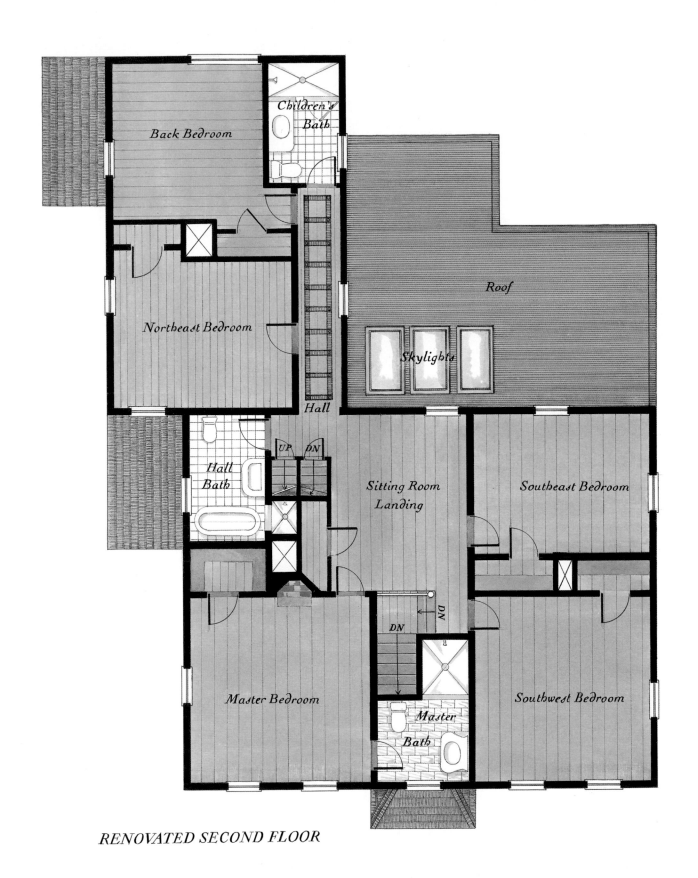

RENOVATED SECOND FLOOR

WORKING WITH A CONTRACTOR

I was very lucky to have the perfect person for my job living and working nearby—a general contractor who is also my brother. George understands old houses and he understands me. He knows from working on the Turkey Hill house what I like.

The contractor is the most important person in any renovation. The contractor transforms the dream—and the working drawings that illustrate it—into reality. Responsible for scheduling and overseeing all the subcontractors (such as the electricians and plumbers), he keeps the job running smoothly, on time, and within budget. In short: the contractor determines the cost and the quality of the project. There are two types of contractors:

GENERAL CONTRACTOR: Commonly known as a carpenter-builder, the general contractor should be an experienced craftsman who functions as the field foreman; he is there, on the job, for you. He tends to work with a partner or a few employees and usually takes on only one project at a time. A potential drawback: a general contractor may devote so much time to on-site work that he ignores crucial paperwork and record keeping, such as change orders or billings. A plus: low overhead on his part, which means lower costs for you.

CONSTRUCTION COMPANY: A larger operation that handles several jobs at once, a construction company maintains an office staff that monitors the various phases of the job and schedules permits and inspections. The company usually retains its own teams of employees and subcontractors who travel from job to job. Some construction companies work with individual homeowners only if represented by an architect. Drawbacks: less personal attention and potentially inferior quality work if the company is handling too many jobs at once.

The most reliable resource for finding a contractor is, of course, your architect. He will undoubtedly want to retain a contractor with whom he has a solid working relationship. The next best bet is a friend or business associate who has recently completed a renovation. Other resources: your local lumberyard and other suppliers who over time have had direct contact with the contractors in your area.

Before getting in touch with any contractors, check out their reputation with local watchdog organizations, such as the Chamber of Commerce, the Better Business Bureau, or a department of consumer affairs.

Select the three most likely candidates and schedule interviews. To ascertain the quality of a contractor's work firsthand, request to see several completed renovations. Because so many bills are paid through the contractor, ask for, and check, bank references.

Next, call the contractor's former clients. Did the job proceed smoothly? Were there unnecessary delays? Did the contractor apply for required permits? Was the job completed to the owner's satisfaction? Did the contractor clean up the site once the job was completed?

FEES: Most contractors charge on a cost-plus basis—cost of materials and labor, plus profit. Some charge a fixed fee depending upon the size of the job, others a percentage of the overall cost of the project.

A contractor should work out a specific contract with you; you may want to review it with your attorney before signing. Be sure the contract covers these points:

PRODUCTION SCHEDULE: This details the anticipated sequence of jobs and which subcontractors will be working on them as well as start and finish dates.

LIST OF MATERIALS: Complete lists, or specs, should specify the quantity, brand names, and style or serial numbers for each item to be purchased for every aspect of the project.

METHOD OF PAYMENT: The general contractor is usually paid in thirds: first upon signing a contract, then halfway through the job, and finally upon its satisfactory completion. Bigger jobs require more payments.

CERTIFICATION OF INSURANCE: This covers workman's compensation, damage and liability, all critical issues because of the risk of injury.

POTENTIAL CHANGES DURING JOB: This is, perhaps, the most important part of

RIGHT: **Although every day I discovered another serious fault with the house, I tried to approach the entire project with a sense of optimism. Even when the prognosis seemed grim (we found plaster ceilings beginning to collapse in the upstairs bedrooms), George could figure out the perfect solution to the problem and envision the final results.**

any contract. Any changes made after signing the contract can be very costly. Clarify all costs and responsibilities as changes occur. Who pays for each change? What is the process for approving changes if the contractor uncovers an unexpected problem that requires extra work or materials?

PUNCH LIST: When the job is nearing completion, the contractor draws up a list of what is left to be done, usually small finishing touches. Hold back 10 percent of the contractor's fee until every item on the punch list has been done to your satisfaction.

Since a general contractor's crew rarely does more than carpentry, he contracts out specific jobs to specialists in land clearing and excavation; foundation and other concrete and masonry work; roofing; plumbing; electrical work; HVAC (heating, ventilating, and air-conditioning); plastering and painting; and so on. Even an interior decorator is considered a subcontractor, although the decorator's fees are usually the responsibility of the homeowner. One of the most important functions of the general contractor is to coordinate the work of various subcontractors. Delays in one phase of the renovation can hold up the next phase, and this can be very costly—and extremely frustrating as well. Some delays, such as illness, can't be predicted, but a general contractor and the sub should be able to send in a substitute worker to keep things moving along. Other delays that can seriously hold up work, such as late delivery of materials, should be anticipated; building in extra time can keep the job on schedule.

The general contractor pays all bills from subcontractors. If he fails to do so, the sub has the legal right to charge the owner directly—even if the owner has already paid the general contractor in full. To avoid this potential problem, the owner should insist that all subcontractors sign a lien waiver with the general contractor before any work begins. A lien waiver relieves the owner of all liability.

All subcontractors should carry their own worker's compensation for their crews. In many communities this insurance is required before a building permit can be issued. Worker's compensation pays for medical expenses and time lost. The cost of this insurance runs between 10 and 50 percent of wages. Subs also should be covered against personal or property loss. The general contractor should ask to see each sub's certificate of insurance when reviewing the estimate for his work.

RIGHT: Because the Adams house was virtually down the hill from where I live, it was very easy to make the renovation site a stop in my daily schedule. I found that these daily visits were very important, for I discovered a lot about the house and was able to plan ahead. I insisted, as did George, on a clean and orderly work site. After each major job, the debris was picked up and removed, and the grounds were kept free of unsightly trash and materials. Dumpsters and a bulldozer are essential in grounds work, as are garbage holes or fill sites for inorganic rubbish.

CODES AND PERMITS

Building codes were written to protect the public from faulty construction and risk of fire. The codes cover every facet of construction, from the quality of the concrete mix in a foundation to the structural strength of framing lumber to the safety of paint.

The strictest national building code deals primarily with fire safety. All dwellings, for instance, are required by law to have at least two means of egress in case of fire. Three regional codes, one serving the western states, one the midwestern and northeastern states, and one the southern states, follow the national code for one- and two-family homes called the CABO code—its initials stand for the Council of American Building Officials. These set the standards for their areas. Building codes are constantly being revised as issues change, especially those concerning energy waste and the environment.

Some communities have specific rules to respond to unique needs: earthquakes in San Francisco, for instance, or hurricanes on the gulf coast of Texas. All inspections are based upon local codes. All structural changes to a house require a building permit that is issued by the local building department. The permit is usually secured by the general contractor.

Typically, the contractor must first get the plans okayed by the local planning and zoning department; the conservation department, which is usually concerned mostly with wetlands; and the sewer or

septic departments. Then he can submit the plans to the building department for its review. Once the building permit is secured, work must begin within a prescribed amount of time, usually six months. There may also be a time limit for completing the job. Extensions usually can be applied for.

The fee for a building permit is based on the estimated cost of the contractor's portion of the job. In my community, the fee is $10 for the first $1,000 of job cost and $8 for each additional $1,000. The fee for the zoning permit is approximately $1 for each $1,000 of job cost.

Plumbing, heating, and air-conditioning contractors must obtain separate permits at rates based on their individual estimates of their job costs. Some communities require permits only for general construction and the mechanical trades; others are more demanding.

In many communities, the building

department will stop work on a job with no permit—or a job that exceeds or differs in any way from the work that was specified in the permit. Changes require alterations in the permit, or a new one.

The town or county building inspector will visit the site periodically to guarantee that the work is safe and follows code. The frequency of inspections varies widely depending upon local codes and the complexity of the work. As a rule, there are at least three inspections: one during the framing; a second before the electrical and plumbing work is "closed in" behind the walls; and a third after the insulation is installed. A final inspection follows completion of the work; if that proves satisfactory, the building department issues a certificate of occupancy.

ABOVE: While Miss Adams lived in the house, she used only the back kitchen door, secured by a single, simple lock, the old latch handle and peeling paint on the door belying the valuables within.

Town law requires that the building permit be posted in a prominent place on the site, usually right inside the most commonly used door. Any other necessary permits (such as permits from the health department, the EPA, or the Wetlands Commission) should be posted nearby.

RIGHT: The surveyor's stake with bright plastic tape marks the boundaries of the property. Poision ivy grows rampant in this part of Connecticut and had to be eliminated. (My method is to pull it out by the roots with gloved hands and use lots of brown soap afterward.)

RESTORING T

re·store: 1. To return something to a former, original, normal, or unimpaired condition. 2. To restitute something taken away or lost.
ren·o·vate: 1. To make new or as if new again; repair. 2. To reinvigorate; revive.
Random House College Dictionary

There is always a debate when redoing an old house whether to consider it a restoration or renovation. It is my understanding that a restoration is a pure, line-for-line replication of a space or object, as nearly as possible to its original state. A renovation is a rebuilding of a space or object, with less attention paid to authenticity than to making it new again. ■ As I embarked

on fixing up the new old house, I realized I had to combine the two. Ostensibly a purist and favoring a restoration, I knew I also had to make this house a comfortable 20th-century home with modern conveniences and amenities. With the help of a good architectural historian, a draftsman, a contractor of choice, and an enthu-

siastic frame of mind, we began the restoration and renovation of the Adams house. ■ Right off, I made a list of imperatives for the exterior. One: All old features that had architectural integrity were to be preserved (the lovely stonework in the basement and around the exterior foundation, the six-over-six paned windows, the wavy glass, and the old doors). Two: New work had

LEFT: **During the sandblasting process, the house looks very poor and bare. Obviously, the paint removal is not yet complete, and patches of old white still remain.**
RIGHT: **Builder's paper, scaffolding, and piles of rubble covered with snow make this view reminiscent of *Bleak House*.**

to match or exceed in quality that of the old house. Three: Wood shingles were to be used for the roofs, and the siding was to be the same old pine as the original. Four: Painting of the exterior was to be done carefully, with no harsh preparation of the wood siding; sanding marks or pitting of clapboard with rough sandblasting was prohibited. Five: All wiring, if possible, was to be installed in conduits under the ground so that there would be no unsightly wires overhead. Six: Paths, edgings of walks and driveways, and driveways themselves were to be made of old materials when possible: old cobblestones, brick, heavy bluestone pavers and native crushed stone. Seven: All new additions—mud room, terrace, front portico—were to conform architecturally to the old portion of the house.

JOURNAL

10/12/87 Dumpster arrived. Kitchen walls ripped out. Kitchen chimney flue cleaned out.

10/13 Stone from gas station on Post Road dumped by Victor. Kitchen demolition continued.

10/14 Ross stripped out back room. Conduit purchased. Discussed project with George.

10/15 Basement cleaned. Partition walls removed. Plaster stripped in first-floor guestroom & study. Plumbers disconnected boiler & capped off water line.

10/16 Old heating lines (cast iron) removed by unscrewing them with a pipe wrench & breaking them with a lump hammer & chisel. House reverberated with the extremely loud noise. Old boiler disassembled piece by piece, some sections weighing 200 pounds. Very dirty work. George & his men couldn't get hands clean for days. Pieces thrown into Dumpster.

10/19 Basement floor dug out to lower the level in preparation for a layer of stone.

10/20 Work continued on basement floor. Debris removed, old farm animal droppings dug out.

10/21 Basement work continued. Found rot in old porch wall. Ripped it out. Larry Weiss came over to review, drop off plans, discuss location of bathrooms.

10/22 More walls in kitchen ripped out.

10/23 Work continued on beams in basement.

10/26 No work.

10/27–10/29 Work continued on beams in basement. Tom replaced rotten beams & posts. Powderpost beetles spotted at end of beams along sills of house.

10/29 George & I visited a Victorian Restoration on South Turkey Hill Road to review it & to find sources for craftsmen.

10/30 Kitchen floor & joists removed. Stone cellar will be perfect wine cellar. Discussed trap door for access from kitchen to wine cellar. Plans made to block up back wall open now to outside. George & I walked boundaries of property.

11/2 Discussed installing new bathroom, ripping down wall, repositioning stairs, new master bathroom. Tree surgeon came. George, Larry Weiss & I discussed kitchen plans. George removed upstairs back bedroom wall. Tom & Ross worked on basement reinforcement.

11/3 Work on basement almost completed. New support columns installed. New cement foundation footings poured for support columns.

11/4 Stripping out back upstairs bedroom completed.

11/5 Began jacking up back kitchen addition to level floor. Jack gave way & hit Tom in leg. George tried to catch it & almost broke his arm.

11/6 Repair of back kitchen wall continued. Rotten sills removed & temporary supports slipped in. Back addition needed more support during leveling process & a come-along attached from an upstairs beam to a tree outside. Ice house ripped down.

11/9 Closed in kitchen outside wall. Took off temporary plywood, resheathed wall. Applied building paper outside. Heater purchased to keep crew warm.

11/11 Shoot canceled due to storm. Worked on replacing floor joists in kitchen eating area.

11/12 Plywood installed in kitchen eating area, but only tacked down so it can be removed for future electrical & plumbing work. Lumber delivered for kitchen area. Sorted lumber & brought it inside.

11/13 Floor joists installed in main kitchen area. Began framing in of hatchway to wine cellar.

11/16 Excavating machines dropped off after lunch. Ross & Tom began work on leveling & resupporting kitchen ceiling. George worked outside, breaking up foundation by back hatchway to the kitchen. Edwin (part-time helper) quit to work in a cabinet shop.

11/17 Ross & Tom continued work on leveling & resupporting kitchen ceiling. Sewer line put in. Excavation went slower than expected because they hit ledge & had to determine how to maintain correct pitch while rerouting. Inspector came & gave approval. Harry Hulse came to discuss heating system— promised estimate for 11/20. Stacey from Eastern Tree came to look at trees—will give us estimate.

11/18 Excavation continued. Underground electrical lines installed. Resupport of kitchen ceiling completed.

11/19 Scaffolding set up for work on back kitchen wall. Two back kitchen windows removed & centered. Small window in back wall replaced with an old one removed from another area. George cemented holes in basement wall where electrical & sewer connections came through. Petrified squirrel found in attic.

11/20 Wall adjoining conservatory to back porch ripped out. Electricians began work upstairs. Kitchen ceiling joists nailed off. Tom framed in kitchen door leading to study, to make it into a wall. Black paper applied to kitchen outside wall. Plywood installed for box around fireplace which is to be cemented.

11/23 Electricians continued work upstairs. Ross removed walls & door frames by stairs landing. Tom straightened out kitchen walls. Framing finished around fireplaces in kitchen. C. Hyatt (tree surgeon) took down big evergreen trees by side porch.

11/24 Upstairs staircase walls removed. Ripped out master bathroom floor. Victor dug out foundation for sun porch & removed walls of ice house.

11/25 Started to frame in walls in upstairs back bathroom. Steve Davidson working. Tom sick.

11/26 Thanksgiving holiday.

11/27 George mucking around with footing for sunporch area. Ground very wet from rain. Tom off.

11/30 Work on back bedroom ceiling continued. New, stronger ceiling joists installed. Completed framing on back bathroom walls. Began furring out walls by back bathroom. George picked up more materials. Arnie's Plumbing Heating stopped by with an estimate on heating system—$24,500. Electricians continued work rewiring house. Tom continued furring out walls in kitchen.

12/1 Work continued on bedroom ceiling. Framing completed around kitchen chimneys. Nailers applied to kitchen walls. Oil tank removed; floor graded to right level. Concrete forms framed for furnace equipment platform. George framing footings for porch addition.

12/2 Permits pulled for new addition. Continued work on forms for porch addition.

12/3 Beam installed in upstairs ceiling for wall between middle bedroom & sitting area. Beam jacked up & supported—straightened sagging roof line. Cement delivered for basement foundation. Truck late. By evening, temperature dropped below freezing— George & Kirk went to house to cover wet cement with plastic.

12/4 Ceiling lowered in back bedroom. Dividing wall for middle bedroom & upstairs sitting room built.

12/7 Ceiling joists in back bedroom finished. Straightened out new bedroom wall & framed closet wall.

12/8 Walls leveled out in back bedroom area. Old door frames & savable items consolidated & placed in front bedroom for new bathroom door. Framed in old bedroom doorway, which used to lead to stairs. Crumbling plaster area on stairway wall removed.

12/9 Wine cellar floor dug 4 more inches for more headroom. Piping under kitchen floor broken up & removed. Framed outside door to basement. Installed new joists underneath laundry room. Stone wall chipped out for support beam. Stairway walls leveled. Patched hole in laundry floor. Removed rotten flooring under new laundry bathroom area & replaced with plywood. More materials purchased at lumberyard.

12/10 Work completed on additional support beam. Post installed in driveway for cable, so area can be roped off. Done due to disappearance of sleigh & to unauthorized dumping of dirt on property during weekend. Work started on building stairs for wine cellar & new back outside door for basement.

12/11 Work continued on basement doors. Ross reframed smokehouse door; repaired door using old nails. Work completed on support beam.

12/14 Masons arrived finally. They had promised to come Monday after Thanksgiving. Work began on new porch foundation. Basement door under kitchen wing removed. Began repair on front porch steps. Columns removed to be repaired or replaced. Stairs removed to be rebuilt with pressure-treated wood—won't rot. Terry finished work on basement doors.

12/15 Masons continued work on foundation walls. Ross continued work on front stairs indoors due to rainy weather. Old porch floor demolished. Terry discovered an old well underneath floor. Beautiful, with a 2 ft. round opening about 20 ft. deep. Side walls worn fairly smooth, probably due to constant use of the water bucket. This also solved mystery of large hook located in ceiling of this room—obviously used to hang bucket on. Tom repairing rot spot in laundry room floor— repairing walls & ceiling.

12/16 Work continued on laundry room and front stairs. Mason blocked in kitchen basement door. Terry removed rot from porch where well was found. Rita, Larry, George & I met with Peter V. (cabinetmaker). Discussed using clear pine, which would later be painted. Larry will meet with me after holidays to discuss final layout so we can send out for accurate quotes. Peter & George went to Turkey Hill to look at cabinets in studio kitchen & molding in new library. Tom & Ross working on sun porch framing & floor.

12/23 Framing of porch continued.

12/24 Christmas holidays—off four days.

12/28 Worked on roof framing of new sun porch. Framing in of side walls.

1/1/88 Holiday.

1/4 Ross worked on porch ceiling. Covered old well opening with plastic to prevent moisture from entering house. Snow shoveled off porch roof to prevent any leaking. Tom worked on master bath—removing wall & floors. Layed down plywood.

1/5 Tom framed in upstairs bathroom to prep for plumbers. Patched holes in upstairs floors. Started to install closet door in upstairs bedroom. Ross worked on leveling porch ceiling. Made plywood cover for stairs to wine cellar. Disassembled old bathroom fixtures. Ripped up floor & fixtures.

1/6 Tom ripped out rest of side wall by stairs and cleaned up floor for plumbers. Ceiling beam in porch area resupported. Ross ripped up floor & removed pipes in upstairs bathroom. Also ripped out remaining pipes in rest of house. Plumbers arrived 7:45—worked until 3:45. Began work in upstairs bathroom.

Rita, George & I met with Larry regarding revised kitchen plans. Decided which cabinet doors to be glass, where drawers to be located & what type of molding to be used. Took pictures of studio kitchen cabinets to send out for estimates. Discussed bathroom fixtures; Larry to research & supply brochures. Larry to revise plans & supply copies to us by 1/8 to send out.

1/11 Ross took down upstairs wall next to stairs. Terry still on vacation. Tom worked on installing header for plumber under laundry room bath. Straightened up basement. Repaired fitted interior doors.

1/12 John worked on kitchen windows. Terry reglazing, repairing, priming. Tom helped plumber cut floor joists in upstairs bathroom. Took down wall where pedestal sink will be installed.

1/13 John made window above future sink in kitchen. Also made duplicate of back kitchen window. Tom worked on plowing out back of existing door casings to aid in installation of Sheetrock. Installed cleats for electricians for hanging fixtures. Workbenches made for window repair & general carpentry work.

1/14 Terry stripping, sanding, reglazing windows. Tom began refitting interior doors.

1/15 Tom sick. Terry cut glass, reconditioned windows.

1/18 George called more cabinetmakers for quotes. Made phone calls all day. Called Willpower regarding roof—they never phoned back. Ordered Porta Potti— Riverside $35/day. Set up appointment with Joe of Armore Wood Roof. Called Shimko Fireplace— talked to service. Called August West Chimney Sweeps; made appointment for Thursday.

1/19 Visited Clearvue Glass re estimate on sunroom door's windows. Stopped in Bridgeport to look at old houses, trying to find old glass for use on windows. Called two leaded glass studios—Renaissance Glass was no help; Paul Petrushonis did not have any glass at the time. Ross furred out kitchen wall and patched kitchen floor. Worked with John to cut outside molding for porch. Terry continued work on windows. Tom sick.

(Continued on page 88)

beam framing gave way to a new system called the balloon frame, constructed with boards that are 2 inches thick. Studs for a two-story balloon-framed house rise from the sill, the thick plate resting upon the foundation wall, to the second-story top plates located just beneath the roof rafters. The studs span a distance of more than 16 feet. Balloon framing was prevalent until the 1920s, when national fire safety codes mandated changes. It was replaced by a method of construction known as the platform frame, which is constructed in levels, one level at a time, with studs that normally measure just under 8 feet (91½ inches.) Platform framing isolates each area, creating cavities that make it more difficult for fires to spread.

During a restoration of an old house, there is seldom a need to replace the framing because of its inherent structural strength. Only sills, which are sometimes virtually level with the soil, are susceptible to deterioration.

LEFT: **For contractors' crews to function effectively, the job site must be prepared for the efficient transport of tools and equipment. For safe access, rotted steps are replaced with temporary ones or a ramp, and wood planks are set down on the soil where a future path may be laid. The planks form a bridge enabling equipment to be hauled from the trucks to the house and minimalizing the amount of dirt tracked in. A portable toilet should be set up for workmen's use if renovation is extensive.**

POST–AND–BEAM CONSTRUCTION

Many historic American homes are not only still standing after 250 or 300 years, but they are still sturdy. The framing is what keeps these houses "young." During the 17th and 18th centuries, our ancestors framed their houses with oak, a wood noted for its strength, and fastened the main beams by notching them into one another, then driving wood pegs through the joints, since nails were a rare commodity. The resulting skeleton is called timber framing, or post-and-beam framing. The beams, designed to distribute the weight out to the posts, which are sometimes as thick as 12 by 12 inches, not only supported the weight of the structure, but withstood wind and snow loads through the centuries as well.

During the 19th century, post-and-

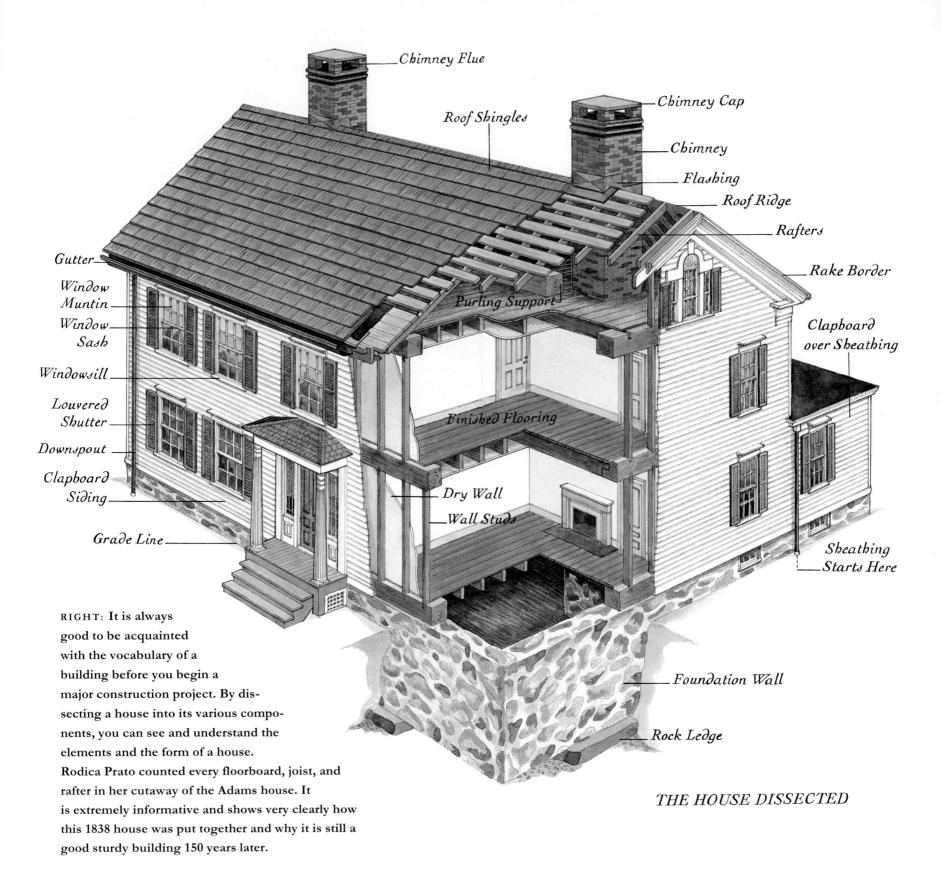

Chimney Flue

Roof Shingles

Chimney Cap

Chimney

Flashing

Roof Ridge

Rafters

Rake Border

Gutter

Window Muntin

Window Sash

Purling Support

Clapboard over Sheathing

Windowsill

Louvered Shutter

Downspout

Finished Flooring

Clapboard Siding

Dry Wall

Wall Studs

Grade Line

Sheathing Starts Here

Foundation Wall

Rock Ledge

RIGHT: It is always good to be acquainted with the vocabulary of a building before you begin a major construction project. By dissecting a house into its various components, you can see and understand the elements and the form of a house. Rodica Prato counted every floorboard, joist, and rafter in her cutaway of the Adams house. It is extremely informative and shows very clearly how this 1838 house was put together and why it is still a good sturdy building 150 years later.

THE HOUSE DISSECTED

CLEARING AND EXCAVATING

Because the land around the Adams house was overgrown with sumac, weeds, and dead or dying trees, I knew it had to be cleared before the restoration could begin. Undergrowth had eaten away at the sills of the house, vines gnawed at the foundation, and dead branches threatened the roof. Since I planned to add a new sunroom, expand the kitchen area, and add a porch, clearing and excavating were necessary.

Specific types of excavation must be done if the following is affected:

SEWAGE: When a cesspool, such as the one on the Adams house property, is replaced with a community-serviced sewage line or with a septic system, the ground has to be prepared and trenches must be dug.

UTILITIES: When gas, electrical, water, or telephone and cable TV lines are to run underground to the house from community-service lines in the street, trenches must be dug.

FOUNDATION: When an existing foundation is sinking or is badly cracked or bowed, it must be repaired or replaced. At the rear of the Adams house, a section of foundation under the old kitchen pantry had rolled slightly and fallen outward, pulling the building with it. George said the rear of the house had dropped as much as 6 inches! In order to build a new foundation to support a new sill, some excavation was necessary.

ADDITIONS: When additions, such as my kitchen expansion and terrace, are planned, the ground has to be leveled and prepared so a new foundation or other support system can be installed. For a wood deck, which requires poured-concrete piers, holes must be dug.

Foundations (and concrete piers) must extend below the frost line. If moisture in the soil freezes beneath a foundation, the ground heaves, pushing up the earth. This can crack the foundation and distort framing in the house above. Also, water pipes laid above the frost line can rupture when water in them turns to ice. Because of the climate in Connecticut, excavated areas around the Adams house had to be dug to over 4 feet below the ground level.

Power equipment can normally be rented by the hour or day: backhoes for digging trenches; bulldozers for removing, pushing, or leveling large amounts of soil; and front-end loaders for moving earth from one area to another—and especially for back-filling inside a new foundation, such as for my terrace.

If the excavator runs into solid rock, or "ledge," underground lines may have to be rerouted or an addition relocated. Ledge can be blasted if necessary. In Connecticut, a contractor licensed to use explosives must get a special permit for each blasting operation. If the ledge blocks every route to the street, blasting may be the only option.

While the machinery is on site, it's a good idea to remove any tree roots or large shrubs with extensive root systems that could endanger underground lines or foundations. We also had several huge stumps pulled up. Finally, the excavator back-fills, packs, and levels all the soil, readying it for later reseeding.

ABOVE: **My old friend, Victor Perkowski, has overseen the excavating, bulldozing, and backhoeing on all my projects. He is at one with his machines in the most poetic sense, never making a visible mistake, never damaging a tree trunk or wall. Working near the foundation with a bucket loader, Victor picked up all the cement refuse, which he used as the base for my new terrace.**

RIGHT: **When Victor had a serious ailment and had to halt his work for a while, Vinnie Palmieri filled in with his machine, an 880D Case backhoe on tracks. He did a lot of the heavy ditch and trench digging for the sewer lines and electrical, telephone, and cable TV conduits so that nothing had to be strung overhead from the street to the house. The trench bottoms were layered with "dead sand," a special mixture used to support sewer lines. Crushed stone filled those sections of trench that ran under the driveway, to prevent collapsing and settling. Trenches were dug so that most of the lines would be under the frost line in our zone.**

ABOVE: Victor Perkowski has a very good array of machines for road work, grading, trenching, and earth moving. It is essential on a large job to hire an expert heavy machinery driver who will carefully reshape the yard or driveway to your plans, with no damage to buildings, trees, and plantings. For trenching, Victor uses one of his two backhoes. Here is his Drott, a backhoe with wheels that also has a 30-foot arm. Stable and strong, it easily and quickly digs trenches for electrical, plumbing, and septic systems.

BELOW: Using the Drott, Victor created an immense hole at the end of the driveway. Everything organic was composted or taken to the dump (burning is not permitted without a permit) and the remaining inorganic refuse was buried in the hole. It is important that such trash be buried deeply and covered with a least 30 inches of topsoil so that a garden or tree can be planted above with no problems.

ABOVE: Photographed from above, the giant Drott looks rather menacing. Actually, it is performing a task in a few hours that would take a man days and days to do: removing several large tree stumps that would have obstructed the construction of the driveway bed. When doing excavating or trenching, it is handy to have a dump truck nearby to cart away stumps, roots, branches, and other debris.

BELOW: A Caterpillar bucket loader being used as a ladder for one of the men so that he can trim the trees with a chain saw. The bucket loader is stable enough to "climb" trees this way, and the driver can direct the pruner as he wishes. Only experienced and capable laborers should attempt such "tricks," however.

REPAIRING THE FOUNDATION

Once we had cleared the overgrown shrubbery and vines from around the house, I realized that we would have to repair faults in some parts of the foundation walls and completely replace others. A waterproof foundation wall is especially important in protecting a wood-frame house against deterioration. And a secure foundation prevents the structure from shifting. Repairs will take care of these routine problems:

CRACKING: Small cracks can be pressure-filled with epoxy cement to give a foundation wall renewed strength. However, the presence of large diagonal cracks could indicate settling problems,

OPPOSITE: **After George tore down the useless additions that had been attached to the back of the house, Victor, with his small Caterpillar bucket loader, effortlessly removed unwanted foundation walls and soil and mounded it all up where the raised terrace would be constructed. Making use of this "fill" saved a lot of money later on.**

As is evident here, rotted clapboard has been ripped off of the house and new sheathing was applied where necessary and covered with protective black builder's felt. I was thrilled to see the last of the old jalousied windows and the door, which dated from the 1950s.

It was during this phase of the renovation process that the house looked its absolute worst. And because this was all happening during bleak November, the house seemed more desolate than ever.

which might require a new foundation.

CRUMBLING MORTAR: If the cement mortar has crumbled, the joints between stones or concrete blocks can be cleaned out with a chisel and then repointed, or filled with fresh mortar.

BOWING: A wall may bow inward when soil—particularly water-impregnated soil—exerts undue pressure against it. To repair, the soil is dug away from the wall. Then a special horizontal jack is hauled inside the structure and extended from wall to wall. Slowly, this jack presses a steel beam placed vertically against the bow until the wall is straight again. Steel or masonry pilasters are installed to buttress the wall, and cracks are repaired.

SETTLING: Gradual sinking over time may not be severe enough to warrant replacing any of the foundation walls. If settling is not serious, a mixture of cement and sand grout can be pumped in under one or more of the footings. Pressure from an air compressor will raise and stabilize the wall. Then any cracks can be repaired.

When taking down an old foundation wall, the adjoining intact walls must not be disturbed. Before the deteriorated section of the foundation has been exposed, the foundation contractor installs a series of temporary screw-jacks beneath a heavy beam placed under floor joists. This is to keep the house from sagging while the faulty material is taken out. The jacks raise the joists an inch or so above the sill so it can be removed and replaced if necessary.

Rotten sills should always be replaced, even if they rest on a perfect foundation. Today's building codes call for the use of

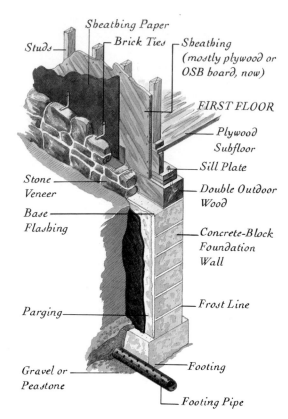

ELEMENTS OF THE FOUNDATION

pressure-treated material when rotten sills are replaced—and whenever wood is joined to any masonry surface. Working in the basement, our crew set a horizontal beam on two steel columns, placed 6 or 8 feet out from the foundation wall, and jacked upward. Great patience was required because, to prevent any structural timbers from cracking, the jack could not be raised more than half an inch a day. When pressure on the sill plate was released, the rotten section could be cut out and replaced with a length of pressure-treated timber. Once that was securely in place, the house was lowered at the same slow rate.

BUILDING A NEW FOUNDATION

In a vintage house, if the sill has deteriorated and must be replaced, or if the foundation must be removed—or if there is no foundation at all—a company specializing in house-lifting can be called in. Steel beams are wedged under the sills through the entire length of the house, and an operator using hydraulic lifting equipment can gently raise the whole building to create needed access. After the work has been done, the building is slowly lowered back onto its foundation.

Construction of a new foundation wall begins with the installation of the footing, an enlarged base formed with cast-in-place concrete running underneath to support the foundation wall. The footing prevents settling, helps distribute the full load of the house evenly over a wide, flat area, and stabilizes the structure. If an existing footing is solid and level, it can be saved and reused.

A footing measures double the width of the foundation wall that is centered on top of it; if the foundation is the standard 8 inches thick, the footing should be 16 inches wide and 8 inches high.

A form for the footing is constructed of plywood or metal panels placed on well-tamped earth along premeasured lines marking the site of the new wall. The sides of the form are braced with wood or metal triangles to withstand the weight of the concrete. After the pouring, the footing is "puddled," or punched with a rod, to rid it of air voids. The surface is roughed up with an iron rake, or a groove is made down its center to bond it with the foundation wall.

Trucks containing ready-mix concrete are equipped with chutes designed to deliver wet concrete to the foundation form. These chutes will carry poured material about 18 feet. If you prefer to avoid the deep tire impressions on the lawn that may result from the weight of a full truck—or have concerns about a garden or underground septic system—consider renting a pumper truck (about $400 to $500 a day, including vehicle and crew). It resembles an oversized elephant with a distended trunk—in this case a 4-inch-thick hose that can deliver concrete to your foundation from the distance of a driveway or the curb.

The Adams house, like many historic buildings in New England, was erected on a foundation made of rocks and stones found on the land. My foundation was repaired with stones of local origin bonded together with dry-mix mortar.

Where new sections of foundation had to be built—at the rear of the house and to support the new terrace—we decided to use concrete block because it is strong, long-lasting, and cheaper than a cast-in-place or poured foundation. Eight-inch-wide blocks are the norm, except in regions such as the desert, where soil tends to shift, or where especially heavy weight is to be supported. In these cases, 10- or 12-inch-wide blocks can be used. The blocks, which are hollow, can be reinforced as needed with steel bars inserted vertically through their openings and grouted in place.

Concrete blocks are secured to each other and to the flooring with mortar cement. Each block is centered, like brick, over the vertical joint of the block below it. This is called a running bond. A concrete-block foundation must be waterproofed, or "parged," with an exterior coating of cement mortar followed by a coating of thick asphalt compound, which prevents moisture from seeping through the wall into the basement or crawl space.

Some builders prefer to work with a cast-in-place concrete foundation. The wall and its footing can be formed simultaneously, but they are usually done in separate steps.

A form for the wall is built on top of the footing to the engineered dimensions and braced with wood or steel framing to support the weight of the wet concrete. When the concrete is firm but not hard, 18-inch anchor bolts are tapped into the top of the foundation wall about every 4 feet and at least 1 foot from the corners. Once the concrete has hardened, the sill—with holes drilled to match the bolts—is dropped over the threaded portion of the bolts and fastened snugly with nuts.

To ensure a watertight joint between the existing and new walls or sections

RIGHT: **A view through the wide double cellar doors into the basement, which we totally emptied. We dug out more than a foot of the dirt floor and brushed down all the stone walls. This entrance was so convenient that it was left in its original location—but both the stonework and the woodwork, including the doors, had to be replaced.**

of wall, many contractors indent the outside and inside corners of the wall before they pour. The indentation is packed solid with a silicone or polyurethane caulk.

After the foundation walls are finished and before backfilling is done, perforated drain pipe is laid alongside the foundation, parallel to the footing, and embedded in pea gravel. The pipe should be long enough to direct rainwater to a dry well (a small underground pit filled with gravel or crushed stone) or to a natural drain field located some distance away from the house.

LEFT: Each mason has his own way of working, and Donnie was especially fun to watch. I learned a great deal about the art of stonework from each of the stone masons we hired, and I grew to appreciate the difficult work and intensive effort that goes into repairs as well as new construction.

RIGHT: Every worker on the site has his own tools and is responsible for keeping them together and intact. After acquainting myself with each profession, I realized that every kit is different. Masons generally carry their tools in leather-handled bags, like this one. A carpenter's work requires a larger investment; most have trucks outfitted to hold all their tools, which are carried from site to site in wooden boxes.

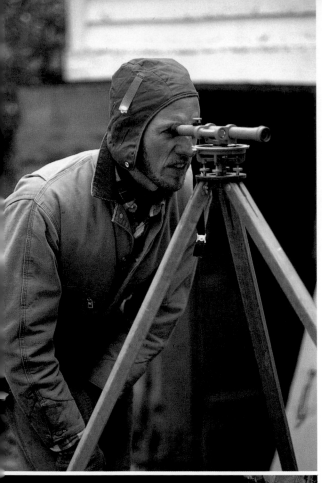

LEFT: Foundation reconstruction began in earnest in November. Dressed for the chilly weather, brother George uses his surveyor's instruments to site the foundation. It had bowed in many places as stones loosened and the house settled. Sills had rotted, causing further havoc. Straight lines and strong foundation walls were created, greatly enhancing the underpinning of the house.

RIGHT: An 8-by-8-inch pine sill plate shows evidence of dry rot and possible insect infestation. George used a hydraulic jack to raise sagging sills and align them with adjoining ones. The mason could then continue creating the stone support structure underneath.

LEFT: Several different masons were hired for the various jobs that needed to be done. One of Donnie's assistants used excavated stones to repair the walls under the sill, taking great care to match the stone patterns of the existing foundation.

RIGHT: New foundation walls were built of concrete block and faced with fieldstone gathered from the property. Since I wanted as much of the stone exposed as possible, the pointing was done carefully so that the face of each stone would not be obscured. The mortar used was a hard mixture of cement and lime.

LEFT: Once the basement floor was dug out to its correct new depth, part of the dirt floor was covered with a cement slab that would bear the weight of the new heating equipment and hot water heaters. A wooden framework was constructed to square off the poured concrete.

RIGHT: A 4-inch pipe was installed under the floor of the new slab to divert excess rainwater running off the roof. George, in his rubber boots, kept an eye on the process to be sure the pitch would be correct for proper drainage.

LEFT: Victor picked up the cement refuse from the excavation work with his bucket loader and transferred it to the site of the new terrace.

RIGHT: George tried to ensure the safety of the crew at all times, and especially when chipping away at materials that could fly up into their faces and eyes. He instructed them to wear protective clothing—goggles, masks, gloves, ear protectors and plugs—when necessary.

REBUILDING THE CHIMNEYS

One reason so many people are attracted to old houses is that they usually have wonderful fireplaces. The Adams house has eight, with flues venting into three chimneys. Ideally, every fireplace should have its own chimney, but if the chimneys are big enough, with well-defined flues leading from each firebox, as many as five separate fireplaces can feed into a single chimney.

When Miss Adams lived in the house, the fireplaces were all boarded up; she was afraid to use any of them. Lack of use didn't prevent deterioration, however. Most old chimneys need to be at least partly repointed, their joints cleaned and refilled with fresh mortar. All three of our chimneys had to be rebuilt, the kitchen chimney from the roof up and the other two from the attic floor up.

RIGHT: Here, the masons are using a level, a plumb line, and a sure eye to lay their bricks. The weather was cold, but the work was so strenuous the men didn't freeze. We did not feel it necessary to fully modernize the chimneys as they were not going to be in constant use. Peering down each chimney from the rooftop, we could verify the condition of the brick and baffles (the brick partitions that create the separate flues merged at the attic floor level). We capped the chimneys with bluestone covers, cut rectangular openings in each, and installed mechanical dampers, one per firebox. The dampers are operated with spring-loaded handles on the sides of the fireplaces.

If you are rebuilding an old chimney or building a new one, keep in mind that its base must rest on its own footing, like a house foundation. Because of fire hazards, neither a fireplace nor its chimney should support any part of the house; the chimney should be separated from all wood framing by at least 2 inches, and the framing should be at least 4 inches from the back of the fireplace. Most chimney structures are built straight up from the basement to the roof. The chimney is then finished with brick above the roof. Any bends of more than 30 degrees will limit a chimney's drawing power and compromise its efficiency. Today's flue-lined chimneys are typically built of 8-inch-thick concrete blocks covered with brick or fieldstone.

THE FLUE: Many old chimneys need to be lined, particularly if they will be used frequently. Flue liners are designed to protect the brickwork from intense heat from the firebox. When careful inspection turned up no major cracks or flaws in my chimneys, however, George and I decided not to have liners installed. There are three types of flue liners:

FIRE CLAY OR TERRA-COTTA: In a chimney reconstruction, the contractor usually specifies a fireproof flue liner made of long-lasting and economical fire clay. The liner is installed in rectangular sections a half inch thick and 1½ feet deep. Corners are curved, and the sections are sealed together with fire-clay mortar.

STAINLESS STEEL: When the chimney is not dismantled, a less costly flexible stainless-steel lining may be inserted into it from the top down—in one long tube that connects to the firebox.

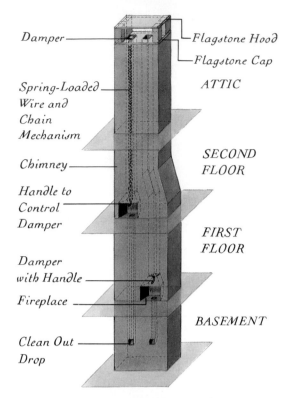

Damper

Flagstone Hood
Flagstone Cap
ATTIC

Spring-Loaded Wire and Chain Mechanism

Chimney
SECOND FLOOR

Handle to Control Damper
FIRST FLOOR

Damper with Handle

Fireplace
BASEMENT

Clean Out Drop

THE CHIMNEY STACK

MORTAR MIX: This is effective when a chimney is intact. To make, mortar is mixed with a base of perlite or vermiculite, the same substances used in garden soil mixes. First, heavy rubber tubing is dropped down the chimney and inflated; then the cavity between the tube and the chimney walls is filled with mortar mix. Once the mix has hardened, the tube can be deflated and pulled out.

To encourage draw and insure that there is room for smoke to escape, the flue opening cannot be less that one tenth the area of the fireplace opening.

The top of the flue liner should extend above the masonry of the chimney by at least 2 inches—preferably 3 or 4. Often fireplace draw can be improved only by building up the chimney another 3 or 4 feet. The best draw occurs when the height of the chimney, from the fire-

box at the bottom to the cap at the top, is at least 20 feet. Fire safety regulations in most communities dictate a chimney height of 15 feet, with at least 3 feet of stack extending above the highest point where the chimney penetrates the roof.

THE DAMPER: To keep out cold air and prevent warmth from escaping, a damper is usually installed inside the chimney, just above the firebox and within arm's reach. Dampers are flat plates customarily made out of cast iron. Before they came into use, the fireboard served as a damper. Made of several planks nailed together, the fireboard was designed to cover the entire firebox opening plus surrounding brick, flushing with the wood mantel to which it was attached by clips or turnbuckles. It was then painted to look like part of the mantel, just as shutters created a complementary architectural effect when pulled shut to seal out the cold.

THE CAP: Rain and snow are the chief enemies of any chimney's mortar joints. To shed water from around the top of the chimney, the mason forms a reinforced concrete cap, or collar (also called a "wash"), around the exposed flue. We capped our chimneys with flat bluestone hoods supported on low columns because I wanted the chimneys to look just as they did years ago. The newest concrete caps have been prefabricated to eliminate cracking problems. If a capped chimney has separate flues, brick spacers called "wythes" are bonded to the chimney walls so the gases from one flue are not drawn into the one beside it. The total area of the openings between columns should be about four times the flue area to make sure smoke will be drawn up smartly by the action of wind blowing through the columns.

To prevent birds and animals from colonizing in a chimney that lacks a chimney-top damper, a mason often installs screening with a half inch or more of mesh over the chimney, creating a barrier without affecting the draw.

THE FLASHING: Because roof leaks often occur where roof and chimney meet, flashing is necessary. Flashing made of 16-ounce copper sheet is ideal; I chose it because it is attractive and long-lasting and because it matches the gutters we selected. One layer of flashing starts just under the courses of shingles that are closest to the chimney and rises up the chimney face. Another layer, called counter flashing, is first embedded in a row of mortar joints around the chimney at the roofline. Then it is bent down to overlap the first layer by at least 3 inches. All the joints between the masonry and the metal are then solidly caulked.

The chimneys in the Adams house rise from the center of the ridgeboard. But in houses where a chimney punctures the roof below the ridge, rainwater or snow may back up against the side of the chimney. To counteract this, masons often add a sheet of bent copper called a "cricket" on the ridge-facing side.

RIGHT: Scaffolding had to be erected next to the house so the masons could haul all their materials up to the roof. A basket hung on a pulley system was raised and lowered for each load of bricks or mortar mix.

SHINGLING A ROOF

I love wood-shingled roofs and, of course, shingle is traditional for an old house like this one. Wood shingles are tapered so that the butt ends visible to the eye are thicker than the ends that are nailed—and hidden—under the course, or row, above them. Shingles are cut in 16-, 18-, and 24-inch lengths and come in bundles containing 25 square feet of coverage. The shingles we used were 18 inches long and varied in width from 4 to 14 inches. Shakes, two to four times as thick as shingles, are somewhat less expensive per square foot since fewer shakes are needed to cover the same area. Shingles are about $1.20 a square foot in the Northeast. Properly installed,

RIGHT: We knew that the roof would have to be replaced, but we did not know until we ripped off the existing asphalt shingles that the sheathing and flashing would have to go, too. The 5-by-5 rough-sawn pine rafters were fine but spaced too far apart. We nailed sturdy spruce ¾-by-4 sheathing over the rafters at 5-inch intervals. Sheathing was used instead of plywood because it permits circulation of air around the shingles, preventing dampness and rot.

Cedar shingles were then nailed on top of the new wood (we used #1 Blue Label Perfections). We treated our shingles with a wood preservative to enhance their life.

The attic was protected with large sheets of plastic. Afterward, the plaster attic walls were patched and painted and the floorboards were cleaned.

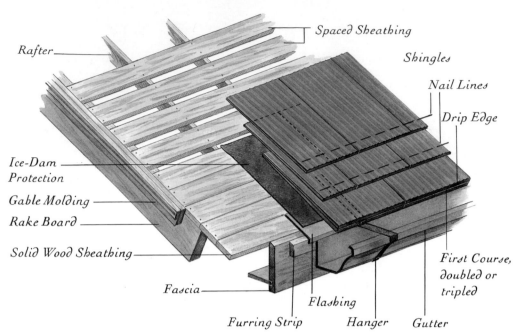

Rafter

Spaced Sheathing

Shingles

Nail Lines

Drip Edge

Ice-Dam Protection

Gable Molding

Rake Board

Solid Wood Sheathing

First Course, doubled or tripled

Fascia

Flashing

Hanger

Gutter

Furring Strip

THE ELEMENTS OF A ROOF

the shingles can last 20 years or more.

Wood shingles come in bundles containing widths ranging from 2 to 14 inches (anything wider is liable to crack). Four bundles add up to 100 square feet of roofing with a 3½-inch exposure. In the 17th century, our colonial ancestors hand-hewed local white pine to make their shingles. Today, most wood shingles are cut from western red cedar, but in the Northeast, white cedar shingles are often the preferred choice. Cedar shingles naturally resist decay, but there are two chemical treatments that enhance their endurance:

AMINO PHOSPHATE is a fire-retardant chemical that prevents shingles from bursting into flame should any burning material land on the roof. This treatment raises the cost per shingle by approximately 25 percent.

CHROMIUM COPPER ARSENATE is a substance applied to add extra protection to shingles in warm, moist climates such as Florida, where wood may deteriorate rapidly. Added cost: 10 to 14 percent.

We were fortunate that in coastal Connecticut neither treatment was required; we simply treated our shingles with a wood preservative for extra life. Old-time roofers claim that the salt air here lengthens the life of any wood, and this may be true since many historic houses in the area remain with shingles intact.

Before you install new shingles, the existing roof may have to be removed. An inspector or local building department representative can tell you how many layers of old roofing material the building code will allow you to retain. If code allows you to keep your existing roof, you will need to be sure there are no deteriorated areas.

Chemically treated wood shingles may be applied directly over plywood or solid board sheathing (the first layer of protec-

tion over the roof rafters) as long as the material is in good condition. Treated wood shingles may also be applied over an existing asphalt or fiberglass roof.

Untreated shingles must be nailed to open sheathing: 1-by-4s or 1-by-6s laid across the rafters like ribs. At the eaves, or lowest roof edges, the sheathing is solid, covered by a layer of roofing felt or moisture-repellant self-adhering membrane such as Ice and Water Shield made by W. R. Grace. This will prevent leaks caused by ice dams, which occur when water freezes and overflows the gutter, creeping behind the roof shingles.

The first row of shingles at the eave is a double or a triple layer, and it overlaps the fascia (the vertically applied board just beneath the eave) by 1½ inches. The overlaps allow rain or snow to run from the roof directly into the gutter.

Roofers install shingle courses from the eaves up to the ridge of the roof. Each shingle is attached with two nails. Noncorroding stainless-steel nails are used to fasten chemically treated shingles; less expensive "hot-dipped" zinc-coated or aluminum nails may be used for untreated shingles. The nails are positioned about an inch above the point where the shingle is exposed and about three-quarters of an inch from each edge. If nails are set too close to the center of the shingle, the wood can cup or warp; nails set too close to the edges may cause splitting.

Solid sheathing is also applied on either side of the roof ridge. A layer of roofing felt goes over this sheathing, which is then followed by a row of shingles. A specially manufactured cedar

ABOVE: Because of its low pitch, the roof over the sunroom needed special treatment. First, fire-retardant paper was nailed to the sheathing, with holes cut out for three nonventing skylights. On top of this, George applied a torch bonded membrane called bitumen, which is a very thick asphalt derivative.

ABOVE: The three-bay garage also needed a new roof. Simple metal-pipe scaffolding was set up for efficiency so that the workers didn't have to haul tools and material up and down ladders. The gentle slope of this roof made the work easy; when the new roof was finished, siding and garage doors were prepped and painted.

ABOVE: George installed skylights constructed with copper framing and special raised curbs by WASCO and put flashing around each one to prevent leaks. Because there was a distance of about 20 inches from outer roof to finished ceiling, George fabricated and installed fixed windows flush with the ceiling, each multipaned to match the sunroom's French doors and transoms. Looking up now, I can see sunlit windows instead of tunnels leading to skylights. The space between each skylight and window also has insulating properties: 1 inch of dead air is worth 3 inches of insulation.

ridge cap is then nailed over the shingles.

Flashing is installed where down-sloping rooflines meet (this is called a valley), and at any junctures between roof and chimneys, vent pipes, or dormers. The best flashing is metal. White metal flashing—aluminum, galvinized iron, stainless steel, or lead—requires a coat of paint on both sides when used under wood shingles because these bare metals may cause unattractive staining. Aluminum flashing with a baked enamel finish is popular with roofers, as it needs no painting. Copper, at least 16 ounces, is the product most used in the Connecticut area for wood roof flashing. Lead-coated copper is most frequently used for flashing exposed to salt air.

Gutters are secured with spikes nailed through the fascia into rafter ends, or with metal hooks supporting the gutter with a strap nailed through shingles into sheathing at the eave. Downspouts are placed at every corner of the house to divert water to drainpipes embedded in gravel around the perimeter of the foundation. The water drains away from the house, ideally to a point in the yard as far from the foundation as possible.

Many roofers specify galvanized steel or aluminum for gutters and downspouts. Copper is another option. Although it is expensive, copper looks beautiful on an old house. It also lasts longer, about 50 years, as opposed to 20 to 25 years.

Building codes require that the attic be well ventilated. Attic ventilation prevents condensation during the winter when temperatures inside and out are out of balance; condensation not only causes shingles to warp, but it can rot out roof rafters as well.

Ventilation also balances summer temperatures. If too much heat builds up inside the attic, it can cause the shingles to buckle. Heat can be released with ridge vents (set at either end of the house under the roof ridges), with soffit vents or midget louvres, or with a combination of these. An attic fan that switches on automatically when the temperature reaches a specific level will also help.

STRIPPING
AND PAINTING
CLAPBOARD

Ordinarily, the older the house the more coats of paint cover its siding. This was certainly true of the Adams house.

We approached several paint-removal companies and discussed various options for removing the cracked and caked paint from the clapboard and trim. Overall sanding was eliminated as a possibility because the sanding discs have a tendency to gouge old board and leave circular marks on the siding. Sand-blasting, with a very fine gauge material, was chosen as the best alternative, and it worked wonderfully. The company we chose, Emilio's Restorations from Bridgeport, was careful and diligent,

removing almost every speck of old paint. The siding suffered very little erosion from the process; it was then lightly hand sanded to smoothness, ready for priming and painting.

Removing old paint is time consuming and expensive, but getting down to bare wood is important in preparing for new paint. All paint adheres best to a freshly prepared and primed surface. Otherwise the paint tends to lift and peel off. A new coat of paint on well-prepared wood should last up to 15 years in a temperate climate. Pigmented stains may last even longer.

One reason that old paint jobs lasted so long was the lead content of the paint. However, since it was discovered in the 1920s that lead paint is poisonous, major paint manufacturers have eliminated lead from all their household paints. During the restoration process, one of my dogs took a liking to the painted floorboards

LEFT: **Sandblasting requires that the workmen wear very good protective clothing and an air-fed helmet to avoid inhalation of toxic dust.**

RIGHT: **The house looked forlorn without its paint and shutters. After sandblasting, the house was washed with plain water and Clorox to kill mold spores. It was advised that the wood age in its bare state for two weeks before being painted. All repairs to the siding and frames were accomplished during this time.**

The new trim around the windows and doors had been primed prior to installation, a good idea since both front and back could be painted easily.

and licked the chipping paint. She developed severe lead poisoning, resulting in epileptic-like seizures. A long course of medication cured her.

Lead was once the base for virtually all paints, especially for those used on the exterior of houses, including the Adams house. Removing lead paint requires special precautions. Before any work begins, spread out plastic tarpaulins to protect the grounds. When stripping is complete, wrap the tarps up and dispose of the debris so that the residue does not permeate the soil. Because lead powder also clouds the air, it's best not to work on a windy day, and no one should eat or drink near the work area.

HAND SCRAPING AND SANDING: This old-fashioned technique, in which workers chip away at the paint with hand scrapers, is the least harmful to wood but takes a great deal of time. However, it is the only way to do some parts of the job, such as stripping narrow window muntins or extracting paint from grooves.

HEAT GUN OR BLOW TORCH: When the heat expelled from the gun or flame of the blow torch is perfectly controlled, the old paint quickly softens into a gelatinous goo that can be scraped off with ease. This method consumes less time than hand scraping because painters can work on large swaths of paint at once, but intense heat is potentially very dangerous when it comes in contact with old dry wood. Some communities prohibit burning off lead paint. Also, flame from a blow torch can scorch wood.

CHEMICAL PAINT REMOVERS: Ranging from mildly caustic to highly toxic, paint removers perform well but, like blow

ABOVE: **During the house painting, all of the windows were papered and taped in preparation for the spraying. This process saves time later because the glass panes will not require a lot of scraping after the painting. This is a view of the western side of the house, with the driveway and two entrances.**

BELOW: **An eastern view of the house during the painting, before any of the landscaping had been done. After the windows were taped, the house was sprayed in sections, transforming its appearance greatly, from a raw wooden edifice to a very bright white home.**

torches, should be handled very carefully. Paint removers are applied with a brush and left for about ten minutes. Once the paint softens, it is scraped off. Multiple layers of old paint may require repeated applications.

SANDBLASTING: With a special air compressor, sand is projected with great force against the painted surface. As implied, the sand literally blasts away the paint. Of all methods, this is the fastest; when the price of labor is to be considered, it can be the least expensive. Sometimes, however. the force of the sand can remove splinters of wood along with the paint, leaving tiny ridges of grain, which is not desirable.

POWER WASHING: Often after a wood surface is scraped and sanded, a chemical such as trisodium phosphate is sprayed on with great force through special hoses. Power washing, which kills the mold or bacteria clinging to residual paint, is not done to a sandblasted surface, because all the old paint has been removed. Power-washing equipment must be used carefully as it can seriously gouge the siding.

After the paint is removed, debris is shaken out into the Dumpster, clean tarps are spread for painting, and any necessary repairs are made.

Paint goes on in three or four stages: a primer is applied, followed by a finish prime and one or two finish coats. The number of layers depends upon the condition of the dry wood; experienced painters can look at the wood and predict exactly how many will be needed. Paint can be applied with a brush or with a spray gun. Each coat must dry thor-

oughly before the next is applied, a process that may take up to two or three days, depending upon humidity. Between coats, the surface should be sanded.

Experts recommend an oil-base alkyd primer followed by latex finish coats. Much has been written about "historically correct" colors. For a mid-19th-century house in a country version of Federal style, white and pale tones such as gray, beige, and light yellow were popular; white with contrasting hunter-green shutters and trim was the most popular

of all. I love this combination and used it on Turkey Hill. The green I used on the Adams house, Hunt Club Teal, is toned with aqua, a shade I developed with Dutch Boy Paints for a line produced for K Mart.

For the Adams house exterior, we chose to use stain, even though it is not as opaque as enamel, because we hoped to avoid a peeling problem in the future. Finally, all of the trim was hand-painted with a brush, using an oil-based gloss enamel paint.

ABOVE: The side entrance looked so pristine and white once the siding was painted. The house appeared like a restored jewel freshly white, with its new roof and Hunt Club Teal doors and porch floors.

INSTALLING CLAPBOARD SIDING

Many of the earliest houses erected in New England were sheathed with long, narrow, beveled hand-sawn boards, which were called "clapboards" because of the sound they made when they were slapped together in a pile. Of all the materials used in 19th-century architecture in the Northeast—brick, stone, shingle—clapboard is still my favorite, partly because it is beautiful and partly because it does its job so well. Their overlap allows them to expand and con-

RIGHT AND OPPOSITE: Most of the clapboard siding was in good condition and needed only to be stripped or sand-blasted to prepare it for painting. Split or rotten clapboard was replaced with siding salvaged from parts of the house that we had taken down. Dominick Adams, one of the carpenters, uses a bevel square to mark the straight edge on one of the remnants of the siding we saved. We did need to add some new 8-inch cedar clapboard to the renovated back of the house. To match up with the existing siding, the boards were exposed 5 of their 8 inches.

The window on the second floor was purchased new and from stock. It was the only new window we bought for the entire house, and I still consider it a mistake, although George keeps reminding me that the egress codes require a window of this width for fire safety. During any remodeling of an old structure, regulations now insist that everything be code perfect.

tract from season to season without disturbing the surface. Today's beveled clapboard is essentially the same as that of old. The most visible difference is that our ancestors' clapboard, made by hand, has a rough finish while new machine-cut boards are usually sanded smooth.

The best wood for clapboard resists decay. Redwood, red cedar, and cypress are ideal; white pine (both Eastern and Western), spruce, hemlock, and yellow poplar are also effective but are less likely to be available. Each clapboard ranges from 4 to 12 inches wide. Remember, though, that with all cut lumber, nominal and actual widths differ; 6-inch clapboard actually measures 5½ inches after it's trimmed.

Clapboard is sold in random lengths from 4 to 16 feet; when you buy a bundle of clapboard, you get an assortment of lengths.

Because I wanted the siding on the addition to the Adams house to match the rest of the building, I chose 8-inch-wide red cedar clapboard. As soon as the boards were delivered, our crew stored them off the ground, under waterproof tarps to avoid warping. Then, to prevent moisture from seeping into the house, every surface of every clapboard was coated with primer. If I had planned to leave the siding natural, we would have used a clear sealer. Some contractors recommend staining or painting the clapboard before it is installed to seal the part of each board to be covered by the one overlapping it. The choice of paint or stain will dictate which side of the board faces outward: paint is applied only to the board's smooth side of the

board, while stain is often used on the rough side.

In the post and beam houses built in colonial times, clapboard was nailed directly over the framing of the house. Houses today, however, are closed in with plywood or fiberboard sheathing to add structural strength and to protect the insulation that is wedged between the studs or vertical framing members. In addition, a wind barrier—called "housewrap" in the trade—is stapled over the sheathing. The clapboard is nailed through the housewrap and the sheathing into the studs.

For extra protection against moisture, 15-pound builders' felt, and asphalt-impregnated paper, may be fastened to the sheathing around every door and

window opening. Then, just before the housewrap is applied, metal flashing and a drip cap are installed above the openings. Once the clapboards are butted tightly against the window and door casings, the joints are sealed with caulk.

A good craftsman, before hammering a single nail, will design the placement of the boards, adjusting them so that the appropriate boards will line up with the top and bottom of the window casings—or, if the windows are uneven, with the casings of the largest window.

Clapboard is installed from the bottom up. On some colonial houses the boards increase in width from course to course so that those at the top of the house look as wide as those on the bottom. This method, which afforded pro-

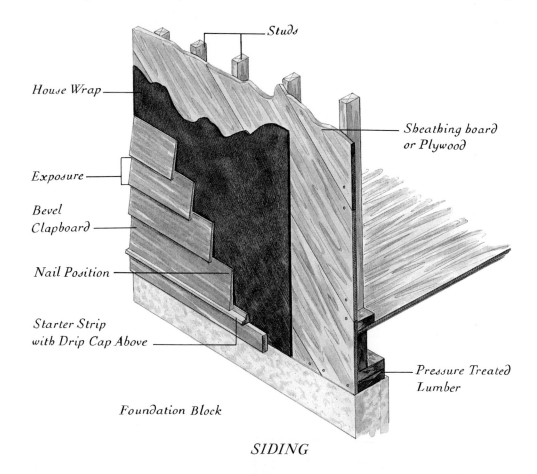

House Wrap

Studs

Sheathing board
or Plywood

Exposure

Bevel
Clapboard

Nail Position

Starter Strip
with Drip Cap Above

Pressure Treated
Lumber

Foundation Block

SIDING

tection from the weather to the more vulnerable rows of clapboard at the bottom passed out of use due to the additional cost. When the house was built, all the clapboards were of the same width.

The first course of clapboard usually lines up with a point lying just below the top of the foundation. Before the first course is installed, though, a starter strip is nailed along the bottom edge of the sheathing so that it will project at a slight angle. Angling the boards, like pitching a roof, helps rain run down and off the house. As the initial course is set in place, it is checked for level. The succeeding courses are all based on the first, with periodic checks all the way up.

The boards are fastened with non-corrosive stainless steel or galvanized nails driven through the board just above the top edge of the board beneath it. Nails are driven in every 16 inches, one into each framing stud. Eight-penny (8d, or 2½-inch) nails are used if the sheathing over the frame is plywood, and 10d, or 3 inch, nails if the sheathing is thicker fiberboard.

For a harmonious appearance, siding craftsmen try to use a single clapboard on each course, reaching from house corner to house corner, or from window or door to corner. Most houses are too large to avoid joints altogether; so carpenters install the clapboard randomly across the surface so that the joints along one row do not line up with those above and below. Usually the joints are made where studs are located so that nails can penetrate something solid instead of just sheathing. To prevent water infiltration, a piece of 15-pound

felt, 2 or 3 inches wide, is installed right under each joint.

Other common old-house sidings:
SHINGLES: Red cedar shingles, which are machine cut, or shakes, which are split on the natural grain and are usually thicker, produce a long-lasting siding. Because shingles are installed individually, they are labor intensive. Some time can be saved if shingles are premounted on 8-foot-long plywood panels—sometimes two courses at a time. Red cedar shingles can be painted or stained, but most people prefer to let them weather to a soft gray.
BRICK: A veneer of brick 3⅝ inches thick makes up the facing for brick houses built today. Bricks themselves are inexpensive, but the labor to lay up a brick wall is costly. Brick lasts a long time, though, and generally needs no more than an occasional repointing of the mortar joints. Brick is available in many

ABOVE: John Minnock and Tom Ball together re-sided the north kitchen wall. Two carpenters can often accomplish a job more than twice as quickly as one; clapboarding benefits from two pairs of hands leveling the material and holding straight, unwieldy lengths.

shades of terra-cotta, plus a range of hues from brown to purplish. If you are matching the bricks of an old house, you will want to purchase old bricks, which are available in building supply lots. These bricks can be cleaned if necessary with muriatic acid.
STUCCO: Often used in the 1920s, stucco is a cementious mix applied over wire lath on outer walls. While the traditional color for stucco is white, color can be added to the mix, and often is. Stucco surfaces can be smooth or pebbly.

CLEANING UP

Cleanup begins the very first day of reconstruction and continues, day after day, until the project is done. Daily cleanups gave our crews an opportunity to retrieve tools that had fallen beneath debris and provided a safe work environment. It also made it easier for George and me to ascertain how the work was progressing when we inspected the site.

For a job as challenging as this one, which generated a great deal of debris, a Dumpster parked on-site is more than convenient. A 30-cubic-yard Dumpster like the one opposite, measuring 8 by 22

feet and 6 feet high, is generally the largest that can be ordered for residential work. It is delivered and picked up by a truck with a bed that tips up, like a dump truck, so the Dumpster can slide off onto the ground. Pickup services include hauling the refuse to the local landfill. Daily rental of such a Dumpster ranges from $5 to $12.

For a single 30-cubic-yard load of debris, the charge for disposal in a municipal landfill can be anywhere from $50 in a remote area to $1,000 in a densely settled community. (Disposal of hazardous material costs more because it must be handled separately and then

trucked to a government-regulated site.)

The contractor is usually obliged by contract to leave the premises "broom clean" when the restoration and remodeling are complete. This means that all traces of plaster, sand, sawdust, and dirt have been removed.

LEFT: Excavation around old houses, especially houses more than a hundred years old, often supplies a great deal of history about a place. Because there was no garbage collecting as we know it today, the family's trash was burned and buried right on the property. "Dumps" were created here and there on the grounds and ultimately covered up. When we cleared and excavated, we had a lot of fun poking through the dirt; several piles of buried "treasure" were found amid the broken chards and glass of the Adams refuse. And bottle collectors found some rather old, rare examples. I was glad when we were finally able to blanket all the sparkling pieces of broken glass with the topsoil that Victor had so wisely piled up around the perimeter of the property when he first skimmed the land.

RIGHT: At the beginning of our renovation, we hired a 30-cubic-yard Dumpster (at an approximate cost of $539 per load). We filled it twice, disposing of the boiler, plaster, lath, pipes, bottles, fixtures, and appliances. It was then replaced with a smaller, 10-cubic-yard container, filled and removed as needed. This way, we could keep the job site tidy. Our neighborhood really appreciated our neat work site; anything that can facilitate good neighbor relations is wise!

RENOVATING

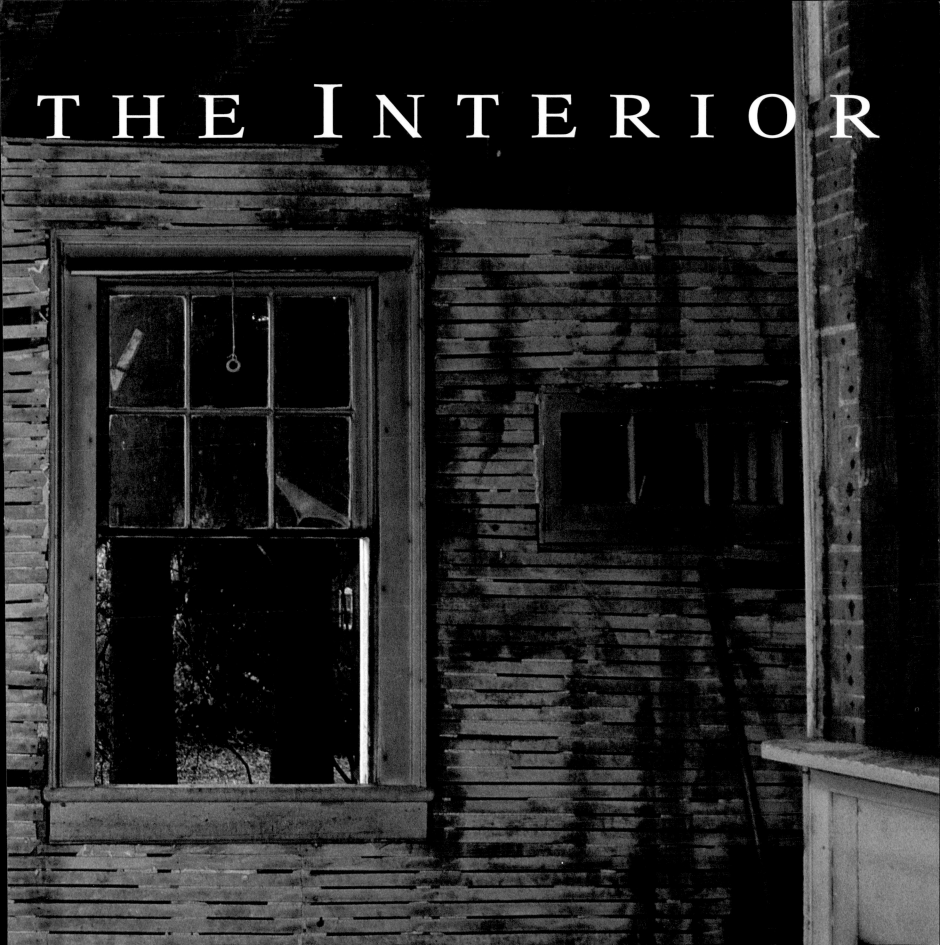

THE INTERIOR

There was a great deal of work to do to bring the interior of the Adams house into the late 20th century. There were too many small rooms and narrow hallways; there was insufficient wiring and plumbing; the kitchen was inadequate for a modern family and had to be enlarged and equipped. Because the Adams house is located on a somewhat noisy and busy corner, air-conditioning was imperative to help screen out noise and pollution. ■ My list of imperatives for the interior included: One: As with the exterior, all architectural features were to be preserved: the original fine proportions of the rooms, the pumpkin pine floors, the original doors, and the original hard-  ware. Two: Old materials were to be used when patching and repairing. Three: All wiring, heating, and plumbing would be installed as inconspicuously as possible while conforming in all respects to convenience and building codes. Four: Blueboard, with its skim coat of plaster, would be used for new walls to match them as closely as possible to the old lath and plaster of the original house. Five: Bathrooms, four full plus a powder room on the first floor, were to be built with fixtures befitting an old house, with no garish tiles or oversized fixtures. Simplicity, rather than showiness, was to be the important feature. Six: All interior woodwork would be carefully scraped by hand to preserve the original profiles of the moldings.

LEFT: **Patsy was our chief plasterer. His years of experience enabled him to achieve smooth, silky walls indistinguishable from the original plaster.**

ABOVE: **An old adjustable square, a chisel, and a wood plane used by the carpenters during the window repairing.**

RIGHT: **Even emptied of its contents, the Adams house continued to surprise us. When a wall was torn down in the kitchen, we uncovered a squirrel's nest, made from pages of a magazine dated 1957, filled with a hoard of nuts.**

Seven: All painting was to be done with oil-based paints. Eight: New woodwork was to be made of indigenous woods and crafted carefully. Nine: The quality of all new work must meet or exceed the old.

JOURNAL

(Continued from page 51)

George met with Coastal Woodworking re kitchen cabinets. Went over plans, showed him studio kitchen at Turkey Hill. Spoke with plasterer Richard Todd re plastering walls. He will get back with price. Called H. Hulse to find out why they were not on the job. Told they were making things up at the shop. Went for a lumber run. Picked up materials. Went to tile store—needed wire lath for bathroom shower stalls. Ross removed rotted ceiling around skylight. Recovered porch roof with plastic to prevent leaking. Worked on wall by stairs. Electrician here 1 hour.

1/20 George went to Lloyd Lumber to get cement for shower work. Researched skylights. Porta-Potti delivered. Heat men came. Ross chopped out stairway beam to make it flush with rest of wall. Tom worked on fitting of interior doors. Terry worked on windows. John mixed & poured cement for shower stall floors.

1/21 Tree men working at house. Trimmed large tulip tree in front, cleared around the house. Trimmed willow by carriage house & the pine over garage. Finished contracted work. Meeting with August Chimney Sweeps. They will get back with a price to clean flues, rebuild tops of chimney, in about 2 weeks. Renaldo cleaned attic. Ross replaced floorboards in attic. Called Armor Wood Roof, talked to service. Heat men came. John installed windows in kitchen. Tom worked on doors. Terry worked on windows. Floorboard replaced in laundry room. New header installed in sun porch.

1/22 Drove to Monroe to look at an old house being demolished to try to find glass. Got name of Richard Kenny. Phoned to find out if glass was for sale. Took sample of glass back. Worked on windows with Terry. Heat men here. Ross made a hole in basement wall for kitchen heat ducts. John cutting out new back window for bedroom off sitting room. Tom sick.

1/25 Talked to Richard Kenny re glass—sample too green. Called Consumers Petroleum about refilling propane tanks. Went to Pella re windows & doors for screen porch. Rough electrical inspection obtained. No heat men today. Terry continued window restoration. Tom patched holes in floors where radiators stood. Ross sick. John framed in upstairs window.

1/26 Snowed. George went to Bridgeport to look at glass. Did not find any. Took Terry up to Monroe—stripped out all window sashes & separated glass from the sash. Electrician & heat men here. John framing in doors in new large window in back bedroom. Tom patching floors.

1/27 Called R. Bohemus at Rings End to find out price for back window for bedroom off sitting room. Called R. Kenny to arrange payment for glass ($300). Called Clearview Glass to find out pricing on screened porch—no one there. Cut up floor patching material for Tom. Discussed lighting arrangements for porch with Steve. Heat men & electrician here. Terry working on windows. Tom working on patching floors. John working on doorjambs on 2nd floor. Ross sick.

1/28 Worked on door frames in bedroom off sitting room. Made frame for back bedroom closets. Terry continued work on window restoration. Ross sick. Heat men here. Spoke to suppliers re chestnut flooring.

1/29 Harry Hulse stopped by to inspect progress on heating system. Requested 2nd payment. John working on the walls in the back room. Terry reconditioning windows. Ross sick. George called Coastal Woodworking to schedule meeting to look at cabinets.

1/30 Electrician working. George checked-in.

2/1 Ordered blueboard. Ross primed outside trim, worked on the fireplace. Tom finished floor patching. Terry still on windows.

2/2 Ross worked on basement walls for duct work for heating system. Tom worked on straightening walls. Drywall people scheduled delivery for Thursday. George visited K Mart in Stratford to research tool for the house. Ross began insulating the kitchen. Sheetrock delivered a day early. George worked on restoring the windows. Saw sample of chestnut flooring & decided against it. Chose clear yellow pine instead. Al Sherman stopped by to give an estimate on clearing the lot of debris. Terry continued work on windows.

2/4 Ross, Tom & John insulating upstairs. Called Armor Wood Roof for estimate for all buildings. Called August West Chimney to follow up on quote. Called Pella Windows re storm windows on porch.

2/5 Blueboarded upstairs ceilings. Followed up on window orders. Work continued on insulating. Armor Wood Roof gave verbal quote of $9,100 on house $5,200 on garage carriage house. Window restoration continued.

2/6 Larry, Rita & I met & went out to look at bathroom fixtures. Rita, Larry & George met with Coastal Woodworking to look at examples of their work. Were very impressed.

2/8 Ross, Tom & John installing Sheetrock all week. Terry working on windows all week. R, R & Pedro scraped paint all week. Children's bedroom insulated. Followed up on quotes for windows & on written quote for kitchen cabinets. Researched skylights. Called Finlia Floor Refinishers for quote.

2/12 Ordered flooring for kitchen & children's bedroom.

2/15 Called Shimko Fireplace for chimney repair quote. Called Stamford Insulation for quote on insulating ceiling above middle children's bedroom. Tom & John sheetrocking library walls & front parlor ceilings. Terry on windows. Renaldo, Renato & Ross scraping paint. Plumbers continued roughing in kitchen & children's bathroom.

2/16 Building inspector gave rough plumbing inspection. Ordered Brosco windows for wall between kitchen & porch from West End Lumber. Marvin ordered doors & windows for porch kitchen from Clearvue. Went to town hall for plot plans. John Ross sheetrocking children's bedroom. Terry working on windows. R, R, R scraping paint. Tom straightening walls.

2/22 Terry on vacation for 2 weeks. Ross out—his truck was broken into. John & Tom sheetrocked children's bathroom. Dominick patching in small areas with Sheetrock. Vinyl pans installed in all showers. R, R, R prepping for painting. John sheetrocked ceiling in old bathroom. Paint arrived from Sherwin Williams.

2/23 Ross out. John & Terry sheetrocking bathrooms, John installing durrock on shower walls. Rita ordered bathroom fixtures from Waterworks. Rita visited Standard Tile in Fairfield to research white tile for bathrooms.

2/24 John continued durrock work in showers. Tom working on sheetrocking master bathroom. Ross on other job. Dominick working on the window restoration. R, R, R sanding woodwork to prep for paint.

2/25 John continued durrock work in laundry room bathroom. Plasterer started work in master bath. Ross on other job. Dominick restoring windows. R, R, R stripping wallpaper in bedroom off sitting room. Renato priming windows. Heating contractors finishing up installation of heating system. Rita researched kitchen appliances at Aitoro & Klaffs. Aimee picked up paint sample cards for meeting with Sherwin Williams.

2/26 Met with Rita & GE lighting people to discuss lighting layout for house. George counted switches & outlets needed for house as well as downlights. R., R, R stripping paint & wallpaper in upstairs bedroom. Renato prepping windows. Dominick glazing windows. Plasterer working on children's bathroom.

2/29 Met with Rita, Alexis, Michael & Shari from Sherwin Williams to discuss colors for house & for special line of Dutch Boy paints. Plasterer working on back children's room. Dominick refinishing windows. R, R, R working on stripping paint in downstairs library. Renato stripping windows. John working on outside trim. Tom working on stripping outside siding off back kitchen wing to prepare for new window in children's room.

3/7 Plasterer continued work on upstairs bedrooms. John & Terry laying out & framing in skylights. Dominick worked on window restoration. Renato helped Patsy repair cracks. Tom sick. Ross on another job.

3/8 Tom applying new siding to back kitchen wall. John & Terry repairing rot on roof over laundry room & sun porch. Dominick worked on windows. Patsy finished bedroom off sitting room & repaired cracks. Scraping of woodwork continued downstairs.

3/9 John & Terry repairing roof. Dominick: window restoration. Scraping of woodwork continued on doors off kitchen. Plasterer began work on master bedroom. Renato continued to plaster cracks in old bathroom.

3/10 Dominick restoring windows. John & Terry repairing roof in preparation for skylight installation. Patsy rough coating master bedroom.

3/11 John, Terry & Tom working on the roof above laundry room. New drains installed. Tom repairing rot on overhang above porch roof. Dominick working on windows. Scraping of woodwork & filling in of cracks in plaster continued. Patsy continued to work on master bedroom.

3/14 Video film day. Crew filmed me walking through each room downstairs, explaining what is being done now & how I envision it to look when finished. John, Terry & Tom working on roof. Dominick working on windows in upstairs hall. Scraping of woodwork continued. Meeting with Coastal woodwork on first pass of kitchen plans. Changes made—island made wider, wine rack above refrigerator removed, bookshelf nest to kitchen sink added on corner cabinet, right window seat removed.

3/15 John & Terry working on roof, Dominick on windows, Renato on repairing plaster walls.

3/16 Dominick replacing all window stops. John, Terry & Tom working on trim & laying out skylights. Patsy working on hall. Aitoro (Rocky) came to discuss appliances for kitchen.

3/17 John off. Tom, Terry & George working on roof & trim. Plasterer working on east bedroom, Renato on plaster wall repair.

3/18 Tom trimming out windows & doors. Plaster working on east bedroom. Dominick working on replacing window stops. Scraping of woodwork continued in west parlor. Met with Rita & Coastal Woodworking to discuss revised kitchen drawings & gave approval for fabrication to begin.

3/21 Dominick repairing windows, sashes, stops. Working on front door windows. Renaldo working on stripping wallpaper off west parlor wall. Woodwork stripped in west parlor. Patsy finishing up east bedroom & rough coated old bathroom. Plumbers finished rough plumbing in old bathroom. Put gas line in under kitchen for oven. John sheetrocking old bathroom wall. Tom replacing trim in master bedroom & bathroom.

3/22 George & Terry making moldings for all rooms. Plaster repairs made in back stairs. Worked on closet between east parlor & library. West parlor next. Dominick working on front door windows. Renaldo stripping wall paper off east parlor. Woodwork stripped in east parlor. Wall at head of stairs sheetrocked & rough plastered. John beginning flooring in back children's bedroom.

3/23 Plasterer rough coating library. Dominick working on front door windows. Tom repairing rot in garage. Terry working on moldings for windows. John framing doors leading from dining room to porch.

3/24 John & Patsy off. Tom & Dominick repairing garage.

3/28 John framing in interior porch doors & windows. Terry cut down transoms & framed transom windows. Dominick replacing rotten garage beams. Tom working on upstairs overhangs for gutter. Renato scraping old paint on front stairs. Old rug removed & discarded. Rita met with Terminex for estimate on treatment of ants.

3/29 Terry finished reworking transom windows & continued to work on trim in upstairs. Dominick continued rot removal in garage area. Garage doors removed so new posts could be installed to replace ones damaged by powder post beetles & dry rot. North East Exterminators came to give inspection & quotation on termite & powder post beetle control. Tom working on trim. John making trim for exterior.

3/30 Masons·began repair of chimneys. Removed all old brick on one chimney, others to be removed & new brick to be installed. Plaster finishing final coat of plaster in library. Dominick working on garage restoration, Terry working on trim. Tom knocked out old brick in fireplace in office.

3/31 Masons continued work on chimneys. Patsy working on rough coating of front parlor. Dominick repairing garage. John hanging doors. Terry—trim. Tom resupported hearth stone in office fireplace—helped Dominick with garage repair.

4/1 Good Friday. Masons worked a few hours lifting brick onto roof. Plasterer worked for a few hours on east parlor.

4/4 Tile men arrived. Will start cement floors. Masons working on chimney—will continue their work while weather holds. Plasterer working on parlor. Tom & Dominick working on garage. Must strip it out so building can be straightened & resupported. John hanging doors. Also nailed off old bathroom floor so that tile men could pour cement floor. Terry installed casings on closets. R, R, R, scraping floors. Sherwin Williams paint mixer delivered.

(continued on page 140)

DEMOLITION

Almost all renovations require some demolition. In the case of the Adams house, we replaced rotted sills and beams, opened up several small rooms to make the kitchen, moved walls to accommodate new bathrooms, and pulled out deteriorating plaster ceilings. At one point I felt as if the whole house was under siege!

Workmen use anything from sledge-hammers and crowbars to picks. The contractor seals off the demolition area with walls made from tarpaulins, plastic sheets, or plywood—whatever works best for the particular situation. Protec-

LEFT: With the plaster torn down from this ceiling, George uses his claw hammer to remove thousands of small handmade nails from the ceiling joists. Demolition is messy, creating an enormous amount of debris. As plaster dust permeates the air and splinters and nails fly in every direction, workers must wear protective clothing. George's winter work clothes include a helmet and mask, plus his work belt. The belt weighs about 22 pounds and usually contains a claw hammer, a punch, a cat's paw, a pry bar, a hive tool, snips, a screwdriver with several bits, a razor knife, two nail sets, a compass, a pencil, rulers, a tape measure, and chalk.

RIGHT: Another example of the sad wallpaper we found in the house; it and the plaster peeled off the lath. After pulling off the rest of the plaster and removing the lath, we resurfaced the entire wall with blueboard.

tive sheeting is also laid down so the floors are not damaged in the process.

At the end of every workday, the contractor makes sure that debris is hauled off to the Dumpster—not only for neatness' sake, but also to help him ascertain what remains to be done.

Of all the rooms in the house, the one most in need of repair was the library. For decades, it had been used as a bedroom and, in Miss Adams's time, as a storage room. A leak in the roof had caused water to seep in under the roofline and through the walls. The corner of the room had rotted away entirely from moisture. Because water damage was so severe, all the corner framing as well as the plaster and lath had to be replaced. Several floorboards in the corner of the room also had to be replaced; we salvaged some from another room because they matched perfectly. Oddly enough, the baseboard was in fine shape.

Certain parts of the area you are tearing down may be worth saving. Before demolition began, I tagged everything I wanted salvaged: beautiful old windows and doors, pieces of molding and trim— whatever I could reuse in some way, even if the piece was only going to be copied.

If a load-bearing wall (one supporting part of the house) has to be removed, that load must be transferred to temporary supports, usually jack posts, to avoid placing undue pressure on the rest of the house. Indeed, without support, some or all of the house could collapse. All exterior walls are load bearing. Inside, partitions running parallel to the length of the house are those that usually carry the load.

Joists rest on, or run perpendicular to, load-bearing walls; a look at the loose joists in your basement or attic will reveal which walls are load bearing.

When any or all of an exterior wall is to be removed, temporary supports are erected just inside the wall; when an interior load-bearing wall is to come down, supports are erected on both sides of the old wall to ensure that the floor system above remains stable. Framed shoring is positioned on either side of the bearing wall to be removed, allowing a good 4 feet of safe working space.

If the removal of all or part of a wall is to be permanent, the opening is spanned by a "header," or beam, constructed of heavy wood or steel. It is supported by large posts or double studs at either end of the opening. If the wall marked for removal contains plumbing or electrical lines, these lines have to be rerouted so they are not severed or damaged when they are exposed.

Demolition occurs in stages, from the outside in. First, anything that is to be saved is removed, such as hardware, trim, millwork, windows, and doors. Then plaster, plasterboard, or paneling is taken down, and any insulation is removed. Finally, exposed framing is dismantled, if necessary.

When the inner workings of an old house are exposed by demolition, problems may suddenly be revealed. Old newspapers, sun-dried brick, cloth, or hay may have been packed in behind the walls as insulation. Animals such as mice or squirrels might have nested there, or insects such as carpenter ants, termites, or powder post beetles that destroy wood by eating or nesting in it. The presence of bugs is a signal to call in an exterminator for an examination and possibly a thorough fumigating.

FRAMING A WALL

Prior to framing in any new walls in an old house, all ceilings and floors must be checked to see if they are level. In old houses like Turkey Hill Farm and this one, they rarely are. An angle of one-quarter or one-half inch can be ignored and new framing is easily adjusted to compensate. A serious sag indicates a structural defect such as a rotted beam; often the cause is a foundation that has settled unevenly over the years, requiring structural work.

Framing lumber should be kiln-dried and perfectly straight. The contractor should weed out any warped lumber, because a bowed stud will show through plasterboard. Small, tight knots won't weaken the lumber, but larger knots could loosen in their holes and cause a structural failure.

LEFT: After demolition, new interior walls were framed in to define additional necessary spaces such as this first-floor bathroom. We used 2-by-4 studs for all new construction. They are usually placed on 16-inch centers, but some of the unusual configurations in this house required slight departures from the norm. Doorways, for example, were not built to the standard height typical of newly built houses. Instead, we matched up our new openings with the beautiful old box-paneled doors existing in the house and used them again.

RIGHT: As each stud is raised into position, it is toenailed into a bottom plate already attached to the floor.

The universal choice for framings is softwood, because it is economical and strong. In northern New England, spruce is popular, but Douglas fir is the usual softwood of choice elsewhere. Most framing is contructed from 2-by-4s that actually measure 1½ x 3½ inches, based upon how the board has been dressed at the mill.

A section of framing consists of two 2-by-4s: a bottom, or sole plate or "shoe," and the other a top plate, with vertical 2-by-4 studs braced between them. The plates are nailed against the floor and ceiling; the studs span the distance between them at intervals of 16 inches, from the center of one stud to the center of the next (actual air space between studs is 14½ inches).

The studs are fastened to the plates with 8d (8-penny or 2½-inch) common wire nails driven at an angle, or "toe-nailed," through each stud. Two nails on one side and one on the other lock each stud at top and bottom. Many workmen preassemble sections of framing on the floor, then lift them into place. Using this method, 16d (3½ inches) nails can be driven directly through each plate into the studs. However, in an old house like

mine, in which no walls are plumb and the ceiling beams are not at perfect right angles, this method was not an option.

If framing is to extend at right angles from a finished wall faced with drywall board, the same technique is used. If walls, ceilings, and floor are plumb, the carpenter usually preassembles the new section and places it in position against the wall. The section can be joined to the wall with construction adhesive or with toggle or molly bolts. Mollies have flexible metal arms that swing open and hold the new framing fast once the bolt has punctured the drywall. The last step is toenailing top and sole plates to the existing wall.

It takes three studs to frame an outside corner. Two of these, set 1½ inches apart with spacer blocks, finish off the end of one wall; the third stud finishes off the end of the adjoining wall.

Framing out a door is more complex. First the doorway location is determined, and the door width and jamb thickness

are marked off on the floor; an allowance for adjustments, ¾ inch per side, is also indicated. Guided by these marks, 2-by-4 studs are nailed on either side of the planned opening, creating the basis for a frame. These "jack studs," or "trimmers," will support the horizontal "header" beam that is nailed on top of them. The header spans the space directly above the door, transferring the structural weight bearing down on it across to the jacks, then down to the floor. Next to the jacks, and nailed to them firmly, is a second pair of studs. When secured to the top and bottom plates, they will ensure the door frame's rigidity.

Sometimes short studs called "cripples" are used to fill in large openings above the header.

When the doorway's rough opening is finally complete, the bottom plate is cut away. Usually it is replaced by a "saddle," or threshold, after the door itself has been installed and the flooring sanded and finished.

LEFT: **A speed square is used to make an angle or square cuts on a joist. Any angle can be accurately drawn by adjusting this tool to a specified mark.**

ABOVE RIGHT: **A metal plumb bob is dropped on a string to mark vertical measurements. This is another old-fashioned tool of the building trade.**

REPLACING THE WIRING

Unless an antique house has been rewired recently by a licensed electrician, it probably needs a thorough inspection and a complete rewiring. Miss Adams made do with the minimum: a single bare bulb hung from each ceiling of the few rooms she used; her kitchen was equipped with two appliances: an outdated range and a small refrigerator. Naturally I wanted the remodeled house to accommodate a full array of appliances and electronics and a security system.

When the old wiring was torn out, we found that it was extremely primitive and patched in a rather unprofessional and seriously dangerous fashion. The material used was called BX cable, installed in the 1930s. We also discovered single wires, cloth-covered and frayed, which were totally defunct by the time we began our restoration. The electrical contractor installed 40 circuit breakers, which he thought sufficient for the size of the house and for the projected usage. Standard duplex outlets were used, placed according to code, and GFIC (ground-fault interrupter circuit) outlets were installed where required in bathrooms and for outdoor use. We put covered outlets outdoors where we thought they might be needed; they are useful if you have machines for hedge clipping and leaf blowing and appliances for outdoor entertaining.

The installation in new walls was a simple matter: the lines were run from the central panel to each room along framing members. But where the parti-

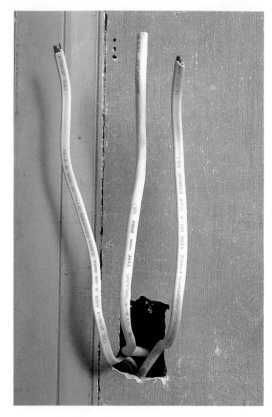

tion walls were left intact, installation was tedious and time consuming. The electrical contractor first cut small wall openings where the switches and plug outlets would be installed. Then, descending to the basement, he had to locate the existing partition walls. After drilling a hole into the wall cavity behind each switch and outlet location, he fed wires up through the hole to those wall openings. Because the entire house was being wired, we could opt for the convenience of having two breaker switch boxes: one in the basement, to serve the first floor; the other in the attic, tied to the second floor.

AMPS, VOLTS, AND WATTS: The minimum power needs for a single-family residence in 1935 was 30 amps; today, an electric range uses at least as much. To make sure the new system could comfortably serve present and future needs, I requested a 200-amp service.

An amp, or ampere, is a measure of flow of electricity through a wire. The flow is pushed by pressure, which is measured in volts; most electrical appliances need only a moderate push of 115/120 volts to operate, but large appliances such as clothes dryers and air conditioners need more, usually 220/240 volts. Volts (the push) times amps (the flow) equals watts (or power). A 100-watt light bulb on a 115/120 volt, 15-amp circuit, for instance, requires less

LEFT: **Virtually all the Adams house wiring was replaced by Romex wire, an insulated wire wrapped in plastic casing that is the basic industry standard. Here, emerging from a wall opening, is a trio of Romex rough wires: the three-wire, which links two switches so light can be turned on or off from two sites in a room; a two-wire, which will power the light from a switch; and a feeder, which is linked to the house's main circuit box that supplies electricity to all lights, switches, and plugs. The importance of having an excellent licensed electrician do the work in a house like this cannot be overemphasized.**

RIGHT: **Sconces, switches, and controls for sound systems, TV sets, and computers are linked by wire to receptacle boxes like this one. They can be either metal or plastic, depending on the type of wiring you use, and installed in walls or woodwork. Some receptacle boxes are made with knock-out sides so they can be enlarged if greater capacity is ever needed.**

than 1 amp: 0.83. A central air conditioner at 5,000 watts on a 220/240 volt, 30-amp line draws about 21 amps. A 7,000 BTU window unit draws 3.64 amps.

Appliances requiring little power, such as lamps, are attached to 15-amp general-use circuits, and larger ones, such as a central air conditioner, to a 30-amp individual, dedicated circuit. An electric range usually retains a 50-amp circuit, and a microwave, a 20-amp circuit. As a rule, the number of 15-amp general-use circuits is computed by house size. Two circuits are allocated to the first 500 square feet of floor area; add one circuit for each additional 500 square feet. By code, a kitchen must have at least two 20-amp circuits.

WIRING: There are three wires (nearly always copper) inside the plastic cable designated for 115/120 volt circuits: a black, or "hot," wire that carries electricity to the fixture or appliance; a white, or "neutral," wire that completes the circuit from the appliance back to the entrance panel; and a bare wire (sometimes sheathed in green plastic) that is the grounding—a safety measure to divert any stray electricity harmlessly to the ground. Inside cable carrying 220/240 volts for three- and four-way switches, a second "hot" wire, sheathed in red plastic, joins the other three wires.

Some electrical codes still insist on armored cable, wiring protected by a flexible steel covering. Armored cable can be used only indoors and in dry locations because the spiral construction of its metal sheathing is not waterproof.

In old houses, utility wiring passed through a meter and then enters the

house through a fuse box, usually located in either the basement or the kitchen, before fanning out to outlets throughout the house. The circuits were intercepted by 15- and 30-amp glass-topped fuses with a fusible metal filament inside each. An electrical overload caused the wire inside the glass fuse to break, or "blow." Identifying a burned-out fuse often required removing each one to determine which circuit was blown; because this can be hazardous, many codes no longer allow fuse boxes. Instead, wiring, which still passes through a meter, is now channeled through a circuit breaker panel, also likely to be mounted in the basement or in or near the kitchen. If overload occurs, the circuit breaker switch flips off. The circuit is reset by flipping the switch back on. Each

115/120 volt circuit is controlled by one switch; 220/240 volt circuits require two. Label each circuit for easy identification, leaving room for extra circuits in case new lines need to be added.

Once the electrical wiring is installed, or "roughed in," and before the wall is closed in, an inspection is made to be sure everything is up to code.

OUTLETS: Wall outlets are installed at least once every 12 feet along a wall; 12 feet is the maximum distance between outlets allowed by the national electric code. For convenience, outlets are usually positioned about a foot above the floor. They should be fitted with protectors, or caps, that can be flipped down to prevent small children from inserting objects into the openings. Wall switches should be installed at least 4 feet from the floor, out of reach of small children. Light switches should be convenient to every entry, to the top and bottom of every set of stairs, and to specific applications, such as kitchen countertops, where it also makes sense to install outlets every 4 feet to serve small appliances, such as a microwave oven. At my house on Turkey Hill, an electrician placed each light switch behind the open door to each room. It is utterly inconvenient and after 20 years I still have not had this mistake remedied.

All outlets in the kitchen, pantry, laundry or utility room, and bathrooms should be connected to ground-fault interrupter circuits, otherwise known as GFICs, to prevent serious injury from an electric shock. The national electrical code states that any outlet within 6 feet of a sink, bathtub, or toilet must be fitted with a GFIC; however, no switch or outlet should be placed within 3 feet or arm's reach of the tub. Most convenience switches are three-way and operate a lamp from two places, at the door and inside the room.

LIGHTING is generally categorized three ways: ambient, task, and mood.

General, or ambient, lighting is often provided by an overhead fixture combined with lighting from other sources—wall lights or standing lamps. If there is no overhead fixture, wall fixtures and/or lamps offer general illumination.

Task lighting concentrates illumination on specific areas where specific functions are performed. Task lighting can be supplied by spotlights, or by lamps in locations near a chair or a desk.

Mood lighting is generally achieved by using dimmers, or rheostats, on existing lamps and fixtures, or on specialized lighting installed on the ceilings, walls, or floors.

The national electric code also covers smoke detection. The code insists that at least one smoke detector should be installed on each floor of a residence. A smoke detector should not be installed too close to any source of smoke or

LEFT: A "two-gang" switch box is double-size with room for more than one switch or receptacle. This one has a plaster ring so that it can be installed in a plaster wall.

RIGHT: Four wires—a Romex two-wire, a Romex three-wire, a cable TV wire, and a telephone wire—all carefully attached to the post-and-beam frame with a staple gun and wire staples.

steam, nor should they be installed at the juncture of a wall and ceiling that is bypassed by the natural flow of air currents. Best locations are the ceilings or upper walls of central hallways, both upstairs and down.

SECURITY SYSTEM: Installing a security system is a wise step today. Most systems have battery back-up in case of power outages. If electrical wiring is exposed during renovation, a security system is easily "hard-wired," or connected with standard cable the same way fixtures and appliances are wired. Otherwise, the wiring must be snaked through wall cavities. A new option eliminates wires altogether. This system connects equipment throughout the house by radio signals.

To warn of the outbreak of fire, the security system can be tied to the smoke

alarms located throughout the house. As a safeguard against burglary, all accessible windows and doors should be protected with electronic devices that sense any attempt to pry them open.

Other devices often added to a system include radio-wave motion detectors that detect the presence of an intruder in a room, electronic pressure pads strategically positioned on the floors, outdoor floodlights that automatically turn on at dusk and off at daybreak, and electronically released, prerecorded, predialed calls for help to police and fire stations. Controls are usually placed near the front entry and are set with a numerical code. A 24-hour monitoring service, connected to the police or fire station, may be available, too, at a cost of between $25 and $50 per month.

Updating the Plumbing

The plumbing in the Adams house was totally outmoded. Because she lived alone, Miss Adams needed only one bathroom. I wanted five, three upstairs and two down.

To save money when new baths are incorporated into an old house, it's best to "stack" them, one above the other so that water pipes can be shared. The least expensive plan, of course, puts all plumbing fixtures—for the kitchen, the laundry, and baths—on the same stack. The price for installation goes up when long piping runs from fixtures to the stack, or when a second stack must serve baths in remote locations, such as at the end of a bedroom wing.

Before investing in new baths, check to see whether the house is served with enough water pressure to accommodate existing needs as well as any additional fixtures. Between 40 and 50 pounds per square inch (or "psi") of water pressure is sufficient for the average home. A municipal water main generally delivers pressure within those amounts. If pressure in the main exceeds 50 psi, the water company may install a water reducer at the point where the water enters the house; excess pressure could damage some pipes.

Most cases of inadequate water pressure occur in homes served by wells that pump water to a holding tank. Maximum pressure is produced for the house when the tank is full, because supply lines are located near the bottom of the tank where pressure is greatest. Therefore, a

ABOVE: **Art Kier, now retired, did all the furnace connections in cast iron and copper. The hot water storage tank, which is part of the furnace, is also a circular that keeps hot water supplied "on demand" to all faucet locations in the house. This is a very luxurious feature, one I wish I had everywhere—no waiting for hot water.**

BELOW: **Solder for copper and brass fixtures and pipes is melted with a small hand-held propane torch.**

holding tank needs to be large enough to meet the needs of your family, with a pump strong enough to keep the tank as full as possible at all times.

Standards for water production from wells are established by states. In Connecticut, a well 100 feet deep should produce 5 gallons per minute for up to four hours. If the well pump falls short of state standards, a new, more powerful submersible pump should bring up the amount of water needed, so long as water underground, called the "aquifer," is available.

Updating the plumbing in an old house often means replacing worn fixtures, installing fixtures in new and existing bathrooms, replacing laundry and kitchen sinks, and adding a dishwasher, and clothes washer, pantry or bar sinks, as well as outside faucets for garden hoses and sprinklers.

It is also the plumber who installs the piping for hot water lines to baseboard radiators and to the domestic water heater that should be sized correctly to serve the whole family. In all cases of plumbing that involves electric hook-ups, a licensed electrician must make the power connections.

All piping used in a residence must be approved by the local building code. Small-diameter pipes (¼- to 1-inch inside diameter, called supply pipes) deliver the supply of hot and cold water. To accommodate a large volume of water, such as that emptying from a bathtub, the inside diameter of wastewater piping ranges from 1½ to 3 inches.

Four choices of piping are possible:
COPPER: Long-lasting, corrosion-resis-

tant rigid- or flexible-tube copper piping is considered the best choice by most plumbing contractors because it is accepted universally by local building codes for hot and cold water lines. It can be used for wastewater lines as well.

POLYVINYL CHLORIDE: Specified for cold water supply and wastewater pipes, PVC is inexpensive, easy to install, and corrosion resistant.

CHLORINATED POLYVINYL CHLORIDE: Permitted by codes to serve hot and cold water supply lines, CPVC pipe is usually specified only for hot water lines because it costs more than PVC pipe. Adhesives need 24 hours to set before CPVC pipe is used.

CAST IRON: The material of choice for wastewater pipes, durable cast iron is normally specified for the lines outside the house leading to a municipal sewer, septic tank, or cesspool. It is also widely specified for indoor wastewater pipes and meets most building codes. Cast-iron piping also masks the noise of water passing through better than any other type of material.

RIGHT: Ricky Renzulli in the basement making sweat-joint connections with silver solder and a torch. Lead drinking water pipes have been outlawed in most states, and plumbers use copper now for water-line connections and heat connections. The support posts, installed after the cellar floor had been dug out and evened, are rough-sawn 6-by-6 native fir. They were set on poured concrete bases that had pads of pressure-treated wood.

HEATING AND COOLING

I don't know when the oil burner in the Adams house was installed, but it was certainly many years ago, and it probably was the first heating system to replace the wood burning stoves. Heating and cooling equipment has improved markedly since the beginning of this century, and even over the past ten years. I took the opportunity to install the latest heating and cooling technology, which required all-new equipment and new ductwork.

Heating, ventilating, and air-conditioning, known in the trade as HVAC, is handled by a special subcontractor. We consulted with Harry Hulse, Inc., heating contractors and decided on a forced-air system, which could be fueled by gas or oil. We chose gas because it enabled us to vent through the side of the house (like a dryer), eliminating the need to vent through the chimney flue as the old

LEFT: These are transition outlets designed to go from round feeder ducts to rectangular outlets. Using stock items saves money in designing a system, yet sometimes special items must be custom-built. The rectangular hole in the floor is a "supply"; it was covered with a pierced cast-iron grille from the Reggio Register Company. Grilles are fabricated in many different materials and in regular or custom sizes. Steel, iron, aluminum, and brass are common materials used. I recently have seen beautiful wooden grilles that look like part of the floor when installed.

system did. The fireplace in the office had been bricked up; we were able to knock out the brick and reclaim it. Before our new forced-air system could be installed, the old oil furnace had to be removed along with all the iron radiators and cast-iron pipes. The contractor installed a high-efficiency gas boiler in a newly prepared area of the basement designed especially for it.

Ours was a customized system utilizing two air handlers, one of which was installed in the basement, the other in the attic. The hot water boiler supplies water to the air handlers through a fixture resembling an automobile radiator, which heats the air that is then forced through the system by a fan. The heated air travels through the insulated ducts to floor registers, where it is released into the rooms of the house. The attic unit does essentially the same thing but forces the air through ceiling registers. During the summer months, the same system is used for air-conditioning.

A well-designed heating/cooling system is quiet and efficient and disturbs as little floor space as possible. There are basically two types of systems:

FORCED HOT AIR: In this system, the furnace and air-conditioning units are housed separately but use the same ductwork to deliver heated or cooled air to each room. The heating aspect is fueled by electricity, gas, or oil, and the cooling by electricity or gas. Air is heated when it passes through a heat exchanger (piping exposed to a heat source). When the heated air leaves the exchanger, it travels, by the force of a furnace fan, through ducts to room diffusers. For cooling to

ABOVE: The duct work for the heating and cooling system, made of aluminum, was very neatly fitted between ceiling joists and wall studs. These systems now take up so little room that one is barely aware of their existence.

occur, a cooling coil, or evaporator, is mounted at the point where the supply duct leaves the furnace and cools the air returning from the rooms. The cooled air is forced by the furnace fan into the duct system. As in the self-contained cooling systems, the condenser is located outside the house.

HEAT PUMP: Operated by electricity, a heat pump works like a reversible air conditioner. In summer, it functions like a normal air conditioner. There is an evaporator unit attached to the ductwork inside that releases cool air throughout

the house and a condenser outside that ejects warm air outside. In winter, the system reverses itself. The evaporator inside becomes a condenser, squeezing heat from the cold outside air, and the condenser outside becomes an evaporator expelling cold inside air to the outside. At a certain point below freezing, however, the pump can no longer extract heat, so it must be supplemented with an electric resistance heating element, which looks like the coil in an electric baseboard heater and which automatically turns on.

Both systems deliver air to the house through rectangular sheet-metal or fiberglass ducts. Metal ducts are conductive and can lose heat to the air around them, so to save energy they are often lined with insulation, especially when the ductwork travels a long distance. Nonconductive fiberglass ducts are energy efficient as installed.

The ductwork leads to floor-mounted diffusers, which are rectangular metal plates with a series of fins to direct the flow of air. Most diffusers are located near outside walls beneath windows or glass doors because these areas are most susceptible to heat loss in winter or heat gain in summer.

Installing diffusers in first-floor rooms requires little effort, only cutting and fitting in the floors to meet the ductwork immediately underneath. Getting ducts to higher floors, however, may necessitate some demolition to run through a corner offset or a closet, and between second-floor joists to second-level floor diffusers. Temperature is controlled by thermostats that are installed on inside

walls (so they aren't triggered by outside temperatures) about 4 feet off the floor.

Since hot air rises, heated air flows naturally through the diffusers at a slow rate, rising to the ceiling and gradually filling the room. Cooled air enters at a faster rate, propelled by the heating/cooling fan in a stream toward the ceiling where it descends naturally to fill the room. Return-air grilles draw house air back into the system for reconditioning. Most new systems utilize zoned heating and cooling. Specified spaces, or zones, are cued in to independent thermostats; zones can be turned off altogether, or

kept at a minimally comfortable temperature when unoccupied.

There are two other heating options: HOT WATER HEATING: Fueled by oil, gas, or electricity, this system delivers heat through baseboard registers from piping rather than ducts.

BASEBOARD RADIANT/CONVECTIVE HEAT: Fueled by electricity, this system needs no ducts or pipes. Resistance wiring in the baseboard units creates the heat. Because cable is thin and relatively stiff, wiring can be snaked behind existing walls. This is an easier task than installing new pipes or ducts. Ther-

mostats can be tied to each room, facilitating energy conservation. However, electricity rates in some areas of the country make this kind of heating prohibitive. Radiant heating systems that use hot water and plastic tubing can now be purchased.

ABOVE: One of the heating contractors soldering a water line leading into the furnace. Installation of such equipment must be done by experienced professionals who are required to conform to strict building codes and practices.

INSULATING

Many old houses are drafty because they were never insulated. Sealing a house with insulation significantly reduces heat loss (and cold air leaking in) during cold days and heat gain when days are hot.

In order to assess the effectiveness of insulation materials, the air-conditioning, heating, and ventilating industry has devised a measure called an R-value. The letter R stands for resistance to heat transfer; the higher the R-value, the more effective the material. Ironically, it is the way air is trapped, or pocketed, that creates effective insulation. Because wood is a cellular material, it has natural air pockets. Softwood, the structural material for most houses, has a low R-value of 1.25 per inch.

There are several insulation materials in wide use:

FIBERGLASS: This is the most familiar insulation material; it is a woolly material made up of thousands of fibers that trap air in tiny pockets with an R-value of roughly 4.0 per inch. As an insulator, fiberglass is about 50 times as effective as stone. Fiberglass comes in three

forms: loose fill that looks like raw cotton; kraft-paper-faced blankets (sold in rolls, often with an aluminum-foil side as an option); and batts that are precut into so-called friction-fit sections. Loose fill is sprayed under controlled pressure into wall cavities and between attic floor joists. Blankets are cut to size and used sometimes in place of loose fill between attic floor joists or floor joists built over a crawl space. Batts measuring 15 by 92 inches fit between 8-foot-high studs on 16-inch centers. We used fiberglass insulation in the Adams house, installed according to code: 3½ inches, or R-11, for walls, and 6 inches, or R-19, for ceilings. For some ceilings, foil-faced sheathing was applied under the blueboard to maximize the R value of the underinsulated space.

MINERAL WOOL: Spun from a meltdown of slag, shale, and limestone and sometimes called "rock wool," this fibrous material resembles fiberglass, is installed the same way, and has similar R-values.

CELLULOSE: Made from finely chopped paper—often recycled newspaper—that has been chemically treated to resist fire and vermin, cellulose is sprayed under controlled pressure, like loose fill, into wall cavities or between attic floor joists. Its R-value is slightly less than that of fiberglass.

POLYSTYRENE AND POLYURETHANE: These two materials, produced of various plastics in the form of rigid foamboards, are ½- to 1-inch thick. They are often used to boost the R-value specified for walls in an old house, as well as for cathedral ceilings and foundations. Molded or expanded polystyrene boards

have an R-value between 3.6 and 4.4 per inch. A board produced by the extrusion process contains many more tiny cells, pushing the R-value up to 5.0 per inch. Polyurethane, which contains even more cells than extruded polystyrene, delivers R-values of between 5.6 and 6.3 per inch. Plastic insulation is also available as a canned foam resembling shaving cream. This material is handy for filling small cavities difficult or impossible to insulate any other way.

Insulation is installed by a specialist whose choice depends upon the community building code standards for R-values. Codes vary from region to region. Installers wear protective clothing, goggles, and respirator masks to avoid touching or ingesting any loose or flying particles when they work with sprayed or blown fiberglass or with mineral wool.

Because heat rises, resulting in a great loss of warmth through the roof, the most important area to insulate is the attic. Insulation is laid between floor joists in an unfinished attic or between roof rafters when the attic has flooring. Insulating an attic alone can generate energy savings of up to 30 percent. R-value requirements range from R-30 in cental and southern states and R-38 in the northern tier of states.

Outside walls, which require R-values of 19 in southern and central states and 21 in the north, are insulated with blankets or blown-in loose fill. To raise the R-value in an existing wall beyond what blown-in insulation alone can achieve, the interior walls must be removed so that foamboard can be installed between

STEPS TO TAKE BEFORE CLOSING IN THE WALLS

There is a very clear-cut method to constructing a space, and the chronology or sequence of steps is one that has become standard, based on common sense and building codes.

1. After all the 2-by-4s are in place and all the roughing in and framing complete, the plumbers install the pipes and water lines.

2. The electrician then guides his wiring throughout the space.

3. The wiring for the alarm and sound systems, plus the telephone and cable TV lines, are all installed.

4. All of this has to be inspected and clearance given before proceeding any further.

5. Once clearance has been obtained, insulation can be installed. For the Adams house, we used fiberglass insulation according to code: 3½ inches, or R-11, for walls, and 6 inches, or R-19, for ceilings. Tom applied foil-faced sheathing over blueboard to maximize the R-value.

the studs. The rest of the space is filled with fiberglass or mineral wool.

To protect the insulation outside wall framing from moisture damage, or "dry rot" (a fungus that thrives on moist wood), additional protection can be achieved in the form of a "vapor barrier." Dry rot occurs when condensation builds up as warm moist air on the inside of the house collides with cold air from outside. The easiest barrier to install is a polyethylene sheet fastened over exposed studs before drywall goes up. If the walls are already finished, and peeling exterior paint signals a moisture problem within, you can visit your dealer and purchase paint specially formulated to create a vapor barrier; apply it to interior walls before putting on the finish coat. Then, to be absolutely certain all moisture is sealed out, fit special foam sealers under any electrical face plates that are mounted on outside walls. These sealers will insure the integrity of the vapor barrier.

Because the main portion of the Adams house was originally constructed with no exterior sheathing behind the clapboard, we thought it inadvisable to add any fiberglass insulation here. Moisture penetrating the siding would collect in the fiberglass and rot the walls. We opted instead to insulate only those sections of the house where we found sheathing boards—the rear kitchen wing, the laundry, and parts of the first and second floors enclosed in the addition. Other spaces were filled with foam insulation. Because George was unable to gain access to the air space above the hall bedroom, an insulation company was called to blow in loose insulation. Com-

ABOVE: **We used foil-faced insulation between the studs and joists throughout the house. It is regulation to install such insulation with the foil moisture barrier facing the living area—here the foil is facing down and into the room. The drywall, blueboard, or plaster is applied over this insulation.**

petitive bids were received from three companies before contracting the work.

Air-leaking spaces around windows and doors are sealed with weatherstripping made of closed-cell plastic or rubber, foam-filled plastic tubing, metal, or fabric. Small crevices and cracks around the joints between windows and doors are packed with caulking compound, a

claylike material squeezed from a tube. Air leaks around electrical outlets and switches are closed with plastic foam, applied from a spray can. Energy savings here: 20 percent.

It seems impossible, but an insulated house may ultimately prove too air-tight. For indoor comfort and a healthy environment, a house should have a minimum of 0.5 air changes per hour. Normally, natural leaks in a house provide 1 to 3 changes an hour.

To help produce air changes, the insulation contractor may install a device called an air-to-heat exchanger. Operating on a low-wattage fan, the exchanger forces stale air outside the house while pulling in fresh air. A maze of baffles extracts the heat from the outgoing air to maintain indoor comfort, while allowing ventilation.

SOUNDPROOFING: Muffling sound between rooms increases the cost of a partition by 15 to 25 percent. None of the rooms in my house was specifically soundproofed, but the insulation George installed helped muffle sound traveling between rooms and between floors. Additionally, he packed insulation around the PVC plumbing pipes to prevent pipe noise from being heard in any part of the house. Engineers rate sound transmission with a figure called the Sound Transmission Class, or STC. An STC rating below 40 indicates moderate to poor sound-blocking performance; 40 to 50 STC is good; over 50 STC is considered excellent.

Insulating an interior wall in the same manner as an outside wall helps reduce sound transmission, providing a moder-

ate STC-38 rating. Half-inch-thick sound-deadening panels, such as Acoustiban, affixed to both sides of a partition and covered with half-inch drywall will raise the STC to 45.

To gain a top rating of STC-55, the contractor replaces the existing wall completely. First, extra-wide plates are nailed top and bottom. Then, every 16 inches on center, 2-by-4 studs are nailed on alternative sides of the plates, rather than all along one side.

This system of alternating studs breaks up direct transmission of sound to the rooms on either side of the wall. To further deaden the sound, 3 to 4 inches of insulation is stuffed between the studs and, finally, a double layer of half-inch drywall is attached to both sides of the wall. Because of the alternating studs, the width of a soundproofed wall consumes an extra 3 inches of floor space.

Incidentally, I have learned that an acoustical ceiling treatment by itself does not reduce sound traveling between floors. The only way to muffle sound from floor to floor is to remove the ceiling and insert 4 inches of fiberglass bat-

ting between the joists, and then to nail resilient metal channels 24 inches on center across the bottom of the joists. The channels break the connection between the joists and ceiling, thus interrupting the movement of the sound waves. Once the insulation and channels are in place, a new drywall ceiling can be constructed.

To reduce sound transmission from room to room, solid-core doors should be used instead of hollow-core doors and fitted with close-fitting thresholds.

To absorb sound within a room, one can install thick carpeting, preferably underlaid with a resilient pad and also with a layer of half-inch-thick particleboard.

Draperies and fabric wall hangings also absorb sound. And, of course, acoustical ceiling tiles can be applied. I did not opt for any of these solutions as they would have interfered with the historic look of the rooms.

ABOVE LEFT: Carpenter Tom Ball cut the foam insulation with a hand saw or with a circular electric saw. In a few places he used quite a bit of this material. The foam is wedged in place; except around the edges, no adhesive is necessary if it is cut to size and squeezed into place.

ABOVE CENTER: Tom cut 2-inch-thick R-max foam insulation to fit wall cavities under windows and in walls where there was no sheathing. He also used the R-max board in the ceilings where new construction was done, sometimes using an X-Acto knife to set a tight fit. Fiberglass batt insulation would not have been appropriate; foam is preferable because it will not retain moisture, which causes plaster and wood to rot.

ABOVE RIGHT: It's hard to imagine that in the 19th century the thin plaster and lath wall was protected from the weather by nothing but the siding. In all new construction, it is preferable to have sheathing or plywood installed under the siding in addition to the insulation.

STRIPPING PAINT AND WALLPAPER

I was lucky that very little had been done to the interior over the years. Most of the woodwork and walls had only two or three layers of paint, and in a few rooms, we found just two layers of wallpaper.

Walls and trim that have been stripped, cleaned, and sealed offer the best surface for applying new wallpaper or fresh paint. In many old houses, the decorative wood trim has been painted repeatedly over the years, usually with

LEFT: **Renato and Renaldo Abreu and their charming father, Pedro, visiting from his native Brazil, helped out with interior wall and trim preparation. The young men are my gardeners during the summer months and all-round handymen when it is too cold to garden. In three weeks, they scraped the peeling paint from the walls and sanded the window and door trim. They used mainly traditional hand methods with sharp scrapers of various sizes that can fit molding profiles and remove old finishes without damaging any fine detailing.**

The paper was so dry that most of it came off with a scraper. Even the paint was so old that it chipped off with very l ittle effort. Stripper was used on stubborn areas. Masks were worn to keep inhalation of plaster and paint dust to a minimum, as undoubtedly most of the paint used in the house contained lead. On very cold days, George provided space heaters to warm the rooms.

oil-based paint, until the fine detailing of the original millwork is often obscured completely.

To achieve a smooth surface, door and window casings, baseboard moldings, and other trim should be thoroughly rid of old paint—or any finish, even shellac—and primed before a new finish such as paint or stain is applied.

Removing old finish is achieved by first brushing on a special chemical solvent to loosen it, then carefully scraping and rubbing with steel wool or fine sandpaper to bare the original wood.

Because such solvents are usually toxic, it is best to have the work done by professionals. When applying these solvents, and particularly when sanding, they wear protective clothing, gloves, goggles, and respirators. They ventilate the work space with plenty of fresh air and keep the area free of matches and any other potentially combustible materials. However, there are now very good paint strippers that are effective and considered worker-safe. It is well worth asking about these when materials are purchased.

Paint remover is applied with a natural-bristle brush wide enough to cover the molding, and then left for about 10 or 15 minutes to soften the paint. The solvent usually penetrates only one or two layers at a time; several layers require multiple applications. Once the paint is softened, it can be scraped off in clumps with a putty knife. To reach crevices, a dental pick may be used. Accumulated paint is wiped off onto old newspapers or rags or plastic drop cloths for disposal.

Old paint containing lead—and most

ABOVE: **We were fortunate in that over the years very little had been done to the interior and most of the woodwork and walls had only two or three layers of paint. Likewise, we found a maximum of two layers of wallpaper. But every now and then something had been painted more heavily, necessitating the use of a heat gun to soften the paint for removal.**

paint over 15 years old does—is considered a hazardous material, so the contractor has to make arrangements for its safe disposal in a government-approved site. Lead-based paint should always be removed with solvents and never sanded

because of the risk of inhaling the lead-filled dust. If the old paint is only one layer thick and in good condition, the painter may simply wash it down with water and a household cleaner such as Spic and Span to dull it, then apply the finish coat of paint right over it.

Once as much of the paint as possible is scraped off, the remaining bits can be removed with fine steel wool or a fine-grit sandpaper as long as a mask is used. When free of paint, the wood is given a final sanding with a very-fine-grit sandpaper to eliminate any raised grain in the wood and to provide a satiny surface. Residual wood dust is wiped off with a tack cloth, which is impregnated with a nondrying oil. A coat of primer is applied before the wood has a chance to dry out.

Professional painters prefer an alkyd-oil base coat as the primer for wood trim. The finish coat can be alkyd-oil, acrylic, or vinyl paint. While some professionals prefer top coats of latex paints, such as acrylic or vinyl-enamel, because they are easy to spread and dry quickly, most would rather work with an alkyd-oil top coat. It provides a smooth finish, washes without losing its glow, and is more chip-resistant than latex.

Trim that is stained or left natural can be waxed or finished with a clear polyurethane, which seals the wood and produces a tough, durable surface.

REMOVING WALLPAPER: In an old house, wall coverings, like paint, may have been applied one layer over the other through the years. There are several types of wall coverings, and the techniques for removing them vary slightly.

114

VINTAGE PAPER: Vintage wallpapers (and non-prepasted modern wallpapers) are removed with relative ease. The old paste is softened with a sprayed, enzyme-laden chemical remover or steam-generating machine still preferred by some professionals. Its long hose is attached to a handheld rectangular metal plate with a pinhole vent that releases the steam. Once the bond between paste and paper is weakened, the blade edge of a putty knife can be inserted beneath the paper to push it back into long curls, making it easy to tear off.

MODERN VINYL WALLPAPER: This paper is produced with a tough polyester fabric backing that resembles cheesecloth with a slightly tighter weave. Since backing and face are tightly bonded, an entire sheet can be stripped off the wall in one steady pull.

VINYL LAMINATED WALLPAPER: When removed, the vinyl face separates from the paper backing, leaving the backing firmly attached to the wall. A contractor may leave the paper attached as a cost-cutting measure, but it is preferable to remove the paper to avoid bubbles that may appear when paint or new paper is applied.

PLASTIC WALL COVERINGS: Produced from 1935 to 1965, these are neither strippable nor peelable, so they are harder to remove than any other wall coverings. To allow sprayed chemical removers or steam to reach the plaster through plastic covering, the worker dimples the material with hundreds of punctures by rolling the surface with a metal-point-studded roller. The covering is then removed like a vintage wallpaper.

ABOVE: **Because the house was unheated, the men scraping off the old wallpaper wore heavy gloves. Here, one of them pushes the dried-out paper, applied so many years before, right off the plaster wall. Steam or water is used to remove paper more strongly affixed to the wall.**

A plaster wall may be nicked in the process of stripping and tear-off, and in the case of very old walls, small clumps of plaster may come off. In both cases, the wall will have to be patched before new paint or paper can be applied. If a leak or other damage is discovered behind the wall covering, more radical repairs may be necessary.

If the wallpaper is attached to drywall, chemicals will loosen it without harming the drywall's protective paper facing. If steam is used, care should be taken not to hold the steamplate too close to the wall. If the protective paper does loosen, the drywall may have to be replaced.

To clean up residual paste after the wall covering has been removed, workers wash down the plaster or drywall with water and a standard household cleaner such as Spic and Span or Top Job. In the past, a mixture of trisodium phosphate, or TSP, and water was used, but today this solution is considered too caustic by the Environmental Protection Agency.

Once the cleansed wall is dry, it must be sealed before new wall covering is applied. In the past, a wall was sealed with "sizing," or glue mixed with water. Since sizing has been found incompatible with modern wall adhesives, an acrylic-resin binder is now brushed on instead.

STRIPPING SHUTTERS: A shutter is one of the most diffucult surfaces from which to remove paint. The Adams house shutters are louvered and were covered with so many layers of paint that the slats no longer pivoted. Because there was so much deterioration, total paint removal was impossible. The best George could do was go over the surfaces carefully with an electric disk sander, removing as much paint as possible. The shutters were then power washed and finally lightly sanded before priming and painting.

If the condition of the wood permits, the easiest and quickest way to remove paint is to take the shutters to a stripping specialist. A paint stripper, who charges by the piece, immerses each shutter in a huge vat containing a caustic solution that eats away the layers of paint. Once the paint is dissolved, the shutter is removed from the vat, washed, and dried. A light sanding is needed before repainting.

INSTALLING DRYWALL

For a historic home like this one, I initially felt that plaster walls and ceilings would be more appropriate than drywall. However, I didn't want us to take the time, or endure the many problems, of repairing or replacing all the old wood lath, which would have been necessary. So George chose a gypsum-based product called "blueboard," a type of drywall that comes in sheets and can be applied directly over old plaster walls and ceilings. Because a blueboard wall is covered by a thin coat of plaster, the effect is very similar to a real plaster wall. Every ceiling was done this way, covering the

LEFT: **Ross Bedard, left, and John Minnock are finishing the stairwell walls with blueboard, developed to replace the more expensive lath and wet plaster process or the less expensive Sheetrock method. We used blueboard to repair or replace plaster walls and ceilings throughout the house. Instead of pulling down the old plaster ceilings that were damaged but still secure, Ross and John nailed the blueboard directly to ceilings, taping and dual coating each surface prior to painting it.**

We left the old carpeting on the stair treads. I was often tempted to tear it off, but it offered the best protection for the wood, which would have suffered greatly from all the heavy traffic. We also covered mantel tops with heavy cardboard; floors were protected with thin sheets of gypsum board or plywood, and resin paper was used to cover all other surfaces.

117

old plaster. Most walls were left intact and merely repaired. New walls were blueboarded.

Before drywall can be applied, all the studs must be in place and deemed perfectly "true," or straight. Contractors use a process called "stringing the walls," or "sighting the studs," to determine straightness. Blocks of half-inch plywood are mounted at each corner, one at the top and another at the base of the frame. A nail is hammered into each block and string is tied from nail to nail. The string is pulled tight to indicate a straight line. If any section of wall behind the string is more, or less, than a half inch away, filler can be added or wood can be chipped off to correct for straightness. (Actually, the "sighting" process begins even earlier, at the lumberyard, where 2-by-4s are "eyeballed" for straightness before purchase.) Once the studs are affirmed as straight, the drywall can be nailed on.

DRYWALL: The term "drywall," which refers to strong, fairly heavy gypsum board, or plasterboard, that is nailed or screwed to wall or ceiling framing, was so named to distinguish it from plaster, which is termed "wet wall." The most common types of drywall are Sheetrock and blueboard.

Traditionally, drywall's hardened core is gypsum mixed with lime, the same materials that make up plaster. At the factory, the plaster-like material is formed into panels that are backed with thick, brown liner paper, and faced with a durable multi-ply, white or cream-colored paper ready for paint or wall covering. The long edges are wrapped with the face paper to make them easier to paint

and the short edges are then filed smooth.

Most drywall panels measure 4 by 8 to 4 by 16 feet. Thicknesses range from ¼ to ⅝ of an inch; the most commonly used panels are ½ inch thick and weigh 68 pounds. The universal height for residential interior walls today is 8 feet, but panels up to 12 feet high are available for older houses with high ceilings. To cover walls higher than 12 feet, the drywall contractor installs the panels horizontally, one above the other.

One problem encountered in drywall application is called "nail pops." If the framing behind the wall warps, the movement of the wood pushes out, or "pops," the nails holding the drywall. These days, the problem rarely occurs if framing is constructed with kiln-dried lumber. To make sure the problem won't occur, though, special annular ring nails are used; these are barbed in reverse so they won't pull out easily. Another frequently used fastener is a 1¼-inch drywall screw. To further ensure that the drywall will not work itself loose from the framing, construction adhesive may be applied to each stud as well.

When two drywall edges are butted together, a shallow valley is created at the seam, or joint. To avoid "telegraphing," wherein the joints show through the paint job, the drywall contractor must tape, fill, and seal each joint.

With the aid of a wide putty knife, the valley is filled with joint compound or Spackle. Paper tape matching the face paper on the drywall is rolled out and embedded in the Spackle, and a thin coat of compound is spread over the tape to fix it in place and prevent its curling.

After it dries, between 24 and 48 hours, a second coat of compound is spread over the joint, extending one inch on either side of the taped edge, and feathered into the drywall surface.

Once the compound has dried, it is sanded and dusted. A very thin skim coat of compound is spread and feathered out about two inches beyond the second coat and then lightly sanded. Often a special vinyl-acrylic primer, called Sheetrock First Coat, is applied at this stage to make the entire surface, including the drywall, tape, and joint compound, accept paint the same way. This gives the walls a plaster look, and far less paint is necessary.

Blueboard is basically installed the way other drywall is, the difference being that after the blueboard is nailed on and its seams taped, the entire surface is then layered with plaster. First, a "brown coat" base is applied, followed by a top coat of gypsum, plaster, and lime. The results are exactly the same as those of plaster, but the process is faster and more economical.

RIGHT: John Minnock is using a nail to locate ceiling joists so that the blueboard can be nailed securely in place. In an old house, the idiosyncracies of beam, joist, and stud placement require a lot of detective work. Electricians, plumbers, and carpenters find that much of their work time is consumed by searching for irregularly placed joists and studs. Yet to do their jobs properly, they must take the time, or the work cannot be done correctly.

SPACKLING AND PLASTERING

Most walls and ceilings in houses as old as mine were made of plaster built up over wood lath. The plaster was applied in three coats—a rough "scratch" coat followed by two smooth finishes. Plaster in some old houses may be as tough, smooth, and beautiful as the day it was applied. In most, though, the plaster has deteriorated over time—especially where wallpaper has been pulled away.

To patch pits or small holes in plaster, Spackle is applied. This putty-like compound made up of vinyl powders and adhesive mixed in water is available in two forms. One comes ready-mixed and cures by drying. It's used to patch plaster walls that are not exposed to excessive moisture. The second type, which has the ability to resist moisture, is sold as a powder and mixed with water on the job. Instead of drying, it sets chemically.

If the plaster is too far gone, new plaster is applied to small areas. In New England, many old-time contractors still build up plaster walls over wire lath, a close-knit diamond mesh. Wire lath

LEFT: The main plasterer, Patsy, created a staging set in every room. When brown-coating and plastering, it is necessary to move around very quickly, and this set gave Patsy the freedom he needed to create a surface that felt and looked like a fine plaster job. Recessed lighting was installed in the entire kitchen area with wall lighting in the form of sconces above each of the two fireplaces.

121

applications take two finish coats of plaster rather than just one. Today, a system known as veneer plaster is used to match a three-coat plaster wall. More often, however, new wallboard is used.

Plaster is made primarily of gypsum, a crystalline material (hydrous calcium sulfate, also used a soil supplement) mined from the earth. In its purest form, gypsum mixed with water is known as plaster of paris. For added durability, pure gypsum is premixed with lime. The contractor adds clean water to the dry mix, stirring until the plaster achieves a smooth consistency. It is then applied to the wall with a flat-edged trowel.

Blueboard, the most common material used today, is a gypsum board covered with a chemically treated blue-colored paper that promotes a bond when plaster is applied. The blue paper distinguishes it from plain gypsum board, which will not bond with plaster. A new alternative is a material made of 10 percent gypsum and 90 percent recycled paper. It is put up with screws or nails and taped with a special coating of joint compound. There is little taping, no blowout, and no bubbles.

The plasterer covers the seams, or butt joints, of the blueboard with a pressure-sensitive fine plastic mesh such as Imperial Gypsum Base, available in rolls. As the scratch coat of plaster is applied over the surface of the blueboard, it seeps through holes in the mesh tape and holds fast to the paper underneath, camouflaging the seams. Once the scratch coat has dried, a second coat is applied. Both coats are spread in gradual sweeping strokes for a seamless surface.

LEFT: Upstairs, the children's wing was comprised of several tiny bedroms. We eliminated walls, and two bedrooms and a new bathroom were created in the resulting space. Plaster walls were cleaned, and cracks were opened up, taped with fiberglass reinforcing tape, and then topcoated with a thin skim coat of plaster. All woodwork was carefully scraped to remove excess paint, and then primed and painted. Walls, too, were primed and painted before the floors were refinished. Electrical outlets were placed appropriately according to code.

TOP LEFT: Some of the original plaster walls needed only minor repairs. Renaldo applied paper tape over a crack in one of these walls and is now spreading joint compound over the paper with a spatula called a tape knife.

TOP RIGHT: Discovering the tools and materials of each of the trades is one of the fascinating aspects of rebuilding an old house. Each artisan uses these materials in slightly different ways. The 16-by-16-inch metal "hawk," very much like an artist's palette, is used to hold the plaster while it is being applied to the wall with a trowel.

BOTTOM LEFT: Patsy's mixing tub, looking very well used, is set on the staging along with his other materials—water buckets, sacks of plaster, and lime. There was a lot of wall area in the kitchen, and it consumed more of Patsy's time than any other room.

BOTTOM RIGHT: The steel trowel Patsy is using to repair cracks is perfectly flat. A taping trowel is slightly curved, 12 to 16 inches wide, enabling the compound to be applied so it is slightly thicker over the tape than along the edges, which are automatically feathered.

TOP LEFT: The original, old bathroom of the Adams house was gutted except for the cupboard and the old woodwork. All the fixtures were rearranged, and all of the plumbing and electrical material was replaced.

TOP RIGHT: Eric Logan, a painter who works with Cornell McNeill, the painting contractor, is a hardworking professional. He did most of the priming and first non-decorative painting inside.

BOTTOM LEFT: Patsy applying a thin top of plaster with his steel trowel.

BOTTOM RIGHT: Coffee Break. George had a midmorning and midafternoon coffee break of 15 minutes each for all the workers. Most men brought their own Thermos jugs and lunch boxes filled with "energy" foods like doughnuts and cupcakes for the breaks.

REFINISHING WOOD FLOORS

Beautiful pine floors are now one of the best features of the Adams house. When I first saw them, it was difficult to imagine that the wide boards which were covered with threadbare rugs and layers of dingy paint could be so promising. Don't assume that the wood floors in your house are irretrievable; you may find that, with proper finishing, they can become your greatest asset.

To decide what course of action to take, clean a 2-foot-square area with fine steel wool and mineral spirits, and then

LEFT: We hired independent floor sanders from nearby Norwalk to grind the floors with heavy-duty professional machines. A rough paper is used to rough sand; then a finer grade smooths out any roughness and ridges. A third paper was used in some places to smooth the pine to a very, very fine surface. This sander was used to surface grind large areas of flooring. There were some problems with the paper clogging the machine because of the high resin content of the wood and the heavy paint coating in some places.

RIGHT: Here an edging tool is used to grind away the corners and edges of a floor heavily coated with paint. I prefer sanding the floors before the final interior painting is done because of the tremendous amount of dust that results. Once the floors are finished, they are completely covered with builders' paper and taped to protect them while the room is being painted and decorated.

sponge away the dirt. When the floor is dry, sand if necessary, apply paste wax, and buff it by hand. In most cases, the wood will come up beautifully. If water has completely penetrated the wood, no amount of sanding will bring it back, but if the water has left only a surface stain, it can usually be removed with a mixture of bleach and water.

MAKING REPAIRS: To begin, the floors should be thoroughly cleaned and vacuumed; protruding nail heads should be reset and splintered, and broken strips or planks of wood replaced. It is best to replace wood with its same species. In New England this is often oak, native pine, yellow pine, or heartwood; in the South and West, pine. Identical floor strips for patching can often be removed from a closet, back room, or the attic.

To remove a strip of flooring, the flooring contractor works with a special electric-powered reciprocating saw. Its blade moves back and forth swiftly and cleanly, enabling him to cut out one strip while leaving adjoining lengths intact. After the board has been removed, a new tongue-and-groove strip is pressed into place and nailed secure.

REMOVING WAX: If a floor has been waxed only and never varnished, a buffing machine fitted with steel wool pads moistened with mineral spirits can remove all the layers of wax, down to the bare wood. The flooring contractor passes the machine over the wood in two directions, with and against the grain.

REMOVING THE VARNISH: If coats of varnish have been laid down, the finish has to be removed with a drum sander, to which rings of sandpaper are attached.

Because of the enormous amount of dust raised by the sander, the operator must wear a respirator mask. Using a sanding machine requires dexterity to avoid gouging the wood. The worker moves back and forth across the floor maintaining an even pressure—making sure the sander is always in motion.

If the buildup of the finish is multi-layered, the operator will usually make several passes parallel to the grain. After each pass the sandpaper is changed, from rough to medium-grit to fine, until the wood is clean and smooth. Between each sanding session, accumulated wood dust is removed with a heavy-duty commercial vacuum cleaner.

If the strip flooring itself is less than ⅜ inch thick, the operator will make only one or two passes, both with fine- to medium-grit sandpaper. If the floor is a parquet (strips laid in a herringbone pattern), the operator will make two passes with the same type of sandpaper before a final sanding with the dominant grain. Once the overall surface of the floor has been sanded, the operator will switch to a smaller machine called an edger, or disk sander, to finish the edges.

FINISHES: Whether or not you want to have the floor stained before a finish is applied is a decorating decision. Newly sanded old hardwood floors of oak, maple, or cherry have a patina many people choose to preserve, but old pine may appear too pale and bland. The finish chosen also depends on whether the floor is hardwood or softwood.

HARDWOOD: For hardwoods, many flooring contractors prefer water-based clear finishes because they dry in less

than one hour, never yellow, and are more durable than polyurethane and less toxic to use. Other contractors still use polyurethane because it resists water and other fluid stains and does not require waxing. Three coats are recommended for high-traffic areas, two for average rooms. Polyurethane is applied with felt pad applicators that push the liquid over the surface of the floor.

SOFTWOOD: For softwood floors, such as pine, many contractors prefer a stain-sealer or a sealer with a compatible varnish or lacquer finish, even though these require periodic waxing. Sealers work better on softwood because softwood fibers are more flexible than those of hardwoods and the sealer penetrates more deeply into the wood.

To make a floor look vibrant and rich after the sealer has been absorbed some floor finishers apply three coats of marine-grade varnish, which seemingly magnifies the wood texture, creating a translucent coating with sheen and depth. If the floor dulls over time, it can be reinvigorated with a coat of wax.

RIGHT: **The laundry room floor is blocked off to allow the final coat of polyurethane to dry without intruders. We sealed the floors immediately after sanding and vacuuming. Once the sealer had dried, three coats of polyurethane were applied over four days. I did not allow anyone to walk on the surfaces for 24 hours to insure proper drying. I used a mixture of ¼ glossy to ¾ satin polyurethane, which gave a mellow but hard finish. It was then waxed with butcher's wax and buffed to a soft sheen.**

RESTORING MILLWORK

I was determined to restore all of the original millwork in the Adams house—the moldings, trim, mantels, cabinets, muntins, balusters, doors, and porches. It is these details that enhance the character of an old house.

"Millwork" is an 18th-century word meaning work from the sawmill: the production of shaped wood house parts ready for installation. Millwork includes windows, doors, and their surrounding casings, as well as moldings, trims, mantels, cabinets, columns, and other architectural details. The modern profiles of many moldings, cornices, and mantels are derived from their 18th- and 19th-century counterparts.

In the past, all millwork arrived from a shop unfinished. Today, most new windows, doors, mantels, and cabinets are prefinished and prestained—or at least preprimed.

Millwork in an old house may be grimy and carry several coats of paint and perhaps a layer of mildew. Even in such a condition, it can be restored with careful cleaning, sanding, and refinishing.

Portions of millwork damaged beyond repair by termites, water, or fire can usually be replaced with exact copies by a millwork company. To reproduce an existing piece, a new metal template must be made to match the profile of the old one. This can be replicated from an actual sample or from a sketch.

At the shop, knives are set into a rotary cutter to match the template. Rotating at high speed, the cutter carves the old profile into new wood as the piece is passed through. It is best, of course, to use the same kind of wood as found in the old house. Most millwork, both old and new, is eastern or western pine or ponderosa pine.

Replicating carvings is possible when the motif is common—a leaf, for example, or a rose or a star. Most millwork firms carry a collection of such decorative motifs. The figure is embossed on the wood by first heating (but not burning) the wood fibers and then pressing a metal reproduction of the pattern into the wood like a mold. The resulting pressed figure looks as if it were actually carved by hand.

It may be possible to find doors, windows, or special moldings that match the originals and are just as old. Country auctions are one source, as are salvage yards; look for the latter in the Yellow Pages under "Building Materials, Used."

Many companies manufacture reproduction period millwork and offer it through mail-order catalogs.

LEFT: **The Adams house had more than 175 broken or cracked panes of glass in the six-over-six windows. To remove brittle glass from soft or rotten frames without breaking the glass is extremely difficult. On a job as nerve-wracking as this restoration, George estimates that a window repairer like Terry can only last on the job about three and a half weeks. Terry, one of the best glazers we know, retired from this particular project after five weeks.**

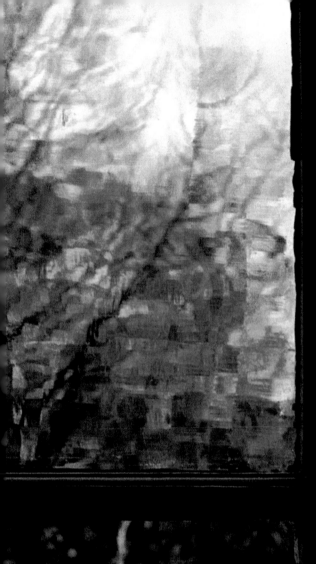
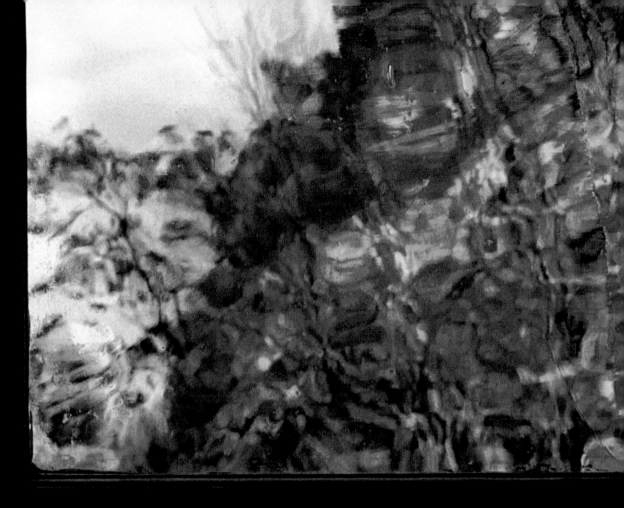

LEFT: The front door and its framing needed heavy scraping and paint removal. Larry used a heat gun to soften the layers of paint, making it easier to remove with a scraper. Heat guns must be used with caution and by a practiced workman. (Some localities prohibit the use of this tool.)

RIGHT: Many moldings in the old house were so far beyond repair that they had to be pulled off and re-created. Here, Tom traces one of the old moldings onto new stock; it will then be cut to the desired profile by using a hand plane and power equipment.

PRECEDING PAGE: A view of the backyard through one of the six-over-six windows original to the house. These windows were rather graceful, and I wanted desperately to save as many as possible. If one had to be moved, it was used elsewhere in the house. Only one window, in the back bedroom, was replaced; fire regulations dictated that it be wider.

The old glass was made locally in the 19th century. Its wavy appearance provides an ingredient of true charm. The glass itself, although full of imperfections, is often more clear and crystal-like than much of the new glass being sold today. Old glass seems to clean better than new, as though it were harder and brighter.

To repair the damaged windows, each sash had to be taken from the frame, then every pane of glass was removed from that sash. The frame and muntins were stripped of paint and repaired, then primed with oil primer. Next, all the panes were reinstalled using new tacks and glazing putty. George found "new" old glass in old buildings being demolished.

CREATING A

NEW KITCHEN

The kitchen has always been the most exciting and interesting room in the house to me. It is the first room that I want to see when I enter a home and the room I am most concerned about in terms of accessibility, function, and utility. It is the room that is most used by the contemporary family and the room that requires the most planning during a renovation such as the one we did at the Adams house. ■ In the house where I grew up, my mother spent most of her day in a bright sunny room that was both kitchen and eating place. All of the sewing was done there, all of our homework was completed around the big, pink, Formica table, all the seedlings were propagated on the picture windowsill above the table, and my father performed small tasks like repairs in the center of the room. It was more than a kitchen— it was the family's room, the conference center, the most important room in the house. ■ Even though it was a long rectangle and the appliances were too small for a family of eight, it was efficient because the work

area was confined to one part, the eating space to another, the sewing area to another. The only inconvenient aspect of the design was that the small "powder" room's door was off the eating area. ■ When I moved to New York, I had a neat, bright kitchen on Riverside Drive. It too was well laid out and convenient, though not spacious enough for a table; we ate breakfast and had

snacks at the counter sitting on stools. It was a narrow room but easy to cook in. Merely turning around from the stove, I could reach the sink and refrigerator on the other side. ■ My kitchen at Turkey Hill, though built on a much larger scale, is based on that

LEFT: The kitchen space during demolition looked like a war zone, but once the exterior walls were repaired and closed in the space looked very encouraging.

RIGHT: Williams-Sonoma sells this very wonderful copper pot rack. Of heavy gauge metal, it hangs from specially installed eyes affixed to the ceiling joists.

139

New York kitchen, with counters separating the work area from the dining area. It is a small workspace, but efficient, and I have cooked many, many meals in that kitchen.

I felt so liberated in terms of square footage when I saw the Adams house space and realized that I could freely design a wonderfully spacious and utilitarian kitchen. Surprisingly, the new kitchen layout was easily conceived. Larry, George, and I met together to determine which walls could be eliminated and which spaces could be altered or expanded to fit my grandiose plan for a large work kitchen with a great deal of convenient storage, excellent heavy-duty appliances, and an eating area that would be both useful and beautiful.

The kitchen was to be as professional in nature as possible, but with the appearance of a cozy country room. The floor was to be pine, and painted and finished with a hard polyurethane. The cabinets were to be painted wood. The millwork would resemble fine furniture, exceeding in quality anything that existed in the house. All appliances were to be heavy-duty and of the finest quality, with stainless exteriors.

There was room for a grill and a deep fryer, for huge side-by-side refrigerator-freezer units, and for two sink areas. Most wonderful was the tremendous amount of wall space that could be fitted with floor-to-ceiling cupboards. I wanted the Adams kitchen to be my dream kitchen, and it is. At least one of them.

JOURNAL

(Continued from page 89)

4/5 Furnace dropped off. Patsy worked in west parlor. Garage roof stripped off. Pulleys attached to posts to straighten building. Tile work begun in children's shower. Electrician wiring garage. Masons worked chimneys. Terry installed base trim & working on floors. John repairing flooring & baseboard.

4/6 Furnace installation started. John & Terry finishing trim upstairs & framing closets. Dominick & Tom jacked up garage support beam. Plasterer working on finish coat west parlor ceiling.

4/7 Masons working on chimney. Rita reconfirmed that survey would begin next week; scheduled exterminators for 4/15. Arranged photo session at Coastal Woodworking to discuss stairway railing & moldings which must be milled. Terry & John working on upstairs trim. Dominick & Tom resupporting garage.

4/8 Insulation men working above children's wing. Tom priming garage trim. Dominick repairing garage.

4/11 Furnace installation completed. Plasterer didn't show. Terry finishing upstairs closets. Masons working on chimney. John trimming closets. Dominick & Tom repairing garage roof to prep for new roof. Tile man working on laundry room shower.

4/12 Kitchen door installed. Roofing started on garage roof. Plasterer finishing upstairs closets. John & Terry finished up trimming out closets.

4/13 John & Terry sheetrocking around new kitchen door. Plasterer touching up upstairs walls. Kitchen cleared so plasterer could start. John & Terry installing porch windows. Rita called phone company to have service switched over to the underground wires. Dominick & Tom continued roofing garage. Tile men finished floor in upstairs children's bathroom.

4/14 Tom & Dominick continued roofing garage. John & Terry installing porch doors & windows.

4/15 Continued installation of porch doors. Attic floor of garage installed. Exterminator sprayed for powderpost beetles & ants. Carpenters removed floorboards in kitchen area. Tile work continued.

4/18 Tom & Dominick trimmed out garage & finished attic flooring. John made new window frame & sill for master bathroom. Terry off for two weeks.

4/19 George picked up marble for master bathroom. Dropped off order for marble basemolding. John & George worked on flashing of porch roof. Tom & Dominick finishing roofing on back side of garage.

4/20 George & John worked on reroofing porch. Tom & Dominick disassembled scaffolding behind garage & began replacing rotten roof boards on front. Patsy & Renaldo plastering kitchen.

4/21 John continued porch roofing. Tom & Dominick roofing garage. Plasterer & Renaldo plastering kitchen.

4/22 Closet Maid people came—decided to use laundry rooms as the location for K-Mart Closet Maid infomercials. Norwall Wallpaper Co. came—paper selected for sitting room bedroom. Discussed border to be produced. Called Sherwin Williams people for last refining of color palette. Color selection should be ready in about 2–2½ weeks.

4/25 Plasterer doing rough coat of kitchen. John installed remainder of porch windows. Tom & Dominick working on garage roof. Tile man working in master bath shower.

4/26 Dominick cutting glass for kitchen cabinets. Tom finishing peak on roof. John finishing the porch roof. Tile man working in master bath shower.

5/6 John working on kitchen floor with Tom. Patsy working on final ceiling coat in laundry. Clearing of land continued. Painters priming upstairs.

5/9 John finished kitchen floor except for hatchway to wine cellar. Kitchen cabinets brought in & placed in general area. Tom helped to finish kitchen floor. Dominick worked on siding around porch. Tile men grouting master bath. Patsy working on laundry room.

5/11 Door between kitchen & porch, cabinets & bar sink area installed. Clearing continued on property. Dominick finished shelves in upstairs linen closet. Tom worked on baseboards in laundry. Patsy finished dining room ceiling. Renaldo working on taping west parlor, closets, cellar stairs.

5/12 Plasterers off. John worked on kitchen sink cabinet area. Renaldo taping in dining room. Land clearing continued.

5/16 Terry framing kitchen windows. Dominick finishing up exterior around porch area. John installing final kitchen cabinets. Painters sanding & priming upstairs bedrooms. Plasterer touching up areas.

5/24 Dominick & Tom built box to protect skylights from being damaged while roof work takes place.

5/25 Masons dropped off block for patio foundation wall. Tom repairing trim in parlor & study & fireplace mantel in dining room. Closet shelving finished. John installing kitchen crown molding.

5/26 Kitchen porch removed —temporary stairs built. John finished work on crown molding; started on base.

5/30 Memorial Day

5/31 Floor sanders started. Masons working on patio foundation. Heating contractors arrived. Moved shingles to roof. Tom & Dominick replacing roof trim. Dominick took apart small side porch—replaced all wood eaten away by ants. John working on base molding. George taping sun porch.

6/1 Gigi & Fabiano cleaned windows for infomercial. Floor sanders working upstairs. Dominick & Tom repairing trim. Masons working on patio.

6/2 Victor back. Filled in around patio foundation. Worked on cleaning up land & burying tree roots. Gigi & Fabiano restacking stones on wall. Floor sanders finished & started to apply lacquer sealer. Sandblasters taping up front windows—will start work today. Patsy finishing up odds & ends downstairs. Plumbers installing shower controls & downstairs toilet. Dominick & Tom replacing trim around roof. John framing skylights.

6/6 Infomercial—B&D Sander, Dap Bathroom. Painter working on upstairs hallway.

6/7 Victor clearing land. Carpenters repairing trim on roof. Painter painting upper hallway. Crew setting up scaffolding outside of back sunroom.

6/8 Infomerical —Rustoleum in Carriage House, Dap outside caulking.

6/9 Infomercial —Sherwin Williams paint — interior. Omni water filter.

6/10 Repair of roof trim continued.

6/13 Roof begun —Victor grading garage side of property. Pulled out tree trunks by porch.

6/14 Roofing continued. Sanders working on side of house with rotary sander.

6/17 Masons working on terrace wall. Painters priming downstairs. Sanders working. Roofing continued.

6/20 Sanders working on house. Masons working on wall. Roofing continued. Electrician working on attic wiring. No painters.

6/21 Roofing continued. Masons continuing work on back terrace. Painters priming downstairs.

8/1–8/12 George on vacation. Larry worked on stripping paint off clapboard butts. Mike the mason worked on foundation wall on east side of hose. D&J Masonry finishing up back patio—setting bluestone.

8/15 Larry still stripping paint. Brad started work. Tom & Brad worked on kitchen porch. D&J Masons grouting bluestone on patio. Mike & helper worked on side foundation wall. Victor grading property.

8/16 Larry stripping paint. Tom & Brad framing porch. Masons working on patio.

8/24 Plumbers installed ice maker, dishwasher, pedestal sink in laundry room bathroom. George installed backsplash of Garland. Larry worked on papering dining room & office floors.

8/25 Larry & Brad sick. Tom worked on siding on porch. Rita & I met with Dennis Rowan re painting exterior, to start in two weeks. He suggested a sealer to remedy our bleeding problem.

9/1 Tom replacing rotten molding around roof. Larry cleaned up kitchen for painters.

9/2 Discussed paint techniques with Marla. John fitting columns for porch, worked on drip edge on new window in sitting room bedroom. Larry stayed late filling nail holes in kitchen. Rita delivered stainless steel to Casey Sheet Metal to be cut for dishwasher.

9/3 Marla, Debbie & Mark started painting kitchen cabinets. Larry filled remaining nail holes & staining cabinet shelves. R & R helped oil cabinets. Renato worked half day, Renaldo whole day.

9/4 Marla & crew finished colored panels, started painting around cabinets. I agreed to make interior cabinet next to the kitchen sink solid blue-green to match veining in slate countertops. Marla left to start another job—Debbie to finish up.

9/6 Larry began insulation of kitchen porch. John doing final fitting of portico columns. Tom finishing siding around patio doors, replacing rotten trim around roof. Debbie painting mantels. Renaldo staining & oiling. Tatko brothers delivered slate countertops. Arrived around 10:00 after 5-hour drive from Upper Grandville, N.Y. Crate weighed over 1,000 lbs.

9/7 George & John installed countertop by bar sink. Tom & Brad worked on the porch. Decorative painters not working. George & John tried to install slate by kitchen sink, but it was not cut correctly. Rita called Tatko Slate Co. to have slate returned.

9/14 Debbie back with assistant. John installing banister on staircase. George & four-year-old son Kirk drove to Tatko Slate Co. Tatko recut one piece while George waited. Returned with it after a 16-hour trip. Tom & Brad worked on porch—installing pine walls. Brad left at 2:45—not feeling well.

9/15 Debbie & assistant working on cabinets. John finished old banister on main staircase. George & John installed recut slate kitchen countertop. Heating contractor finished last details of furnace. Rita called gas company to have furnace & range turned on; scheduled for 9/20. Dennis Rowan Painting company worked on sanding, caulking & prep. Rita, Ross Roy Advertising & Dick Roberts had preproduction meeting for infomercials.

9/16 Painters began priming exterior; finished about ⅔ of spraying. All windows covered with plastic. Patio covered with drop cloths. Marla & crew of four arrived to finish kitchen painting; worked on kitchen doors— keeping the old look & making them look a little fresher. John began work on office bookshelves, measuring & planning materials list.

9/17 Dennis Rowan painters finished priming exterior of house. Began sanding garage doors.

9/18 Debbie returned to work on kitchen cabinets. Began work on island.

9/19 Exterior painters sanding & caulking. Debbie, Mark & Ted finished painting & waxing kitchen cabinets; shelves returned to proper places. Debbie finishing painting island & touching up old doors. Interior painters painted parlor mantel, touched up ceiling in entrance hall. Started prep of banisters. Bliss working on props for infomercials.

9/20 Debbie & Ted finished cabinets. Interior painters worked on sanding & prepping banisters. Began stain kill in areas of kitchen. John sealing countertops with Ston-yl, continued work on bookcases. Exterior painters finished up sanding of house & began spraying on stain. Garage doors primed.

9/21 Interior painters began painting kitchen.

LEFT: Looking from the kitchen cooking fireplace toward the stove, the room appears crowded, busy, and very workable. This is how I like a real working kitchen to be: tools are accessible, everything in view is usable, worthwhile, and pleasing aesthetically with no unnecessary ornaments or chotchkies. Antiques or old kitchen gadgets, crocks, copper pots and kettles, baskets, and all-new good equipment are sufficient decoration for today's kitchen and cook. The stove we chose is a six-burner Garland restaurant range with a griddle, open-air broiler, and over shelf. The hood, fabricated by Vent-a-Hood, is stainless steel.

The copper hanging rack is a special-order item from Williams-Sonoma. The heavy grid enables one to hang more pots than usual. The double kitchen sink is the largest Elkay kitchen unit available. A double sink rather than a single is desirable if pots, pans, and dishes are to be stacked and drip dried or soaked. I prefer using large cutting boards on top of the maple counters of the island; this helps protect the counter and also makes cleaning up easier. A cutting board can be washed in the sink and dried in the sun, whereas the counter can never be scrubbed as well.

The windows were left unadorned. Curtains or shades are completely unnecessary in a room like this unless there is a great deal of bright light, in which case I would use venetian blinds.

The island and the small cupboard next to the stove are movable, designed as pieces of furniture rather than built-ins.

The urn is filled with culinary herbs; they live quite well in a bright sunny window, with periodic sojourns outdoors for a dose of direct sunlight.

PLANNING THE KITCHEN

Miss Adams had many interests, but cooking was not one of them. In her kitchen she had a little refrigerator, a small table, a stove, and a sink—nothing more. But to me, a kitchen should be a place to cook, eat, write, talk on the telephone, visit with friends. So we decided to replace Miss Adams's spartan arrangement with a combination family room and country kitchen.

To get the space we needed, we opened up five small rooms, several pantries, and a half bath, all part of a later addition to the 1838 house. We removed all the interior walls of the first-floor addition—none were structural—and kept only the chimney. The chimney has two fireplaces, back to back. One now services the working portion of the kitchen, where it can be used for grilling and hearth cooking; the other faces the eating area.

The large space resulting from the demolition accommodates not only the kitchen and eating room, but also a glassed-in sunroom. A small but very useful mudroom added outside the kitchen door serves as the entrance to this busy part of the house.

Everyone's concept of the perfect

LEFT: **In designing the kitchen, I took into account the demands of a large family, the availability of restaurant equipment, and the appeal of the 19th-century architecture of the house. My aim was utility and convenience in a beautiful and spacious area.**

145

ABOVE: When I first saw the Adams house kitchen, it looked like this. The fixtures had been placed with no regard for aesthetics, convenience, or utility; the refrigerator jutted out into the room, the stove was yards away from the sink, and there was no counter or storage space. The floor was covered with layers of linoleum, the fireplace was boarded up; no lighting of any kind was evident except for the overhead fixture.

ABOVE: As demolition proceeded, five small rooms were merged into one large and very promising space. Even though our plan called for such an area, it was not until the walls were removed and the old plaster stripped that its feasibility was evident. At last there was light and room to move about and a place for proper placement of equipment and furniture.

ABOVE: After the studs were straightened, the wiring and plumbing installed, and the walls and ceiling spaces insulated, the plasterboard was put up. What an immense difference this step makes in construction, for all at once the room has real form and one can see the entire space clearly. The recessed lighting in the ceiling turned out to be a great idea, affording good, basic illumination for this large kitchen while remaining very inconspicuous and subtle.

kitchen is different, but regardless of individual preferences, there are some general principles to keep in mind.

The first step in planning the arrangement of the kitchen is to decide what kind of equipment you want for cooking, cleanup, and refrigeration.

There are several issues involved in selecting kitchen appliances: space, the way you cook and entertain, the style of your kitchen, and, especially in the case of refrigerators and dishwashers, energy efficiency. Appliances are discussed in "Selecting Appliances" (page 150).

COOKING: At least 3 feet of counter space on either side of the cooktop or the range is ideal; up to 5 feet is better.

REFRIGERATION: At least 18 inches of counter space on the side of the refrigerator where the door opens, or on both sides if it is a side-by-side, is desirable.

CLEANUP: The key to cleanup convenience is having enough counter space, a minimum of 2 feet on either side of the sink and dishwasher if you can.

Besides cooking, cleanup, and refrigeration, it is often convenient to set aside special areas in the kitchen for supplementary activities.

MIXING: I find it convenient to keep all the equipment I need for mixing everything from cookie batter to salads in one spot, at least 3 feet wide, near both the sink and the refrigerator. This is the place to insert into the countertop a marble slab for rolling out pastry dough and

a maple cutting board for chopping and dicing. In the Adams house, we decided that the best location for the mixing center was the large island.

EATING: In planning the eating area, try to allot 9½ square feet for a round table with a diameter of 42 inches for four to six people, or 9 by 12 feet for a rectangular table 36 by 72 inches. Whatever the size of the table, the rule of thumb is 3 feet of breathing space around it. If you don't have the space for a full-scale eating area, you may be able to fit in a breakfast nook or a cantilevered counter with barstools underneath. If standard chairs or stools are used at a counter, the eating surface should be 30 inches high, instead of the usual 36

ABOVE: All of the cabinet work and special millwork was created by Coastal Woodworking in Bridgeport, Connecticut. The well-trained craftsmen at this large and very modern facility build the basic structures in the shop shown here and transport them in pieces and sections for final installation on the spot.

ABOVE: When the cabinets and cupboards arrived, I was very pleased. Viewing the work in pieces in the shop, I had found it impossible to appreciate how very beautiful they would be. Fitting them into the fresh space took more than a week. The cabinets were leveled and screwed together, doors hung and fitted, and ceiling and floor moldings applied. The fitting crew is extremely important; they make the whole scheme come together.

ABOVE: A view of the eating area. Some of the top cupboards were constructed with glass-paned doors to be used for storing and displaying the more visually appealing china and glassware. Others were made with paneled wooden doors for storing things like light bulbs, less attractive serving dishes, cooking equipment, and less frequently used small appliances. During the whole installation the floor was well-protected.

inches. Allow 20 to 24 inches along the counter for each place setting.

SERVING: About 3 feet of counter space close to the stove and within easy reach of the eating areas is ideal.

PLANNING: A desk 3 or 4 feet long with a telephone, shelves, and storage can serve not only as a place to make shopping lists and plan menus, but also as a home office.

ENTERTAINING: A bar sink and a 24-inch-wide undercounter refrigerator, perhaps with a wine cooler or dishwasher, situated just outside the main kitchen area, such as a pantry or family room, are very useful if you entertain large groups frequently.

RECYCLING: Another area that should be near the kitchen, if not in it, is a recycling center, with separate containers for cans, glass, and plastic, or whatever is recyclable in your community

LAYOUT: Most kitchen planners recommend that the three basic work centers—for cooking, refrigeration, and cleanup—form a triangle. According to a study conducted by Cornell University, for maximum efficiency the sides of this imaginary triangle should add up to between 12 and 22 feet.

The work triangle theory is not an unbreakable law—especially these days, when an island and supplementary appliances, such as a wall oven and microwave, are no longer considered luxuries—but it is a useful guide.

Efficient arrangements of the work areas tend to fall into one of four categories.

ONE-WALL PLAN: When there is very little space, the ideal pyramid dissolves into a straight line, with the sink at the center. Keep the range or cooktop at least 18 inches from the end wall to leave room for counter space.

CORRIDOR PLAN: Two facing walls at least 64 inches apart allow for the classic triangle, with the sink in the middle of one wall and the refrigerator and range on the opposite wall, with counterspace in between.

L-PLAN: This is the pattern we used in the Adams house. The range is on one wall, with the sink, counters, and the

LEFT: The mudroom entrance, designed by Maggie Daly, was a perfect solution for a busy family: a convenient place to hang outdoor clothing, store muddy shoes and boots, and place groceries while unloading the car.

ABOVE: Looking out the mudroom door, over the back steps toward the garage. It is very easy to transport packages from the driveway to the house.

refrigerator and freezer on the adjoining wall at a right angle. We put our island parallel to the stove wall. Another L-shaped option arranges the major functions along one wall with a counter or peninsula projecting out at a right angle. To be really useful, an island should be at least 2 feet wide and 6 feet long, with storage underneath.

U-PLAN: The most spacious arrangement, this should have a base at least 8 feet long, where the sink is usually placed, and two "legs," at least 4 to 5 feet in length, one with the cooktop, the other with the refrigerator. In a really large kitchen, one of the legs can be a peninsula rather than a wall, and quite often there is an island between the legs.

The distance between the island and each leg should be about 4 feet so that oven and refrigerator doors can be opened at the same time without bumping into each other.

However the cooking-cleaning-cooling triangle is arranged, there should be a way for people to enter the kitchen without passing through the work area.

ORIGINAL KITCHEN

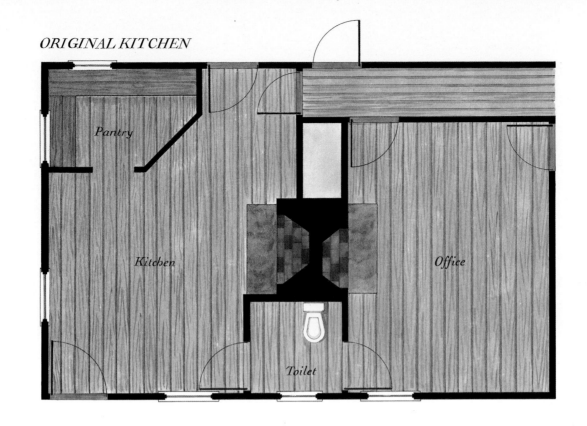

Pantry

Kitchen

Office

Toilet

Ice Maker

Dishwasher   *Refrigerator Freezer*

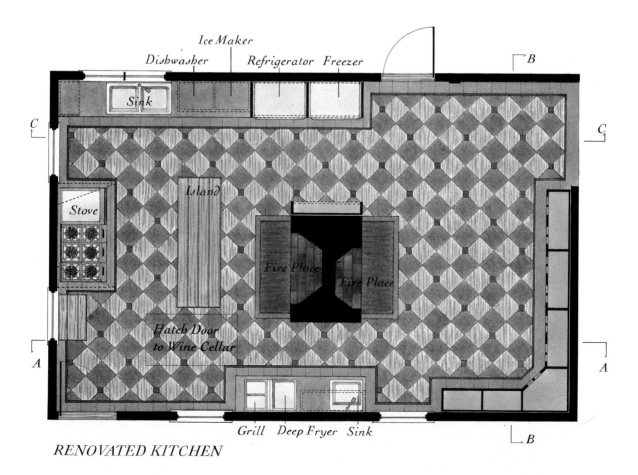

Sink

Island

Stove

Fire Place

Fire Place

*Hatch Door
to Wine Cellar*

Grill   Deep Fryer   Sink

RENOVATED KITCHEN

149

SELECTING APPLIANCES

Storing food, cooking, and cleanup are still the fundamental functions of a kitchen—just as they were in the 17th century. But how different the experience is today!

REFRIGERATORS: Industrial designers have given us separately cooled vegetable crispers and meat trays, continuous ice-cube makers, access in some doors to cubes and ice water, automatic defrosting—and plenty of storage in the unit itself and in the door.

Refrigerators with freezers above or below the cold storage area measure from 28 to 33 inches wide while those with freezer cabinets alongside, in the so-called side-by-side configuration, are from 31 to 48 inches wide. The most common choice is 36 inches wide, 68 inches high, and 24 inches deep. This model contains about 25 cubic feet of storage space—comfortable for the food needs of a typical family of four.

Refrigerators designed to be built into a wall of cabinets have the compressor above or below the unit, thus saving on depth; these are offered in 30- to 48-inch widths, too. Modular, separately built-in refrigerator and freezer units, though, can easily span a distance of more than 6 feet. Specialized undercounter coolers for wine and ancillary undercounter refrigerators or freezers measure 24 inches wide, and are particularly suited to a bar area or pantry.

Even refrigerators labeled "energy saving" may have significantly different energy demands. The U.S. government puts out a useful book on energy-efficient appliances; check your local bookstore or write the U.S. Government Printing Office. The higher initial price results in long-term fuel savings.

Refrigerators present an additional environmental problem. At present, all residential refrigerators commercially available in the United States use chlorofluorocarbons, which damage the ozone layer when they escape into the upper

atmosphere. If you are discarding an old refrigerator, be sure its CFCs are recycled; your appliance serviceman should be able to help.

STOVES AND OVENS: If you have a large kitchen and entertain frequently, a restaurant range with six burners, double ovens, and a griddle is ideal. I chose a Garland model for the Adams house. Weighing 400 pounds, it may require extra support under the floor, and must have an insulated wall behind it. Most restaurant ranges stand alone, but some new ones intended for residential use

ABOVE: **For the Adams house, I chose all stainless-steel appliances: a Garland commercial range, a Gaggenau deep fryer and grill, Elkay sinks and faucets, and two Sub-Zero refrigerator-freezer units. The stainless steel is easy to clean, and its subtle sheen works well with the blues, greens, and ochers of the woodwork and the copper trim on the floor.**

have extra insulation in the sides so that they can be inserted between cabinets.

Traditional range and oven combinations (20 to 40 inches wide) are still popular, but some people prefer to separate the elements: a cooktop dropped into the counter, plus separate undercounter or wall ovens. Drop-in cooktops can be as narrow as 18 inches for four burners and a griddle. Some come with a downdraft ventilating system that eliminates the need for an overhead hood.

SINKS AND DISHWASHERS: Dishwashers are proven water savers. Nearly all are 24 inches wide, half the width of a typical double-door base cabinet. Narrow models, 18 inches wide, can be installed in a bar or pantry area.

Kitchen sinks in stainless steel and enameled cast iron are available with one, two, or three bowls; some have built-in drainboard and strainers or cutting boards that fit into or over the bowls. If you often cook with friends, it is convenient to have two sinks with separate faucets so that one person can scrub pots and pans while the other washes dishes or rinses vegetables. Some new faucets regulate the temperature of the water to within one degree, with digital readouts to prove it.

I don't use food-waste disposals; they are noisy and ecologically incorrect. Some communities bar disposal because of the strain they place on the sewer system; I find an equally serious strain is placed on septic systems and cesspools. If you have even a bit of property, there is a much better destination for your nonmeat food waste: the compost pile.

ABOVE: As a serious cook, I prefer copper-fabricated kitchen pots and pans. Mine are tin lined—I still have a source nearby for retinning if necessary. However, because fewer and fewer people know how to cook with copper (it is essential to always keep liquid or oil in the bottom of the pan, for example, and retinning must be done when copper starts to show through), I keep a supply of high-quality stainless-steel pots available for others who cook in my house.

To clean copper, I use a French product, Copper Brill, a paste that I buy at Dehillerin in Paris that polishes up quite beautifully. In humid weather, or near salt air, no amount of polishing will keep copper shiny. Scouring powders made especially for copper are also good, and for those of us who cannot use these commercial products, there is always the old standby, baking soda, lemon, and salt.

ABOVE: We used an American chestnut kitchen table in the dining area. It is large enough for eight, but normally just six chairs are set around it. These chairs are Hitchcock pillow backs.

LEFT: The mantels were treated with the same care and fine craftmanship as the rest of the millwork: nice, simple detailing. Drawers had to be fitted, and much planing was done to make sure the poplar sides slid well on the wooden runners. No metal fittings were used in the kitchen. Fine brass hinges were used on the cupboards with handmade wooden knobs for the pulls. A custom crown molding was installed; it hid the irregularity on the tops of the cabinet work and made everything seem level and perfect.

RIGHT: The second sink area is set in the same counter as the grill/deep fryer. This is handy for cleanup, as well as for an informal bar area. The mantel is shaded subtly, as is the rest of the woodwork, with soft variations of the original colors of mustard, blue, green, and gray.

CHOOSING COUNTERTOPS

I have very specific preferences when it comes to choosing counter materials for kitchen use. I used mottled gray-green hand-honed slate from New York State, especially cut by Tatko Slate Products in Middle Granville, for all of the counters and backsplashes above the sink and stove in the old house kitchen. This satiny smooth stone makes a beautiful counter, and one which will last forever. After installation, I coated the surface with Ston-yl, a penetrating sealer that works well on all types of stone.

STONE: Stone counters are now very popular and I think very beautiful. In addition to hand-honed slate, I like marble and granite. The stone must be at least an inch thick and is very durable if treated well. No cutting can be done directly on this kind of surface and it must be immediately cleaned after use

LEFT: **The Gaggenau grill and deep fryer were a wonderful addition to this kitchen. Set right into the honed slate counters, they can be easily cleaned. An old marble-top baker's table, purchased at a local tag sale, is a good place to roll out pastry. The graduated rack in old blue paint hanging on the wall is a tobacco sorter.**

ABOVE RIGHT: **A view of the new kitchen looking toward the back door. The large hole in the floor is the hatchway that leads down into the wine cellar, a basement space that had no real access and was previously unusable. Unheated, it is the perfect location for wine storage.**

with a warm wet rag. These counters are prone to chips or cracks if heavy objects are dropped on them or knocked against the edges. White marble will stain with berry juice or acetic liquids, so these should be wiped off immediately. Wiping with few drops of Clorox diluted with water right after spilling will help.

WOOD: Not long ago, butcher's block was very popular for counters, but I really do not care for its appearance. After one year of hard use, even the very best butcher's block will be scarred, and the finish seems very uneven. I prefer to have counters made of tiger or bird's-eye maple, with boards 3 to 6 inches wide and 1½ to 2 inches thick. These can be glued and bolted through the entire width of the counter with long metal rods; the surface should be sanded, smoothed with steel wool, and then very lightly oiled. I still use individual cutting boards for heavy chopping and cutting.

CORIAN AND AVONITE: These synthetic stonelike materials are excellent. Although not as hard as stone, they are less prone to chipping or breaking. Although manufacturers claim that you can cut on these surfaces, I make a habit not to, as they do scratch; a portable board should be used.

FORMICA: It is the most widely used counter material and the least expensive. Formica is easy to clean and makes a very good working surface. Again, it requires a portable cutting board.

TILE: I do not like tiles as a counter surface. I find that the grout is a problem, staining with age and use, and the tiles themselves offer a rather uneven and unsatisfactory surface on which to work.

LINOLEUM: This can make a very good surface. When used carefully and edged with a hard material such as steel, it will last for many years.

COATED METAL ZINC: This is a great surface, terrific for rolling out pastry and working with bread doughs.

Lighting

Most people feel more comfortable under incandescent light than fluorescent. New-style fluorescents, however, approximate very closely the glow of incandescents and use less power. They also last longer: deluxe warm white fluorescents last from 9,000 to 20,000 hours compared to 750 to 1,000 hours for ordinary incandescents

OVERALL ILLUMINATION: For a space between 75 and 120 square feet, ceiling lights should provide at least 80 watts of fluorescent light or 200 watts of incandescent. For larger space, increase the light level accordingly.

TASK LIGHTING: Tubular fluorescent under the cabinets and downlight over the major work areas are helpful both for safety and for energy conservation. For the desk, a lamp should suffice; for the dining area, consider a downlight, chandelier, or track light.

CABINETRY

Because I am an inveterate collector and like to display my dishes and glassware, I wanted plenty of cabinets with glass doors in the Adams house kitchen. I thought Shaker-like wooden cabinets with glass doors, including a whole bank of floor-to-ceiling storage wrapping around a corner in the breakfast area, would be utilitarian and beautiful. I wanted everything to work perfectly; as meticulously as fine furniture. I found a superb

LEFT: This is the work area of the new kitchen, an excellent space not only for cooking, but also for preparation. The island is generous in size, yet narrow enough to get around easily. In my newest kitchen project, in Lily Pond House on Long Island, I built an immense island measuring 13 by 7 feet, with stove, dishwasher, sinks, drawers, and cupboards. I find that its sheer size slows me down—I spend too much time just walking around it.

The counter of this island is tiger maple, a wonderful hardwood that remains stable. Some woods tend to "move" or warp, and should be avoided at all costs when building fine cabinetry.

Open shelves are very useful, not only for display, but also for utility, as objects are readily at hand. I keep frequently used small appliances right on the countertop. Wider-than-normal windowsills are great to hold wooden spoons, metal spatulas, and strainers. The copper bottle holder was made in the 19th century. The sconces are old, their mirror reflectors and glass hurricanes casting a lovely light.

cabinetmaker from Coastal Woodworking in Bridgeport, Connecticut, to design and execute the work. I had admired painted cupboards in a friend's kitchen and decided that I would create a painted finish. The cabinetmaker and I opted to construct the cupboards from clear pine with poplar drawers and runners, and birch plywood interiors and shelving. Because they were going to be stain painted, the difference in the woods would not be discernible to the naked eye. The clear pine was the least expensive of the woods of choice; the clear poplar is a very stable wood and an excellent material for drawer interiors.

The shelving was made from ¾-inch thick birch plywood. Also very sturdy and completely stable, it took the paint very well.

The space was measured so that the

LEFT: **The huge cupboards hold large batter bowls, dough bowls, and platters. The shelves in the upper cupboards are moved up and down easily thanks to holes drilled in the uprights; pegs are inserted wherever desired, the shelves placed on top of them. This system looks more pleasing than the metal strips and clips usually used for this purpose.**

Two-inch brass hinges were selected to hang the doors, with three pairs used for each long door to prevent warping.

The doors are self-closing with magnets on right-hand doors and frames; the left-hand stationary doors are latched with little brass releases. These upper cupboards make excellent storage for decorative dishes and glass.

cabinets would align perfectly with the window trim. The cupboards were fitted with old glass salvaged by George from a 19th-century house in Bridgeport. Hand-turned wooden pulls appropriate to the Shaker-like appearance of the cupboards were made on a lathe for the drawers and cupboard doors.

National Home Builders Association guidelines recommend at least 72 running feet of wall cabinetry. My feeling is that 120 feet is more realistic. We have this in the Adams house, plus the space in the base cabinets, drawers, and shelves in the island and the hanging rack above it.

Base cabinets are usually 24 inches deep and 30½ inches high. The 4½-inch-high toeplate on which the base cabinet sits and the countertop, which is 1 or 2 inches thick, raise the counter to the standard 36 or 37 inches. If you are tall, you can boost the work surface to a more comfortable level by installing a wider toeplate or countertop, or add an additional drawer. The widths of base cabinets vary, starting at 9 inches and continuing in 3-inch increments to 48 inches.

Wall cabinets usually start 18 inches above the countertop to leave room underneath for storing canisters and small appliances. They are about the same width as the base cabinets, 30 inches high and 12 inches deep. In the Adams house, we built the cupboards to the ceiling and planned to use a kitchen ladder to reach the highest shelves. Often, though, I have used the space above cabinets to display some of the kitchen things that I've collected. You can also install extra storage there for oversize pots and pans.

Cabinet manufacturers are now making available many kinds of specialized storage: shelves that roll out on tracks, drawers with slots for cutlery or tailored for knives or spice jars, corner base cabinets with lazy Susans. These comprehensive storage systems stand in for the old-time pantries.

Nearly all the major manufacturers provide varied storage options, but they do not all build their cabinets with the same attention to quality materials and details, or with the same range of styles or finishes (usually painted, stained, or polyurethaned wood, or a plastic laminate). Since cabinetry accounts for 40 percent of the total cost of the typical kitchen project, selecting a finish you will be happy with is very important. There are three options:

CUSTOM CABINETS: Designed and made by a local cabinetmaker, these are the most expensive. Everything from the choice of wood to the depth of the shelves to the finish on the hardware is done to your specifications.

CUSTOM-MANUFACTURED CABINETS: Produced on special order by cabinet companies with the same materials they use in their stock work, but with modification specified by the designer. These

ABOVE LEFT: An earlier inhabitant had created a pantry in a small room off the original kitchen by installing this primitive shelving. This pantry was one of the five rooms that ultimately became the new kitchen.

ABOVE: Shallow open shelves are great for displaying canned goods and preserves. I also store many of my culinary spices, herbs, and condiments in glass jars; these shelves offer a perfect place to keep them. I find that I use things more frequently when I see them out in the open.

usually take at least four to six weeks.

STOCK CABINETS: The standard cabinets that kitchen showrooms have in stock are often quite good, but you should check to see how the shelves are installed and what materials were used on the sides and backs of shelves and drawers.

One way to upgrade a well-made stock cabinet—or an existing but serviceable cabinet—is to install better quality hardware. In fact, no matter what kind of cabinets you select, pay special attention to the hardware, as this is one of the details that will be important in the overall effect.

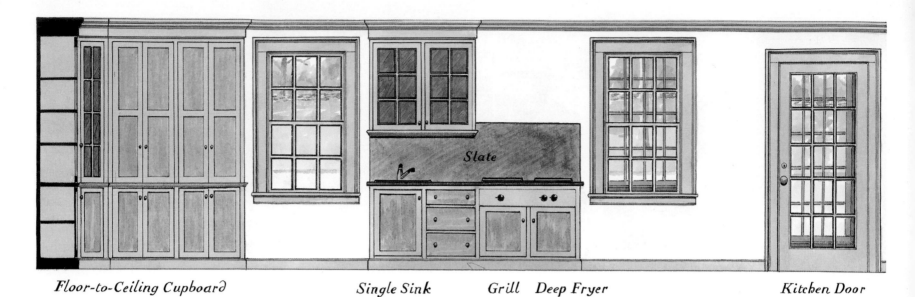

Floor-to-Ceiling Cupboard   Single Sink   Grill   Deep Fryer   Kitchen Door

KITCHEN - WEST WALL - ELEVATION A-A

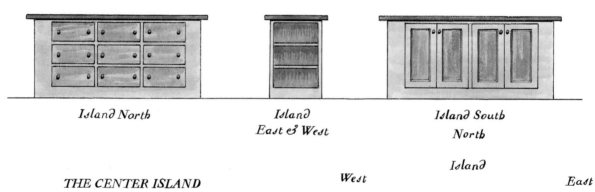

Island North   Island   Island South
                            East & West   North

                                                        Island

THE CENTER ISLAND   West   East

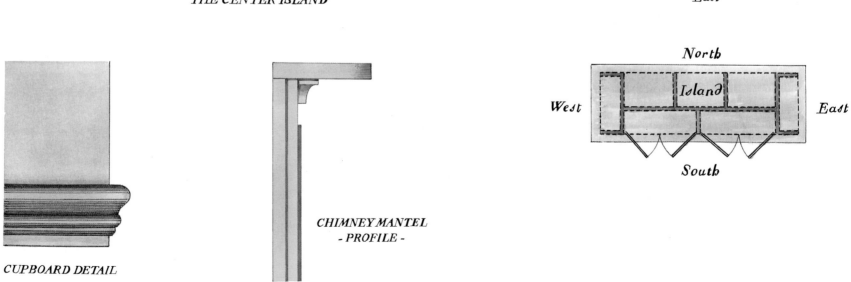

CUPBOARD DETAIL   CHIMNEY MANTEL
                            - PROFILE -

160

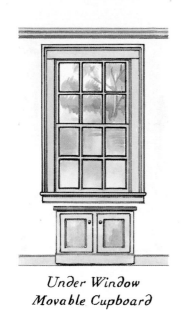

Under Window
Movable Cupboard

Door to   *Door to*   *Floor-to-Ceiling Cupboard*
Basement *2nd Floor*

KITCHEN - DINING AREA - SOUTH WALL - ELEVATION B - B

       Dishwasher *Ice*   *Refrigerator*   *Freezer*   *Door to Sunroom*
Double Sink   *Maker*

KITCHEN - WORK AREA - EAST WALL - ELEVATION C - C

REFINISHING THE CABINETS

The cupboards and woodwork in the new kitchen were painted and designed by a friend, Marla Weinhoff, a decorative painter and designer from New York City. The colors we chose were combinations of ochers, blues, and greens. Marla's method of finishing the pine and poplar of the cabinets was complicated, giving an amazing, delicately shaded appearance to the wood. The interiors of the doors, as well as all the exterior surfaces, were treated to her process.

Once the cabinets were installed, Marla finished the interiors, using a mixture of tung oil and raw umber artist's oil color to stain and seal them.

For the door panels, she mixed powdered artist's pigments in tung oil to create transparent tints in several shades of green, cobalt, and ultramarine blue. Marla treated each panel as a separate painting, brushing and rubbing the stains into the wood to enhance the grain. Every color was used on every panel but in differing proportions and values.

On the exterior surrounds, Marla wanted to suggest the layered look of the distressed paint on the kitchen doors. First the wood was sealed with tung oil and allowed to dry overnight. Then she and her team applied satin-finish oil-based paint in three colors—khaki, camel, and green—brushing on the colors together and blending them to achieve the visual effect of old paint. This opaque treatment contrasts with the transparency of the powdered-pigment stain on the panels.

For the final step, she applied three coats of clear butcher's wax on all the stained and painted surfaces, and then buffed them well.

ABOVE: Marla applying color to the door panel fronts. She and two assistants worked very long and hard for almost two weeks applying the finish to the cupboards. Working with the neatness and efficiency of laboratory technicians, this crew and Sherry Ringler, who did the kitchen floor, were not only gifted artisans, but efficient and professional. Since the kitchen gets such a tremendous amount of wear and tear, it is of utmost importance to use finishes that are not only decorative, but hard, durable, and long-lasting.

LEFT: Careful of appliances and wary of the slate counters, Marla and her team effectively divided their labors and completed the job step-by-step. The finished project expresses a great deal of personality; each door was done in a different shade of the overall tone, and the interiors were painted in many different shades, ranging from light blue to a deep teal. The fireplace mantel area was stained a rather dark grayish black, reiterating the mottled gray slate of the counters.

RIGHT: Marla's tools were collected from all over the world: brushes from Japan, Italy, and France; paints, tints, and colored powders from a variety of suppliers, and rags from everyone's discarded laundry.

Painting a Diamond-Patterned Floor

Old copper pots and kettles were an important element of my picture of the Adams house kitchen, and I wanted the finish of the wide-board yellow pine floor to pick up the copper theme. My first idea was a painted checkerboard with every other square done in copper paint. But Sherry Ringler, who was introduced to me by a friend and quickly became an important part of the decorative team for the old house, suggested an alternative to my original idea. Sherry, an accomplished decorative painter from Springfield, Ohio, who has a very good sense of what is right for a project and will not allow a client to proceed when she considers the direction misguided, cautioned that the copper paint would not look vibrant enough. She won me over to her idea: a checkerboard turned on its side to create a diamond pattern, with areas of natural wood alternating with areas antiqued in the same tones as the cabinets, accented with small squares of copper leaf where the diamonds intersected. A copper leaf border around the edge would be the finishing touch.

Sherry is an extremely competent draftsman and can mathematically lay out a complicated pattern so that it fits a space correctly and accurately. The initial stages of her work—devising the plan, laying out the design, taping off all necessary areas, choosing the correct materials to use, mixing her colors—took her longer than the painting itself.

Sherry and her assistant measured the entire floor and decided to use squares

approximately 12 by 12 inches, set on the diagonal, which read as diamonds. After removing the protective paper and cleaning the floor well with a tack cloth, they determined the exact center of the room, then measured off the area to be painted in diamond patterns, leaving a border about 9 inches wide.

To strike the grid for squares set on the diagonal, it is necessary to ascertain the length of the hypotenuse, the diagonal line drawn between opposite corners of a square; in this case the hypotenuse is 17 inches. Standing on adjoining, not opposite, sides of the room, they used a chalk line to snap a set of diagonal lines across the floor, then a second set of diagonals at a right angle to the first. The result was a perfect diamond grid.

Sherry then taped along the edges of each diamond that was to be left natural, using a single-edge razor blade to trim tight corners. (She says Anchor Brand masking tape is best because it is sticky enough to allow very little seepage, yet releases with little residue.)

1. Working from the edges to the center of the room, Sherry applied a mustard-color base coat to every other diamond. She used three parts Benjamin Moore 1048 to one part mineral spirits. She also painted a base coat on the border and let the floor dry overnight.

To match the color of the cabinets, Sherry mixed two glazes—a mauve (Benjamin Moore 1193) and a fern green (495)—into Benjamin Moore satin Impervo,

thinning the blend with mineral spirits.

Using two cotton gauze rags that had been washed and dried to eliminate lint, she wiped on the green glaze, then randomly streaked the mauve through the wet green, working with the grain of the wood. As she went around the room, she also glazed sections of the border.

Once the glazing was complete, she removed all the tape. Four hours later, when the last glazes had dried, she applied satin polyurethane thinned 3 to 1 with mineral spirits to the entire floor. She used a smooth nap roller, then a 4-inch varnish brush in the direction of the grain to remove brush marks and bubbles. The doors were sealed with plastic and the room left to dry overnight.

2. The next morning, after the vents in the kitchen were sealed to prevent drafts, Sherry used a draftsman's compass to mark a small square of 1¾ inches at the four corners of each large square.

3. At this stage, she taped the edges with Scotch Safe-Release masking tape, a brand that comes off with almost no residue, good when seepage is not a problem. Each square was coated with Rolco quick gold size and allowed to dry for 1 to 3 hours.

4–5. Sherry then applied the copper leaf, tamping it down with a brush.

6. She removed any flecks from the leaf with a clean tack cloth and a Dustbuster, then gently peeled away the tape.

The whole floor was given three coats of satin polyurethane, with overnight drying time between coats. It took two more coats of low-luster polyurethane to get the quiet glow we wanted. The extra finish has also helped protect the copper leaf, which has stood up to extremely heavy foot traffic.

DECORATING

Eastern Turkestan

THE ROOMS

As the restoration/renovation proceeded, my thoughts often turned to the decoration. It occurred to me that the house would lend itself well to a total decoration plan, and I envisioned a basic 19th-century interior rendered comfortable and elegant. I wanted a contemporary approach to the graceful art of period design, utilizing careful choices of antiques and reproductions. One day I had a brainstorm: I would gather together a fine group of decorators and artisans to design each of the rooms individually, while maintaining the central theme of a 19th-century farmhouse adapted to the myriad requirements of a modern, busy family of the 20th century. To achieve this, I would form a "showhouse" committee to benefit a local charity. The decorators, designers, and artisans were very enthusiastic about working on the project. ■ The beneficiary of the showhouse was Paul Newman's camp for children with blood diseases, the Hole In The Wall Gang Camp in northeastern Connecticut. I think that his involvement played a major role in the success of the entire event. He was an active participant, and both he and his wife, Joanne Woodward, contributed time and effort to the publicity and the gala. ■ Each designer was given a room to decorate, along with a small list of requirements, reminding each of them to coordinate the design with those of the adjoining rooms, and to use furniture and objects that would complement the 19th-century theme.

LEFT: **An American 19th-century convex mirror graciously reflects the finely detailed upstairs hall sitting room, which was fashioned out of the catacomb of halls and the unlit bedroom of the second-floor landing. Sometimes it is a good decorating idea to leave one or two lighting fixtures in a room unelectrified: the original candle light is an appealing feature.**

RIGHT: **The trompe l'oeil cupboard bookcase depicting beautiful books and collectibles was delightfully executed by Eva Llanos for Suzanne Miller's upstairs sitting room landing.**

ABOVE: The second-floor landing was a difficult area to renovate, but the final solution worked very well, and made the stair and landing serviceable and safer than before. Doorways were eliminated, giving the area more wall space on which to hang pictures. The ceiling was defined with moldings.

ABOVE RIGHT: The Hole In The Wall Gang Camp and its founder, Paul Newman, were the inspiration for the showhouse. During the final stages, Paul offered almost daily support of our effort and this kept up everyone's enthusiasm.

We tried hard to work out compatible color palettes, degrees of formality, and an overall sense that the house was a whole, and not just a series of unrelated rooms, a typical syndrome of the popular showhouse. Each designer understood that this was to be a joint venture and that the artisans, often overlooked, were to receive equal attention. This house was to be a celebration not only of fine design, but also of fine craftsmanship.

I found that many friends and neighbors were enthusiastic about being involved in such a project. A small committee headed by Karen Tarshis was set up to run the entire showhouse. We also ran a series of seminars to attract visitors to the area for an extended visit, to learn and study a variety of techniques while visiting the showhouse and other interesting sites in the neighborhood. The range of subjects included Decorating

with Antiques and Flowers, Decorative Painting Techniques, The Fine Points of Hiring a Painting Contractor, and Elements of Design and Planning.

The showhouse was a great success, raising several hundred thousand dollars. It engendered a great deal of good will in our community and helped rekindle the townspeoples' interest in the architectural history of Westport. I know that the workmanship and craftsmanship of the project were stimulating to those who viewed the house.

WORKING WITH A DECORATOR

Design professionals may be either decorators, whose tasks mostly involve selecting furniture, accessories, wallpaper, fabrics, and paint colors, or interior designers, who are usually also qualified to make interior construction decisions, particularly if they are certified or licensed. All competent design professionals have had special training and, as experienced visual thinkers, should know what will work in a room. They also usually have access to resources unavailable to most consumers, mainly "to the trade only" fabric and furniture design showrooms as well as specialty shops.

A designer or decorator can be expected to have good rapport not only with suppliers, but also with contractors, painters, paperhangers, cabinetmakers, carpet installers, and upholstery and curtain makers to ensure that you receive top-quality products and workmanship. Hiring a professional can be a sound investment. The decorator saves you time and money by doing the legwork for you. Further, the professional you hire will be equipped to handle problems that arise on the site and to prevent costly mistakes.

The ideal design professional is patient and totally comprehending of your personal taste and needs. Knowing what pleases you, particularly what you feel comfortable with, the designer may be able to present ideas or solutions you might not even have considered. The best way to find a design professional is through word-of-mouth referrals from friends whose homes you have admired.

Many department stores carrying home furnishings also have in-house design staffs; the design fee is included in the price of purchases. A final resource is decorating magazines and books.

When interviewing designers and decorators, it is helpful to learn about their education, approach to problems and challenges, and the kind of work they've done in the past. Most important, you will discern how each responds to your needs as well as to your time and budget constraints. Trust your judgment; hire the person with whom you feel most comfortable.

There are many ways to work with a decorator. You can hire a designer solely for a consultation, which should include approaches to your design problem as well as a roughed-out floorplan and suggestions for color schemes and furnishings. Deeper involvement includes access to resources, visits to showrooms, and the selection of fabrics and furnishings.

When you decide on a design professional, it is a good idea to draw up a contract or simply a letter of agreement, stating how payments will be made.

The American Society of Interior Designers (ASID) defines six different forms of possible compensation:

FIXED OR FLAT FEE: The designer will quote a total fee that covers a full range of services from concept to installation, exclusive of expenses.

HOURLY FEE: You will pay for the time the designer devotes to your project. Depending on the services required and the designer's reputation, expect to pay $50 an hour and up.

COST-PLUS: The designer purchases the products and furnishings you've chosen at cost, adding such services as carpentry, upholstering, and picture framing. You will be billed from 15 to 40 percent more, depending on your agreement.

PERCENTAGE FEE: Similar to cost-plus, this arrangement covers all goods and services purchased or specified for your project. For example, ASID guidelines state that "if the net cost of furnishings is $30,000, a designer might charge 20 percent of that as compensation for design services."

RETAIL BASIS: The designer obtains products and furnishings at the net price accorded professionals, then bills you at the retail rate. The 35 or 40 percent differential is the designer's commission.

COST BY SQUARE FOOT: The fee you are charged is determined by the square footage of the rooms.

BELOW: Choosing the right fabrics in a color palette designed to fit a room is a complex and time-consuming effort.

THE FRONT HALL

The front hall welcomes visitors as they enter and sets the decorative and emotional tone for the entire house. Although the front hall in the Adams house is small, its proportions are perfect—and I love its sturdy staircase leading to the newly designed landing. Once the old stair carpet had been removed and the stairs sanded, I couldn't decide whether to refinish them and leave them uncovered or recarpet them. Virginia Pierrepont suggested an ingenious idea: a trompe l'oeil stair runner.

When we discussed the walls, we concurred at once on a faux wallpaper, patterned after damask, in a pale celadon green, a favorite color of mine. The finished result was subtle and soft, with just enough highlighting to delineate the design.

Stenciling the walls is a tradition that goes back to colonial days when wallpaper was difficult to obtain and extremely expensive; it's still a wonderful way to personalize a wall.

We mounted a row of plates—some old, some less old—at the top of the walls; drawing the eye upward, and visually expanding the space. We decided to keep furnishings to a minimum and, instead, emphasize the unusual and beautiful hand-painted decoration.

FAR LEFT: This picture of the front hall gives a good idea of the condition and lack of decoration evident in the old house while Miss Adams was tenant. The wide-board floors were covered with very dingy old carpet (in actuality, it helped preserve the floors, making sanding and refinishing quite easy). The old louvered screen doors, painted dark green, were in great disrepair. The side lights, one of the interesting architectural features of the house, were covered with dark louvers, and the only light that penetrated the hall was from the transom over the door.

LEFT: Looking down the center stairway: the split stairs were dangerous and were changed when the upper hall was redesigned.

RIGHT: The newly decorated front hall and west parlor look fresh and light. Rugless and refinished, the pine floorboards are a fine feature of the house and add to the fresh feeling. Much more daylight is in evidence in the absence of shutters, and the windows admit a great deal of lovely, soft light.

All hardware was cleaned, polished, and left unvarnished. We painted the walls and trim the color of heavy cream.

Stenciling the Walls

To create her stencil, Virginia first researched damask patterns in several textile design books dating from her grandmother's era. She selected a motif that she thought would best suit the wall and copied it onto a piece of drawing paper. She fine-tuned the drawing until it was just the right size to fit into a 12-inch square. Then she placed a sheet of acetate film over the drawing and traced the design with an indelible marker. Using an #11 X-Acto blade, she carefully cut out the stencil, making sure every stroke was within the traced outline.

To prepare the pre-primed walls for stenciling, Virginia and her assistant, Caitlin Nammack, rolled on Benjamin Moore's Wintergreen Eggshell latex, warming it slightly with a hint of raw sienna and yellow ocher. (The trim was painted with Benjamin Moore Satin Atrium White Satin finish. The front door and window frames were painted white, with Benjamin Moore Satin Impervo Alkyd low-luster enamel.) They then measured the walls, and, using a chalk line and blue chalk, laid out a grid of 12-inch squares. The squares were outlined with 1-inch-wide masking tape. As she did with the faux runner, Virginia decided to stagger the pattern checkerboard style, with one motif in every other square.

The corners of the stencil were attached to the wall with masking tape. Virginia and Caitlin daubed, or pounced, paint through the stencil using a #2 natural bristle stencil brush. They used a special color acrylic, a fast-drying paint with a plastic-resin binder, in graphite

gray tinted slightly with ultramarine blue plus a quarter-cup of water so that the glaze would become somewhat translucent. Virginia prefers acrylics for stenciling because they are easy to work with; japan colors dry more slowly.

They worked from the center to the edges in a circular motion, keeping the brush as dry as possible. They dipped only the tip of the bristles into the paint, never covering more than one quarter of the bristles, and then blotted the brush on a damp paper towel to remove any residue.

Once the paint had been applied, Virginia dabbed at the image gently with cheesecloth for an even texture. Then, after removing the stencil, she and Caitlin, working freehand, added highlights in white and shadows in blue-gray with tapered artist's round brushes.

To give the "wallpaper" an iridescent shimmer, Virginia used a special glaze composed of ⅓ cup of #242 silver and

#10 aqua metallic powder blended, both found at Pearl Paint in New York City, and ½ gallon of Golden Acrylic Matte Medium diluted with ½ cup water. After removing the masking tape, Virginia applied this glaze to the wall with a 2½-inch-wide soft bristle brush. Finally, she rubbed the glaze lightly with a clean cheesecloth to give it a subtle sheen.

LEFT: The woodwork, plainly painted an eggshell cream, and the sanded, finished and painted staircase contrast beautifully with the stenciled walls.

RIGHT:

1. Caitlin drew the design of the stencil on acetate before cutting it with a knife.
2. Virginia used a "pouncer" to apply paint to the wall through the stencil.
3. Virginia refined the stencil with freehand painting. This technique avoids a static look and creates a much more "hand-painted" appearance, highlighting the original design with color and depth.
4. After glazing the wall with a very light application by brush, Virginia then softened the finish with a cheesecloth rubbing.

Painting a Stair Runner

Runners manufactured on Wilton looms, which were invented in the mid-18th century to produce velvety carpets with intricate patterns, were very popular during the Federal period. Virginia Pierrepont chose a simple triple-dot design, a motif that would have been commonly used at the time.

To demarcate the edges of the runner, Virginia's assistant, Caitlin, pressed 1-inch-wide masking tape against a penciled border. Within these boundaries, she brushed on a coat of Benjamin Moore's Satin Impervo Black alkyd paint cut with 4 tablespoons of Satin Impervo White to dull the hue slightly.

While the paint was still somewhat gummy, she took a 12-inch-square piece of rabbit-wire mesh and pressed it firmly into the paint to simulate the texture of carpeting. While the mesh was in place, she used a blunt #2 hog-bristle stencil brush to apply a taupe japan glaze lightly over the surface to bring out the woven effect. Japan color is a pigment mixed in a resinous varnish that contains no oil; to make a glaze, it is mixed with oil paint and a thinner such as turpentine or mineral spirits.

After removing the mesh, Virginia and Caitlin dotted every fourth square with the triangular triple-dot motif, using a narrow point-tipped artist's brush called a round. The design was staggered over alternating rows, as on real carpet.

Finally, Virginia hand-painted faux gold rods at the juncture of each tread and riser, then finished it off with faux fringes at the bottom.

ABOVE LEFT: **All the balusters (spindles) were removed for cleaning and repainting. The stationary newel post was cleaned in place and painted to match the woodwork. The old rug was also left in place until all the construction was completed; this protected the soft pine stair treads.**

ABOVE: **All the plaster and lath was removed from the stairwell and powder room walls so that the plumbing, heating, and wiring could be installed.**

RIGHT: **The newly finished floors and freshly painted woodwork accentuate Virginia Pierrepont's beautifully painted walls and stair runners. A standard-size decorative grille set into the understair wall provides for the intake of air into the heating system. The woodwork was scraped and sanded before being primed and painted with two coats of eggshell enamel.**

THE EAST
PARLOR

Designer Robert K. Lewis loves old houses, and he particularly appreciated the fine lines and gracious proportions of the Adams house. He knows a great deal about historic buildings (when I asked him to decorate the east parlor, he noted that 15-foot-square rooms are typical of the Federal period), but he keeps his history in perspective, maintaining that a room can be true to its past and still be comfortable and modern.

In 1838, when the Adams house was built, there were people still alive who had fought in the Revolutionary War. By then the Empire style was all the rage in cosmopolitan centers, but here in the backwater of the West Port of Connecticut, even a prosperous family would probably have adhered to the design tenets of an earlier era. With that in mind, Robert's room recalls the mood of the years around 1800.

Because a parlor was typically the best room of a house, it usually displayed a family's finest furnishings and ancestral portraits. This was the period of the American portrait, the painted reflection of the newly powerful and prosperous middle class. Robert selected a pair of enormous portraits; their scale gives the room a distinctly contemporary feel. He installed cornices and picture moldings to highlight the portraits, suspended the pictures in the traditional manner from chains, and positioned recessed spot-lights to suffuse them with halos of light. In their plain gold frames, they look magnificent against the white wall.

Robert decided against faux finishes for the parlor. After pulling down the peeling floral wallpaper that encrusted the walls, he decided to simulate the whitewash used in the 19th century. He accomplished this by mixing 1½ cups of

FAR LEFT: **Robert Lewis is a very well informed designer who does intense research into the history of each room he works on. For the parlor he studied Connecticut transitional architecture and the social history of early houses.**

LEFT: **A view of the east parlor when Miss Adams lived in the house. Robert transformed the room with his style and grace.**

RIGHT: **To the left of the doorway leading into the parlor from the center hall, Robert Lewis placed a Newport drop-front desk (late-18th-century mahogany) and filled it with memorabilia. The writing papers were designed by his wife, Joy Lewis. (She even made an engraving of the Adams house for our showhouse letterhead.) The French polychrome tin soldiers from the American Revolutionary period, manufactured in either France or Newport, wear uniforms of the King's own grenadiers.**

The painted Dutch armchair is part of a set from the early 19th century.

LEFT: The portraits that dominate the east parlor, dating from 1820 to 1830, are of Connecticut gentry, a man and wife from nearby Essex. Through the open window of the gentleman's portrait, one sees the Connecticut River, his ship, his bank, and his church. In her portrait, his wife sits beside her beautiful table with the marbleized top and decorated base. Her house is seen through the open window.

The pictures are hung authentically on antique brackets specifically designed for picture moldings.

The window treatment is typical of Robert Lewis: an unusual documentary toile de Jouy simply transformed into drawn-up festoon blinds. (The fabric was also used for the slipcovers, upholstery, and table cover.) Attention to detail is evident in the cording used to work the shade and the beautifully decorative brass knobs affixed to the wall.

Contemporary lighting, both fixtures and spots, are an unusual and very effective feature of Robert's design.

The tea service, copperplate-engraved transferware, was made in France circa 1825.

Spackle into each gallon of white Devoe interior latex flat paint. Robert didn't want a barnlike stucco finish, though, so he brushed on the whitewash in even horizontal and vertical strokes with a 6-inch-wide bristle brush.

He painted the trim in a pale biscuit, using Benjamin Moore's Satin Impervo oil, #OW13.

ARRANGING FURNITURE: "A room is most alive," Robert says, "if the furniture layout is not absolutely rigid." He always provides some anchors—often a sofa and a big wing chair for reading—but keeps the other chairs and tables small and portable, so they can be moved around to facilitate conversation.

The most inviting arrangement should make its major impact as you enter the room. For this reason, Robert placed the pieces comprising the focal point of the room—the Sheraton sofa flanked by the twin portraits—in full view of the door. Instead of the usual 17-inch-high coffee table, he set a 29-inch-high tea table in front of the sofa. Besides being historically more correct, the table offers a place to display beautiful objects and to serve tea.

Another of Robert's visual tricks was to pull the sofa a foot or so away from the wall to draw the eye into the room; all the furniture against the walls created a stiff unlived-in look. All furnishings should relate harmoniously to each other in terms of scale, no single piece upstaging another.

ESTABLISHING A PALETTE: Color is perhaps the most essential element in decoration. More than any other, it enhances mood and is the clearest visual statement

ABOVE: From 1824–1825, the Marquis de Lafayette, who had served with Washington during the Revolution, toured the United States. A wonderful black-and-white toile de Jouy commemorating his visit is used throughout the east parlor. Printed from an old copperplate, the toile, called "Lafayette" or "Hommage de L'Amerique à la France," depicts France as a seated female figure crowned and carrying the shield of France, accompanied by a figure clad in armor. Homage is tendered by Indians, one carrying the flag of the first Union. The exotic American flora and fauna include alligators and deer.

about the personality of the room. I generally prefer a soft palette of grays and greens and was pleased when Robert chose to work with a subtle neutral palette. I felt it suited the gracious mood of the room.

The starting point for a color scheme can come from almost anything—a rug, a painting, a piece of fabric. Here it was the black-and-white toile used for the curtains and upholstery. Robert warmed up its crispness with the biscuit-hued woodwork and a sandy-golden "sweet grass" matting on the floor. In the 1800s similar matting was laid down in fine houses during the summer, when Oriental rugs were rolled up and removed to storage.

Neutral hues tend to expand a room visually, while dark colors make it feel smaller and cozier. Many psychological studies have been made to determine the way people react to certain colors. Most people find "safe" colors such as white, beige, linen, or taupe easier to live with than more vivid colors. In general, you can choose bolder, brighter colors for rooms in which you spend less time and for accents, such as pillows.

ABOVE: A close-up of one of the antique andirons.

RIGHT: A framed 1845 lithograph, *Surrender of Cornwallis at Yorktown*, depicts Cornwallis, Washington, Lafayette, and others, including the grenadiers also represented by the period tin soldiers. Marching from Newport, the French grenadiers participated in this decisive battle of the war.

The early-19th-century Liverpool pitcher on the mantel, with a black copperplate-engraving transfer pattern, commemorates Lafayette's last visit to America.

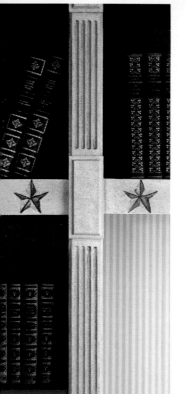

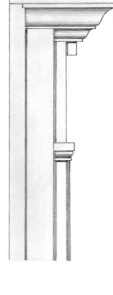

THE LIBRARY

Interior designer Justin Baxter planned the library as a comforting retreat—the perfect spot to curl up with a novel and a glass of sherry on a midwinter evening or to read spring planting catalogs. He used built-in bookshelves and down-filled furniture, including a sofa with plump cushions, a club chair, and a Victorian slipper chair, and a palette that plays off deep tones against creamy ones. He began with the largest single element in the room, the Chinese needlepoint rug. To that he added a sumptuous array of color and pattern: raspberry silk damask and leopard-print velvet on the chairs, a pale yellow ribbed cotton on the sofa, a silk and cotton stripe at the windows, another stripe on the wallpaper, and a tapestry throw pillow. To provide a background for this exotic mix, the woodwork was painted a light celery color.

USING PATTERN: In an old house, wall coverings with small-scale patterns, such as the narrow stripe in the library, can create a warm atmosphere at the same time that they camouflage irregularities in a wall. (Stripes can also introduce a trace of a color that would be too strong in a larger expanse, and they make rooms look taller, which is often desirable.)

The simplest way to coordinate fabrics with wallpaper is to select a single color from a patterened wall covering and use that shade for the upholstery or slipcovers on one or more of the large pieces of furniture in the room or for the window dressing. As counterpoint, use a constrasting solid, like the raspberry in the library. For pillows, trimmings, lamp shades, and such, try smaller patterns that pick up one of the solid colors.

Texture also plays a role. In the library, the softness of the velvet contrasts with the silk damask and the nubbly surface of the needlepoint.

Bring home samples of all the patterns you are considering and spread them out next to one another. Squint at them. If one pattern jumps out, discard it. A rule of thumb is to stick with two, three, or four patterns that melt easily into one another, creating a unified look.

ABOVE LEFT: The mantel, seen in profile below, was greatly improved by the addition of simple but elegant moldings and fluted pilaster woodwork. Reflected in the mirror is a continuation of the star theme, a glass and bronze hanging star fixture.

Faux marble on the fireplace surround lightens the whole. Simple clay-potted orchids adorn the mantel.

BELOW LEFT: The fluted pilasters around the bookcases and the beautifully painted stars add a subtle touch of finery. Raphael Serrano, a decorative painter, shaded the woodwork a lovely celery color; from a distance the gold-highlighted stars look applied rather than painted.

RIGHT: A contemporary but very fine Chinese needlepoint rug, wonderfully upholstered and fringed side chairs, and a very simple but lavish balloon shade give the room a great sense of comfort. Reading lamps (brass wall sconces) are perfect for curling up with a book. The stepped bases of the bookcases are a clever handling of the small space, acting as end tables while still serving as ladders.

THE DINING ROOM

The dining room of the Adams house is peculiarly shaped, with almost no wall space, many doors (nine, to be exact, including closets), and poor woodwork. Furthermore, the room is long, front to back, and has no windows, making it the most difficult room in the house to decorate. Artist Wendy Stone came up with a wonderful visual solution to bring lightness into the room and open up the space: a wall mural.

Wendy wanted to base her mural on the China trade that had begun in the 1830s, the same period as the construction of the house. In those days, clipper

RIGHT: When I bought the house, the fireplace was in disrepair and the wooden doors for the beehive oven and wood storage were broken.

The floors were intact, though under a covering of 1930s linoleum. We kept the lovely chair rail but removed the molding at the height of the door frames. Luckily, the plaster, quite badly cracked, had not pulled from its lath and was reparable.

The view at left is into the west parlor.

FOLLOWING PAGE LEFT: Bob Hoven was like a whirlwind. He came with a crew of painters from his New York studio and in just two days wood-grained the fireplace surround and paneling, stippled the woodwork and doors, and glazed and spattered the dining room walls. Everyone had a specific job and worked with great concentration. The results were even better than expected.

ships traveled up the Pearl River to Canton, unloaded cargo, and then waited in Wampoa Harbor for the crates of tea bound for Britain and America. In a book of decorative art of the China trade, Wendy saw *A View of Wampoa*, a scene painted in the European manner by a Chinese artist named Youqua, which had probably been sold to a seafaring captain as a souvenir. This picture and other similar paintings she saw at Connecticut's Mystic Seaport Museum served as the models for her mural. The final painting made this difficult room one of the most interesting in the house.

The dado wall was painted a darker shade of green-teal, which contrasts well with the pale celadon of the glazed walls above. The moldings and doors were all painted a simple off-white. The brick-painted floor, a clever and simple decorative painting technique, is wonderfully useful in the well-trafficked and well-used central room.

We left untouched the saddle in the doorway of the west parlor, which was worn all the way down to the floorboards by more than 150 years of foot traffic. It's wonderful to keep traces of the families who lived in the house throughout the decades.

ABOVE: Walter Jaykus carefully applying a large sheet of theatrical supply canvas to the wall in the dining room where the mural would be painted.

PREVIOUS PAGE RIGHT: R. N. Potter, a New York designer, furnished the room for which she had commissioned a large crew of talented artisans. She used a 19th-century D-end dining room table in mahogany, a 19th-century Continental smoked globe hanging light fixture, a Federal gilded convex mirror (c. 1830, American), and a figured mahogany chest of drawers. Portraits, porcelain plates, and fine candlesticks were used for decoration.

RIGHT: Wendy Stone was inspired by the China trade for her mural subject matter. In a primarily unheated interior, and under a great deal of pressure to finish before deadline, she worked very long hours on the painting. In the 19th century, a mural would have been applied directly to the walls, aging as the plaster aged. The canvas we used will help prevent this.

Painting the Mural

Wendy decided to paint her mural on canvas tacked to the wall rather than directly on the plaster. For such an expensive and time-consuming task, she wanted a smooth base on which to work. Also, in the event a future homeowner would choose to remove the mural, it could be taken down with little or no damage to the painting itself. Wendy told me she could have painted it on the floor and then hung it, but would have risked cracking the paint.

Wendy had anticipated that the artist's canvas would shrink and had compensated with a piece 2 inches wider all around.

Paperhanger Walter Jaykus first primed the walls just as he would for a standard wallpapering job. With a 4-inch-bristle brush, he applied a coat of Benjamin Moore's #3 sizing, a compound made of glue and latex that acts as a bond but won't penetrate the canvas. Sizing has to dry overnight; it should not be sticky to the touch.

The next day, Walter applied over the sizing a quick-drying clay-based wall-covering glue (less runny than water-based paste) with a 6-inch-wide wallpaper-paste brush. Applying glue to the wall rather than to the canvas is another anti-shrinkage strategy. Walter folded the canvas over on itself in thirds, like a letter. Working from left to right, he spread the canvas across the wall, pressing it against the adhesive with a clean wallpaper brush, squeezing out bubbles as he went along.

He then pressed all the edges flat with

a seam roller. Wendy chalked a scaled-up grid onto the canvas. Using thinned acrylic paint in a sepia tone and artist's brushes, she delicately outlined her design over the grid. She then wiped off the chalk lines.

For the large expanse of sky, she brushed on an oil glaze base, using a mixture of white artist's oil paint, "flatting" oil, and turpentine. This base ensured that later subtle colorings in the sky would blend together well. Under the mountain range, which reached across the horizon line of her painting, Wendy washed in the water, slowly and painstakingly building up and then smearing her glazes with brushes and rags and even her fingertips. Then she added the landscape and clipper ships. When she was finished, the effect was slightly faded, as if the mural had been painted years ago.

RIGHT: Completed, the mural gives a great serenity and sense of depth to the dining room. Even interrupted by doorways and closets, the painting evokes the feeling of the great French documentary wallpaper of the past two centuries. Set above the dado, little of the view is lost to the eye, and the harbor of Wampoa is clearly illustrated.

THE ANTEROOM

The anteroom links the dining room, sunroom, and front hall. At the eastern end is the laundry. I wanted the anteroom to blend with the surrounding rooms, especially with the dining room because, with its floor-to-ceiling china cupboards, the anteroom serves as an extra pantry.

Artists Fiona Prichard and Wendy Stone decided to center the room with a faux Oriental rug that would pull together the colors used in the nearby rooms. They poured over books on Samarkand carpets from Central Asia. In their favorite, *Oriental Carpets and Rugs*, by

LEFT: **Another fine decorative trompe l'oeil effect used by the designer was the hand-painted Oriental rug on the dining room floor. Fiona Prichard, the artisan commissioned to paint the rug, did much research and planning to execute her task: to paint a complex design and preserve it for posterity with hard top coats.**

This is a good view of the newly installed glass-paned door and window transom leading into the sunroom, as well as of the skylights. What makes these unusual is that they were installed in two layers, the first being the plain glass skylight and the sashes seen here, made from specially ordered windows designed to match the others in the house.

RIGHT: **Lisa Breznak used just a very few simple materials for her brick-patterned floor: cellulose sponges cut to exact size, green-tinted stain, and papertowels for cleanup of any mistakes.**

Stanley Reed, they found an Eastern Turkestan pattern of the exact same date as the house—with all the same muted colors as Wendy's mural in the dining room. Wendy pointed out that the rug also tied in with the China trade.

Painting a Faux Brick Floor

Fiona and Wendy wanted to create the impression that their rug was resting on an old brick floor. Artist Lisa Breznak brushed over the area a layer of McCloskey varnish mixed with a tiny amount of dark green oil.

When the varnish had dried, she cut two cellulose sponges into 7-by-3½-inch rectangles and daubed turpentine-thinned dark green oil-based paint in a herringbone pattern all over the exposed floor to simulate worn brick.

Finally, to protect her work, she covered the floor with several layers of satin polyurethane.

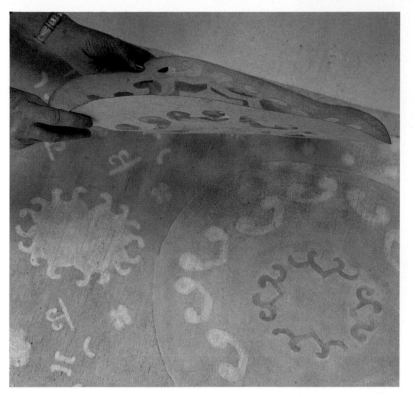

LEFT: **The view through the laundry room door into the anteroom and storage cupboard beyond. The carpet was painted right on the pine floorboards. The cupboard was original to the house, and I decided to keep it because it was useful and because the space really could not be used for anything else.**

ABOVE: **Close-up views of Fiona's work in progress. It was hard on her arms and knees to work in such a painstaking fashion on the floor, but Fiona's perseverance paid off in a superb final product.**

Painting a Faux Oriental Rug

Translating the complex Turkestan pattern from paper to floor proved time-consuming. Fiona's husband helped with the computations; the photograph was magnified so that the repeating motif could be measured. Because the rug was hand-knotted, none of the motif was truly precise; adjustments had to be made to every design. Fiona decided to eliminate some. Even so, she ended up with 20 motifs, each of which had to be translated to a stencil. Unstenciled areas would be filled in with freehand painting.

The wide-plank flooring in the space required special preparation. Fiona blocked off the area to be "covered" with the rug and filled in the deep crevices between the planks with Phenoseal, a vinyl sealant, and the shal-

lower cracks with Dap (vinyl Spackle). She would not normally do this, she said, because she likes to preserve the integrity of the wood, but in this case she had to have a smooth surface for the rug.

Fiona and Wendy sanded over the rug area and laid down two coats of gesso, followed by a coat of Benjamin Moore's latex paint in eggshell finish, #Base 1 3191A, Color 253, the color often used as an undercoating on walls. Instead of working with a brush, Fiona used a natural sponge to get a silkier texture.

The pattern was outlined on the gesso, with specially mixed oil-based glazes used on each stencil.

To achieve the worn look of an antique Oriental, Fiona daubed the painted areas when they were still semidry with a piece of linen to give the rug a walked-on effect.

THE OFFICE STUDY

Joel Clark Gevis came to the Adams house with a deep respect for its architecture, an appreciation for today's artisans—and a sense of humor, too. He loved what he called the "quirkiness" of this passageway between the dining room and the kitchen, which Dr. Adams had used as his office when the house was a school. The little fireplace, one of three emanating from the west parlor chimney on the first floor, had been peculiarly chopped off by the creation of a small hall between the study and the parlor. (The hall houses an exterior door

LEFT: A coarse sisal rug, bound with cotton twill tape, was used as a floor covering for just about half the room. The bookcases, built partially to conceal some water lines, are used to house not only books, but also decorative objects and some small collections.

The Federal armchair, embellished with an unusual Bennison fabric covering, is perfect for the Federal desk.

RIGHT: In his room plan, Joel combined some elements of the turn-of-the-century Arts and Crafts movement with the Federal influence. The scroll-arm buttoned-back chair with ottoman and casters is a fine example of Joel's talent for mixing periods successfully while still creating a comfortable, livable home.

I like the way he hung the small picture in the window, and how he lit the room with graceful mid-19th-century French sconces.

to a small porch on the west side of the house, one of three original exits on the first floor.) Joel and I agreed that we'd keep the fireplace and the hall the way they were.

Striped walls are a classic motif of the Federal period. Joel updated the tradition by making the stripes in the office study very wide—as wide as the vertical molding between the bays of the built-in bookcase. Joel's subtle palette enlivens the room: olive putty for the bookcases and a butter yellow alternating with cream for the walls, which were hand-painted by artist Greg Giesey. By using both a roller and a brush Greg achieved stripes that are soft yet straight, mellow and slightly textured. Greg added a wonderful surprise: a pale blue ceiling (Benjamin Moore HC-171), which gives the room a lift. The trim was painted in Benjamin Moore HC-98 Eggshell Olive.

Floors were sanded, sealed, polyurethaned and then waxed with butcher's paste wax.

Painting a Striped Wall

Stripes are the easiest of all patterns to master. Greg first prepared the walls by priming them. He then rolled finish coats of a Benjamin Moore cream flat-finish latex, Navajo white (which would also be the color of every other stripe). Using a ruler, he measured off 4-inch-wide stripes around the ceiling and marked lines on the walls with a chalked plumb line. He then covered every other stripe with two strips of 2-inch-wide masking tape.

With the tape pressed in place, Greg painted the entire wall surface—one wall

BELOW AND RIGHT: Tape covers the areas that will remain white, providing a straight edge difficult to achieve freehand. It also allows the painter to attain a texture similar to that of the contrasting wall color, also applied with a roller.

FAR RIGHT: Joel hung a 19th-century convex mirror above the mantel, located a single sconce (the match to the one on the opposite wall), and strategically hung small pictures here and there on the walls. Two myrtle topiary trees in moss-covered pots reiterate the simplicity of the room.

at a time—with three coats of flat latex in Benjamin Moore's Butter shade, using a standard roller. When he was satisfied with the density of the paint, he pulled away the tape and corrected the stripe edges with a 2½-inch natural bristle brush. After the paint had dried, he wiped off the chalk lines.

THE WEST PARLOR

In the basically symmetrical Adams house, the two front parlors have the same classic, perfectly square proportions. In decorating the west parlor, Lisa Krieger created a highly interpretive overview of 19th-century tastes by drawing from both the classicism of the Federal period and the romanticism of high

FAR LEFT: One of two rosewood upholstered parlor chairs, covered in a neoclassical fabric, drawn up to the wrought-iron and marble center table.

LEFT: Lisa chose a bold and very unusual color palette for her room, but because she used it in a late-19th-century fashion, muted by the fabric and painted floorcloth, it worked well within the entire house.

ABOVE: Before restoration, the west parlor was as dismal as the rest of the house. The mantel had been boarded up to conserve heat, and the millwork was so crude that we decided to tear it out and start again with a fireplace surround of much more importance. The doors, though simple, matched all the others and were retained.

LEFT: **Lisa likes to introduce a major piece of furniture into a room as a focal point. This secretary, an "abattant" made of bird's-eye maple dating from the late 19th century, fits well on the west wall. The iron planter and the delicate iron flower scale holding pansies, Victorian favorites, contribute to the "conservatory" air of the room. Plants, a fountain, and the urns repeat the theme.**

ABOVE: **The fireplace frieze features three sunburst carvings, accented by vertical breaks across the entire mantel front and sides. A shelf projects approximately 7 inches from the wall, allowing sufficient space for the display of objects, if desired. The pilasters, slightly tapered, remained simple and representative of the transitional period of the house. The fireplace surround was painted to mimic a bold domestic marble; the firescreen was from the designer's collection. The cutaway shows the upper part of the parlor mantel, including the shelf.**

RIGHT: **A detail of the trompe l'oeil, faux marble floorcloth.**

Victorian sensibility. She also wanted to create a room that appeared as if several generations of the same family had made changes over time—from 1838, when the house was built, until the turn of the century.

In an eclectic design, melding the architecture, gardens, and decorative arts of the 19th century, Lisa created a beautiful "conservatory-parlor." Steve Bielitz, attempting to bridge the two styles of architecture that seemed to be the basis for the Adams house, designed and built a mantel that has both Federal and Greek Revival overtones and elements.

Painting a Floorcloth

Lisa asked artisan Pam Asanovic to design the canvas floorcloth for her parlor. The canvas floorcloth—known in the 19th century as the "poor man's" rug, possibly the earliest form of floor coverings used in America—and stenciled floors served both useful and decorative purposes. They created a covering for the soft pine floorboards, especially like those in the Adams house, helping to preserve them. Painted floorcloths were usually used in well-trafficked areas such as hallways and parlors. The large floorcloth Lisa designed covered about 90 percent of the room. Keeping the furniture and other objects of the room in mind, Lisa made the design simple and geometric, simulating marble in various

colors. She also marbleized the baseboards to give an elegant aura to the floor area.

Pam purchased canvas from a theatrical supplier, since art stores don't carry 12-foot-wide canvas in the 12-ounce weight that she needed. In addition, theatrical canvas, which is used for backdrops, is less expensive.

Pam did most of her work at home. She laid out the canvas in her attic, stapling its edges to the floor to keep it taut. After applying two layers of gesso, she rolled on a base coat of cream-colored latex paint in an eggshell finish.

Pam mimicked the kind of specimen tablet once shown to clients to help them select marble. She worked out her

plan on graph paper and then transferred it, to scale, onto the canvas.

With 1-inch-wide masking tape, Pam masked off all the areas that were not to be decorated, pressing the edges of the tape firmly to prevent any paint from leaking through. Then she brushed on teal, her dominant color, in latex paint and dabbed it lightly with cheesecloth while it was still wet to achieve a slight texture.

Using real pieces of marble as models, she painted in gray-and-white marbling with oil pastels. To achieve the subtlest possible effect, she worked with an almost dry bristle brush, adding blushes of green. After each stroke, she wiped the brush clean to prevent any residual paint from building up in the bristles. Veins were added to each piece once the base colors were set.

Marbled borders were painted the same way, in four tones of ocher and raw umber, with black veins.

Pam accented the corners of the rug with a Greek motif called an anthemion, a floral form that looks like a palmette. She traced the motifs, then painted them in maroon-toned acrylics, outlining each one in two shades of gold metallic paint.

Once the floorcloth was complete and the masking tape had been removed, Pam brushed on several coats of a satin-finish water-based varnish usually used on floors. Because this type of varnish is slightly rubbery, the floorcloth can be rolled up without fear of cracking.

Finally, she removed the staples and turned under the edges of the rug so they would not ravel, gluing them down with heavy-duty epoxy.

Marbleizing Baseboards

Marbling is a time-honored method of adding interest to potentially mundane architectural trim. Like wood-graining and other faux finishes, marbling was extremely popular during the mid-19th century. On the west parlor fireplace and baseboards, Lisa asked Pam to replicate the primitive marbling she had done on the fireplace in her own home. Lisa and Pam did not intend to imitate any specific stone, but to create a playful "marble-like" decorative surface ("faux faux," according to Lisa) in the tradition of certain artisans of the mid-1800s. This black-and-white marble, however, does resemble stone found in the 18th century in Pennsylvania.

Pam prefers to work in oils because they are more durable and dry more slowly, giving her time to work on the detailing—and time to experiment. If she makes a mistake, she simply wipes it away with turpentine on a paper tissue.

Faux painting, especially on baseboards and floors, is hard work, but the experts devise all methods of sitting and kneeling to avoid fatigue. Neat work habits are essential to avoid spilling or splattering; covering the floors with paper or dropcloths is extremely important, as is taping off those areas that one wishes to protect.

1. Pam used small and medium disposable foam brushes to undercoat the wooden baseboards, thinking it neater to paint with foam than bristle. She mixed her paints in recycled glass jars with screw tops. For the undercoat, Pam brushed on two layers of flat white oil-based paint. As each coat dried, she lightly sanded it with a fine 220-grit sandpaper.

2. After two coats of oil paint, and sandings between and after, she wiped the surface clean with an oily tackcloth, an impeccably pristine base on which to create her marble veining.

3. After the base was ready, Pam began marbling in sections, laying down a white oil glaze composed of a third each of flat white paint, glazing liquid (available at any paint store), and mineral spirits. Then she blotted each section with cheesecloth and daubed certain areas with pale gray to simulate marble's natural tonal variations.

While the glaze was still wet, she drew on the veins, one at a time, freehand, with a black oil pastel crayon. As she drew each vein, she turned the crayon from its tip to its side, creating an undulating stroke. Striations of violet were added alongside the black strokes to accentuate them.

4. With a soft 3-inch-wide natural-bristle brush, Pam stroked lightly over each vein, on a diagonal, gently blurring the black and violet into the surrounding glaze. Between strokes, she wiped excess paint off the brush so as not to mix the crayon colors into the paint. Once the veins looked "soft" enough, she went back over them with black for extra definition.

As a last step, Pam applied three coats of nonyellowing water-based stain-finish varnish to protect her work and give it a sheen.

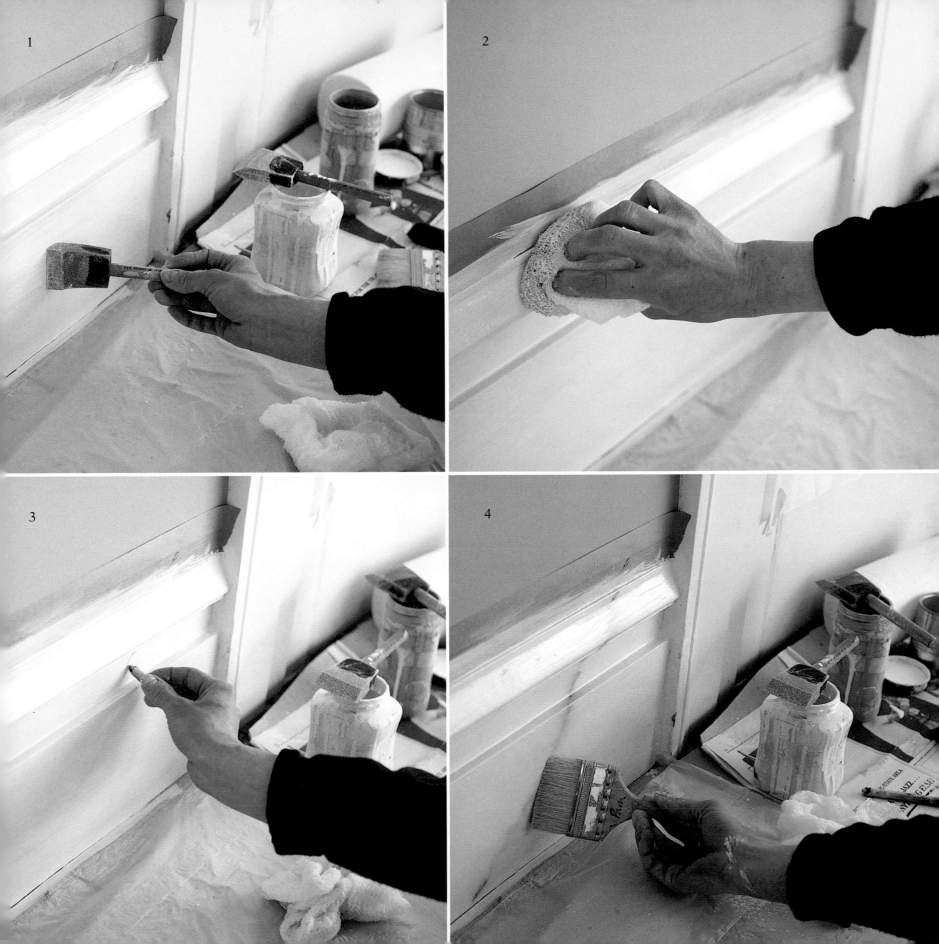

Window Dressing

Lisa wanted a period window treatment for the west parlor and decided on a swag with ball fringe, the swag held in place on an antique curtain tieback.

When you are choosing a window covering, consider the location, orientation and view of the window, as well as its size and shape. Some windows are so beautiful it is a shame to hide them; if privacy is not a concern, they may be best left unadorned unless rugs or fabrics need to be protected from strong sunlight. A poorly proportioned window can be disguised or camouflaged with a clever treatment.

CURTAINS: Curtains are the easiest and most traditional of all window dressings. They tend to be made of lightweight fabrics and are often unlined. Simple, unaffected, and informal, they may be gathered on a rod or pole or hung from loops. They can tie back to the sides of the window or hang free. Café curtains are two sets of short curtains, one installed above the other. Sometimes curtains are accented (and the rods concealed) with a valance, a short curtain that runs along the top of a window.

DRAPERIES: Draperies are installed on rods or rod sets with pulley-and-cord mechanisms to pull them open and closed. Draperies are usually made from heavier, more luxurious fabrics than curtains and tend to be more complicated in their construction, detail, and ornamentation. The part attached to the rod can be pleated, with hooks or clips inserted into the pleats and attached to rings running along a track inside the rod, or gathered.

ABOVE: **Lisa Krieger and John Curry draping gauze to simulate the final swag that John would sew. Pattern making is especially important when it comes to window treatment, just as it is for a dressmaker creating high fashion. If the swag is too deep it can obscure the window, too shallow and it can look very skimpy. These variations can be altered at will when working with a "muslin" or "gauze" as John did. Lisa used a satin from Clarence House for the swag, with a ball-fringe trim found at André Bon.**

SHEERS AND CASEMENTS: Lightweight, transparent, plain-woven, or lacy, these are usually used under draperies. Sheers can be left closed to diffuse the light when draperies are open.

Full, flowing curtains or billowing draperies extending beyond the sides of a narrow window make it seem wider. Short windows appear taller when capped with a valance or a pelmet, a fabric-covered box installed across the window header.

The only time curtains look pleasing ending at the sill rather than at the floor is when the window is recessed—and even then it's best to use some form of window shade or a swag.

SWAGS AND JABOTS: A swag is simply a length of fabric gently draped, garland-style, across the window header. Ends hang slightly, usually one-third to one-half of the way down the top sash. Jabots, also called cascades or tails, are tailored versions of swag ends, and may extend all the way to the sill; they can be very elaborate, and are often trimmed.

ROMAN SHADES: Wide pleats distinguish this shade from the roller type. When the shade is down, it is flat; when it is pulled up, by cords linked to a pulley, the pleats layer behind one another.

PLEATER SHADES: Self-pleats, which look like honeycombs when opened, allow these shades to pull up so tightly they become virtually invisible at the top of the window. The standard width of a pleat is 2 inches. Pleaters come in a wide range of colors. Some are pierced to allow for extra ventilation in hot climates, while others have wider double- or triple-comb pleats to prevent heat loss in colder locales.

BALLOON SHADES: The hallmark of balloon shades is their soft, pouffed panels which may be shirred or gathered at the top and ruffled at the bottom. Balloon shades are usually pulled up with a cord.

AUSTRIAN SHADES: Similar to balloons, their panels tend to be tighter and their scalloped folds more exaggerated. Like Romans, the shades usually pull up by a pulley.

When buying fabric for any soft window dressings, remember that the fuller, the better. Curtains usually require fabric measuring double the width of the window, and draperies or pouffed shades can take triple, depending on the complexity of the treatment.

WOODEN BLINDS: Used instead of curtains or shades, venetian blinds are slats of wood separated evenly from one another by special tapes. Blinds can be slanted two ways to filter light, and raised or lowered by means of a cord. They can be made in many colors and wood grains. Often a decorative valance is used to conceal the blind when it is drawn up.

RIGHT: The swag complete, attached on the right on a hidden brace and on the left by an antique curtain tieback in brass. Embossed and highly decorative, this brass tieback offsets the asymmetry of the swag. The window to the west had a similar treatment, but the tieback was placed on the right. A simple, elegant treatment such as this dresses up a window but does not obscure the view or the beautiful window with its old glass panes. I also prefer such a treatment so that the woodwork is exposed.

THE POWDER ROOM

Perhaps the most charmingly decorated of the rooms was the tiny understairs powder room, executed by Deirdre and Nora Humphrey. One of the "lost" spaces in the Adams house, it was made from a little-used closet under the front stairs. Because it backed up to the kitchen, I asked my plumbers if I could convert it into a tiny powder room. The plan was not a problem for them, and they punched back under the stair treads to gain extra space for the toilet alcove.

The Humphreys, a mother and daughter design team, decided to play up all the surfaces and the vanity, with leafy patterns to make the room feel both cozy and elegant. For the ceiling, walls, and vanity, they created a damask stencil just as Virginia Pierrepont had, tracing from an actual remnant of antique fabric. After painting the background in a creamy tone with semi-gloss latex, they stenciled the damask pattern at random, painting it in a darker, taupe hue.

Cabinetmaker David Bishop designed and built the corner vanity. For the top, he made a template, which he transferred to a piece of laminated poplar. After cutting out the top with a scroll saw, he measured its curved outer rim and cut a strip of the poplar for a skirt. To make the strip pliable enough to bend around the rim, he scribed its back at vertical intervals with kerfs, made with a blade less than ⅛ inch wide which won't saw through the wood. He cut the rim into scallops and then Deirdre drilled circles into each one as a whimsical touch.

ABOVE: This very, very small space was barely large enough to accommodate a sink and toilet, but we managed, and nicely, to install a skirted corner sink and a perfectly proportioned toilet atop a handmade, quilt-inspired patterned tile floor. It was hard to believe that what I had thought of as useless space could be put to use so well.

FAR LEFT: Working with the original drawing of the tiles, Nora's daughter Deirdre laid out the pieces as if she was working on a puzzle.

LEFT: The toilet, called St. Thomas, with a lovely fluted base, is made by the Bostonia Company. The subtle stenciled walls are based on a fragment of old brocade. The "pictures" are fragments of antique children's clothes, which were carefully matted and framed.

Designing a Tile Floor

The pattern for the scattered leaves on the tiled floor was taken from an 1850s appliquéd quilt that Deirdre and Nora had seen in a book. They had twelve quilt squares enlarged to the desired size at a Photostat shop and cut out the shapes.

Because they wanted a random effect, they decided to make a template of the entire floor and use the leaf shapes in an overall pattern. They cut the template from kraft paper and, leaving room for a border adapted from a Chinese Export porcelain plate, traced the leaf shapes onto the paper leaving about ⅛ inch between the tiles for grout. Both leaf and background pieces were numbered.

Ceramist Richard Rudich rolled out a clay slab the size of the template, transferred the design onto the clay, and numbered each piece. The tiles were cut out, and after green and cream glazes were applied, they were fired.

The pieces were traced onto the floor to be sure they fit; any necessary adjustments made with a tile cutter. Deirdre then spread mastic, a setting powder mixed with water, onto the floor with a metal-tooth comb working on one section at a time, as mastic sets quickly. Following the numbered plan, she pressed each tile into the mastic using toothpick-like tile spacers, checking periodically with a flat board to be sure they were level.

After the tiles had set 24 hours, Deirdre spread a taupe-colored grout over the surface with a damp sponge to fill the joints. Excess was removed with a damp cloth; and the tiles were buffed with a clean dry cloth.

THE LAUNDRY

I decided early in the restoration/renovation to make one of the first-floor rooms into a laundry-sewing room. The modern family has a lot of wash and a lot of mending. When I was growing up, sewing, too, was a common household activity and we always sewed and fitted right in our family kitchen. Having an entire room devoted to these endeavors was a real luxury for me.

The laundry, along with the kitchen, was the work center of the early 19th-century farmhouse. Virginia Cooper, a painter, wanted to turn back the hands of time and paint the room as it might have appeared 150 years ago. She decided on the popular motif of hand-painted checkerboard with a "night into day" border taken from the painted phases of the sun and moon found on pocket watches and grandfather clocks of the era. I've always loved checkerboard, so when Virginia described her plan, I was delighted. And because the women of this house spent so much of their time

LEFT: **The border was so much fun to paint, Virginia decided to create another sky, complete with more suns, moons, and stars, on a plywood screen, which she set up to hide the washer and dryer.**

RIGHT: **Two of the great moon faces painted by the artist. The images of the moon were chosen from watch and clock faces of the 18th and 19th centuries. Studying examples from the period, I was overwhelmed by the variety and number of such moon images.**

doing chores, I was especially pleased that the Adams house would have a laundry that allowed for dreaming rather than drudgery.

Painting a Checkerboard Pattern

The room is sunny, with two big windows. After reviewing the layout, Virginia and her assistant, Marlowe Monfort, took exact measurements of each wall so they could determine which size squares would fit the room without overwhelming the space. Virginia decided to work with 10-inch squares; tens are easy to multiply and the size is pleasing. When a row of squares could not be completed, she hid the truncated squares in an unobtrusive, inside corner (one short row is concealed behind the appliances).

To guarantee even rows of squares from ceiling to floor, Virginia painted a border around the room just below the ceiling. She adjusted the width so that seven rows of 10-inch squares would fit between baseboard and border.

Virginia had Marlowe test checkerboard grids on paper on a scale of one to ten. This was a good exercise; it took some careful plotting, but Marlowe devised a balanced checkerboard for each wall. She discovered by trial and error that she had to "cheat" some squares in the corners by as much as an inch, but the irregularity was unnoticeable to the naked eye.

Before measuring or drawing any lines at all, Marlowe rolled two coats of PS 55, a stain-resistant primer, onto each wall, followed by two coats of Benjamin Moore's White Buff flat latex—the same color used for the lighter squares.

After the paint had dried, she transferred her sketched grids, blown back up to full scale, onto the walls. Marlowe first established a plumb line on each wall, and then, because each wall was uneven, she visually corrected the vertical lines just the slightest bit so that the grids would appear straight.

Working from the baseboard up, she measured off and drew the horizontal lines to complete her grids, checking each line with a carpenter's level.

To eliminate confusion, once the grids were drawn, Marlowe penciled an X on all the squares to be painted black.

Painting a Border

A collection of clock faces at the Grandfather and Pocketwatch Museum in Bristol, Connecticut, inspired Virginia to snap Polaroids of her favorite sun and moon faces for a night-and-day border.

For the border's "sky," Virginia blended seven shades of blue in separate trays to reflect the blues from darkest midnight through night into dawn, morning, afternoon, dusk, and back to night.

Working with a 3-inch foam brush, she softly applied one shade to each section of the border, lightening her stroke as she reached the edge of a section and feathering it into the next section.

She blended the edges with a dry roller, using a separate roller for each shade.

After drying overnight, the border was sanded unevenly with 220-grit sandpaper to sprinkle the sky with "stars" and age the paint.

To create the suns and moons, Virginia traced circles, half-circles, and crescents, on the blue ground, then painted in each shape with metallic gold or silver paint with an artist's sable brush.

The next day, when the paint was dry, Virginia blotted on a bit of flesh-toned latex with a paper towel so that slivers of the gold and silver would shine through.

She then traced the features on each face, and using artist's colors and a fine brush, she gave each sun and moon its own personality.

1. Ready to paint, Marlowe rolled out 1-inch-wide masking tape outside the borders of the X'd squares, pressing the tape firmly with an old credit card so that paint would not seep underneath onto the lighter squares.

2. Using a 3-inch-wide foam brush, Marlowe filled in the X'd squares with a thin coat of Benjamin Moore's Shark's Tooth Off-Black latex paint, working from the edges into the center. She treated each square as if it were a painting. She allowed the paint to dry completely before removing the tape.

3. The squares, both black and buff, were sanded with varying degrees of pressure (and three grades of sandpaper—coarse 60, medium 120, and fine 220-grit) to wear away the paint in spots, as it might have been worn by time.

4. All edges of the squares were blurred to soften the geometric effect.

THE SUNROOM

Originally several small rooms and jalousied porches, the new sunroom added an important element to the house: a bright, sunny room where one can sit, read, relax, or converse while enjoying a view of the outdoors with a vista of the most private and quiet part of the property.

ABOVE: A view from the sunroom to the unfinished stone terrace beyond.

RIGHT: The windows, made from stock French doors, allowed for two walls of well-proportioned muntins in keeping with the other windows in the house. The floor is mottled green slate 12-inch squares, which, once installed and grouted, were sealed and waxed to a low luster.

Susan Colley, the designer, covered the stone floor with a sisal rug and introduced the liveliest fabrics from Clarence House and Rose Cumming.

Small framed botanical prints, work surfaces and shelves, and relaxed cushioned chairs give an air of informality and usefulness to the room in keeping with the custom of bringing antique garden ornamentation from the outdoors in.

THE BACK STAIRS

I was fortunate that the Adams house had a back staircase. An additional egress in a house of this size is good not only for safety, but also for accessibility. In my house on Turkey Hill Road, the back stairs were blocked off when a bathroom was built on the second floor and I have always missed the ability to creep secretly upstairs or down when guests are sleeping. The Adams house back stairs are steep but not uncomfortably so. Though it turns sharply and is really not spacious enough to carry large objects up or down, it is convenient.

The back hallway presented us with an enormous design challenge. Faux-finish artists Linn Cassetta and Jane Crawford thought the confined stairwell with its sharp turn was a "squirrely" sort of space to work in—plus it was in lamentable shape. Furthermore, the stairway is very visible from the kitchen, so the design had to work with it. When Linn and Jane visited me in my kitchen at Turkey Hill, they fell in love with my collection of copper molds and pots. I told them a copper motif was being used in the Adams house kitchen, so they suggested applying copper leaf to the stair risers, tying in the small copper squares of the kitchen floor.

The back hallway also had two distinct perspectives—from the upstairs landing and from the kitchen. To create a harmonious connection between the two, Linn and Jane added a verdigris finish to the lower half of the walls and softly glazed the upper walls and ceiling.

LEFT: The back stairs were in quite bad disrepair when I found the house. In some places, the treads made of soft yellow pine were very worn and even cracked. George repaired the more serious problems but left the unevenness and wear as signs of old age. The treads and risers (also of soft pine) were sanded and scraped to remove the old paint and finished to prepare the surface for the application of paint and copper leaf.

RIGHT: The designers, who are also talented artisans, colored the walls a verdigris-textured greenish blue on the lower half and a glazed paler blue above and on the ceiling. A faux painting of a potted topiary plant graced both turnings in the staircase.

Linn and Jane took their inspiration for this potted double standard myrtle topiary from one that was living in the small office. The pot is suitably mottled, and the undergrowth of ivy a lovely touch.

The hanging lamp offers just enough light for the back stairwell to reveal the trompe l'oeil shelf, white dainty cloth, and potted topiary. The old glass makes beautiful shadows on the walls and ceilings.

Of course every stairway should have light switches at the top and bottom. I like to have dimmers put on at least one of the switches so the light can be used as a night light.

FOLLOWING PAGE LEFT: In the upstairs back hall there are several doors opening onto the landing. On the left is the back stairway; the door was removed from this opening. To the right is the attic stair ascending to a full third floor, as yet unfinished except for the two small rooms used for storage.

Trompe L'Oeil

Trompe l'oeil ("fool the eye") is meant to elicit a double take as it plays with truth and illusion. Linn's "no-maintenance" myrtle topiary, crafted with brushes instead of pruning shears, is a witty and personal substitute for a framed painting in the stairwell.

To create her topiary, Linn sketched from the real thing: a potted topiary she placed on one of the stair treads. First she painted on the wall an extension to the existing ledge as a shelf for her display. Then she penciled in the topiary in its mossy, cracked terra-cotta pot, with an embroidered linen cloth draped over the edge of the shelf.

She applied a thick coat of gesso inside the penciled outline to give her a clean white surface to paint on.

Linn prefers to build up her paint in many translucent layers. She works with artist's oils thinned to a watery consistency with gumtine (a refined turpentine) and japan dryer. Oils impart a subtle richness to the surface, but they dry slowly without the japan dryer.

Beginners may prefer painting with watered-down acrylics because they are easier to work with and dry more quickly; since acrylics are opaque, a base coat of gesso is unnecessary.

Copper Leafing

Less expensive and thicker than its fragile gold cousin, copper leaf is also far easier to work with.

1. To prepare the stair risers, Jane first rid them of dirt and loose paint with 80-grit sandpaper, smoothed them with 220-grit, then painted them, using a 3-inch bristle brush, with two base coats of Benjamin Moore's coffee-colored #1159.

2. For the next stage, readying the risers with a highly toxic size, or bond, for the copper leaf, Jane donned a respirator mask and latex gloves. Using another 3-inch brush, she applied Rolco Quick Dry Synthetic Gold Size to each riser. Drying time for the size fluctuates with temperature and humidity; it usually takes from one to three hours. To test, Jane tapped the size with her knuckle; a dry pop or snap indicated when it was properly set up. (If the size is too sticky, she told me, the leaf melts into it and loses its shine.)

3. To apply leaf, Jane worked with her bare hands, but white cotton gloves work well, too; beginners should always use gloves because fingerprints emerge on the leaf after it is varnished or as it ages.

Copper leaf comes in 5-inch squares affixed to a tissue backing. To apply, Jane pressed each square into place and removed its backing, working from the top to the bottom of each riser and allowing narrow overlaps between squares. (A professional gilder can align squares edge to edge, but this is extremely tricky since leaf easily wrinkles and tears.)

4. Once all the leaves were in place, Jane gently smoothed every square with a soft white cosmetic brush, then burnished them with a silk-wrapped cotton puff.

Jane wanted a series of shimmery diamonds on each riser to match those on the kitchen floor, so she cut out a template from cardboard and penciled in the diamond shapes.

Inside each outline, she daubed fast-drying Quick 15 varnish; the varnish would block the darkening agent, an acidic solution that Jane applied to age the rest of the stair risers.

When mixing up this highly toxic solution—¼ teaspoon of foul-smelling barium sulfate powder stirred into 1 cup of water—she once again put on a respirator mask and latex gloves. (We also opened all the nearby windows to give her plenty of ventilation.) She mixed the solution in a wide-mouthed glass jar because it was so strong it would actually melt plastic. Quickly but carefully, she brushed it onto each riser. Once it was dry, Jane applied a durable double coat of polyurethane to protect the leaf from peeling.

To highlight the entire stairwell, Jane outlined its edges in bright copper. What a glorious finish to an incredibly painstaking job!

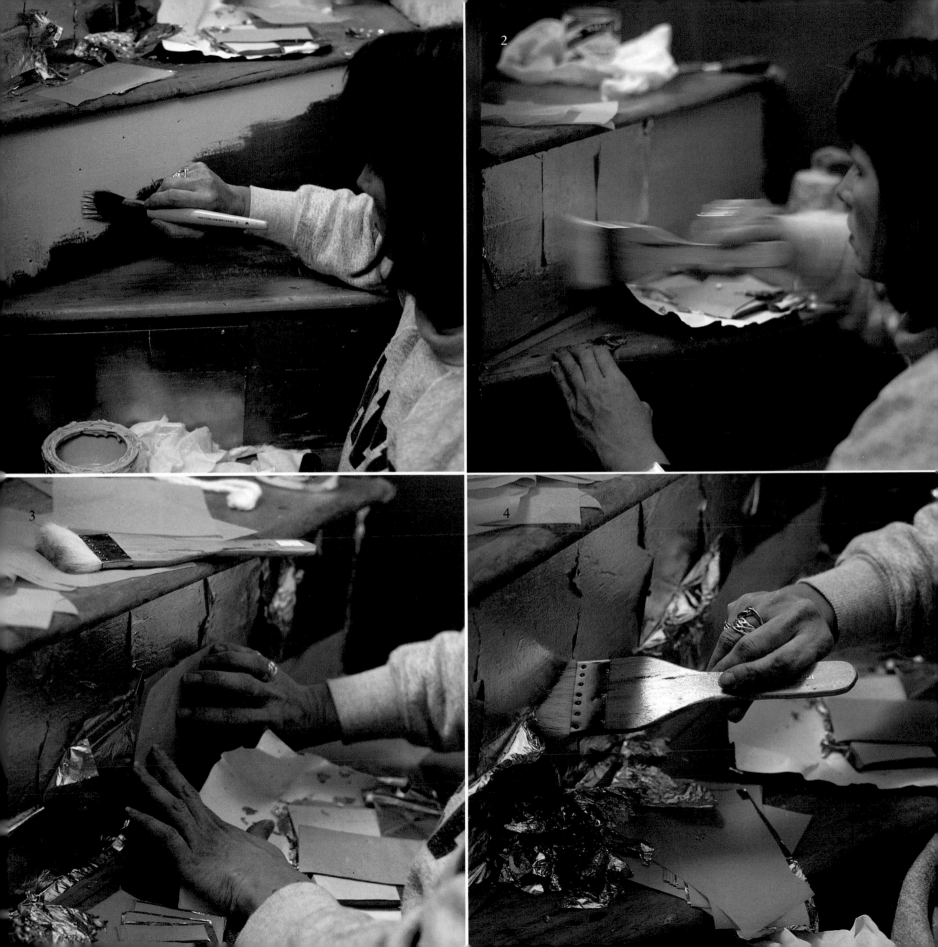

THE HALL BEDROOM

Rosemary Casey is a wonderful designer and I was glad she said yes to my invitation to decorate the hall bedroom. Rosemary wanted to do a feminine bedroom, but I challenged her to do a man's bedroom instead. In response, she dreamed up an irresistible man: a collector, a traveler, a naturalist, a true individualist—and one who loves the sea.

Rosemary likes rooms to be spare and spacious; she disdains clutter. Here she painted the walls gray, the color of the sky this man might encounter when sailing on an overcast afternoon. Gray expands the room and provides a wonderful background for furnishings and objects, among them a twig chair by James Graham and a pair of marine paintings, one by Antonio Jacobsen, the other by artist Robert Newell of Norwalk, Connecticut.

Rosemary enhanced the twig motif by fashioning branches she picked up in the woods into drapery rods; a fern-and-leaf fabric was casually gathered onto the branches and allowed to fall gracefully to the floor without tiebacks. The simplicity of the pine floors was perfect for Rosemary's scheme; a needlepoint rug was the only accent.

Custom-Paint Colors

When choosing the color for a room, I work very closely with my paint store. Stan, of Gilbert's Paints in Westport, has been my longtime ally in altering existing shades to fit my mood and the particular rooms in which they are going to be used. When I find a shade on a chart that appeals to me, often it is too dark or too strong or too light. Stan will work with me at the paint mixer to inject pigments into the base colors until just the right shade is achieved.

Paint colors are certainly just as important as furnishings in decorating a room. Professional colorists can be found, with their own methods of mixing unusual and unique shades. Often your local paint store dealer will be willing and able to perform this task, as mine has been.

LEFT: The low-ceilinged bedroom was transformed into a comfortable and charming room. Unique touches, indicative of Rosemary's personal style, include this natural branch curtain rod. The fabric chosen was from the collection of Cowtan & Tout.

RIGHT: A twin iron bedstead placed along a wall makes a daybed that is comfortable for daytime reading and nighttime sleeping. The nautical portraits go well with the leaf-patterned fabric (a ship pattern would have been both repetitive and dull, Rosemary thought). A white coverlet is spread over a dust ruffle of the curtain fabric. The detailing of the pillows and ruffles is again indicative of Rosemary's careful but understated elegant touches.

FOLLOWING PAGE: American and English antiques complement the Federal simplicity of the house and this room in particular. The floor is certainly the nicest feature of the room, and Rosemary respected it by covering only a portion of it with a needlepoint rug. The extraordinary twig chair was made by James Graham. The bamboo dressing table goes well with the light wood of the twig chair. The walls are painted a flat gray, the woodwork an eggshell white.

THE HALL BATHROOM

The first people to live in the Adams house had no bathrooms at all; they made do with ewers, wash basins, and chamberpots. In the early days of indoor plumbing, everyone shared one bath, and when I bought the house there was still only one usable bathroom, probably dating back to the 1920s. To me it was not really surprising that a house of eighteen rooms should have only one bathroom because I grew up in such a house and we were a family of eight. But today, with emphasis on sports and exercise, it is terribly important to most contemporary families to have more bathrooms. Having a shower, a tub, and spacious sinks and storage for cosmetics, toiletries, and towels is a great pleasure. I prefer old-fashioned fixtures to modern ones, and it was my intention to create bathrooms with an antique style.

Karen Tarshis and Rose Adams decided to re-create the look and feel of a room in a late-19th-century Federal home. Wainscoting of fir with a chair rail, architectural elements of the period, were installed and painted a pure cream color in an antique satin finish (the formula, Benjamin Moore half Linen White, half Decorator White). The walls were painted the same shade, but they were ragged with one part glaze, one part linseed oil, and one part green paint. On this very pale background, decorative painter Diane Voyentzie used artist's oils to render the very delicate sprigs of flowers, seemingly strewn on the walls and ceiling.

ABOVE: We found the old tub in very good condition. It was carefully cleaned, the enamel buffed, and the exterior iron was spray-painted white.

RIGHT: The sink with brass fixtures is a pedestal from Waterworks in Westport. The floor was installed using the small hexagonal tiles so popular from the turn of the century to the 1920s. Simple brass sconces and towel racks were chosen to coordinate with the tub and sink fixtures.

Creative Windows in Westport made the wonderful full-balloon pouf in a pale washed linen floral-print design to harmonize with the needlepoint rug. It was beautifully made with pinked edges, an unusual and clever alternative to overcasting or piping, and lined with lace dipped in tea to achieve an aged look.

The bamboo table and chair reiterate in part the antique furnishings in the hall bedroom. A floral needlepoint rug adds warmth and a bit of formality to the room.

The walls were retained, but the fixtures were eliminated except for the old footed tub, which was in excellent condition. The walls were scraped, the woodwork was prepared for paint, and the linoleum floor was torn up. The old iron stack waste pipe was removed and another smaller, "to code" pipe was installed within the walls along the water lines.

The floor-to-ceiling closet was made smaller, the bottom half used to conceal the pipes for the tub, which was moved from under the window to against the wall. The new toilet and sink were installed in the original positions.

Renovating Bathrooms

Enlarging or adding a bathroom in an old house means stealing the space from somewhere else, in my case one of the numerous but cramped upstairs bedrooms. We turned one small bedroom into a bath for the children. When planning a new bath, try to choose a room over the kitchen or a downstairs bathroom, so the plumbing can be stacked; it is far easier and cheaper than bringing up new lines. In most new bathrooms, contractors like to bury the pipes for all three fixtures in one wall, known as the water wall, with all waste pipes sloping toward the main sewer pipe.

The minimum-size bathroom that accommodates the three basic fixtures—bathtub, sink, and toilet—is 5 by 7 feet. Twice that size is more reasonable, especially if you want to have a bidet, dressing table, or storage for linens. SELECTING FIXTURES: Before settling on your layout, it is wise to pick out the fixtures, since they don't always conform to

standard measurements—especially if you decide to use period fixtures. The most common bathtub size is 5 feet long, 30 inches wide, and 16 inches high. (If you choose a longer or wider model, you may want to have the faucets midway along the side.) New tubs range from a 39-inch-square bathtub to a 7-foot-square whirlpool. Bathtubs come in fiberglass-reinforced plastic, enameled steel, and enameled cast iron, the most durable.

Shower stalls usually measure 3 feet square; they may be built and tiled on-site or prefabricated of plastic. Take care to have the shower head installed at the right height for you and your family, and see that towels racks are accessible. For me, one real luxury is a steam unit installed in the shower with a built-in seat and specially vented door.

Toilets require at least 36 inches in width, 26 inches in depth, and another 30 inches of space in front to move comfortably. A bidet measures about 12 inches across, 26 inches deep, and 11 inches high. New toilets have an ecological advantage over older ones: they generally require only 1½ gallons to flush.

The pedestal sinks that were the rule in old houses are still made today; we

used them throughout the Adams house. However, you may prefer to depart from history and install a basin, or lavatory, into a cabinet called a vanity. The enclosure offers storage space and conceals the waste pipe under the basin. Lavatories are available in enameled steel, enameled cast iron, and vitreous china, or in plastic molded into the countertop. If two sinks in one counter are installed, allow at least 24 inches between them.

The light in the bathroom should be glare-free: a shielded light overhead and frosted lights on either side of the mirror work well. For safety, recessed lights over the tub and the shower are best.

If the room is used by elderly people and your floor material is tile or marble, scatter rugs on thin rubber pads will help prevent accidents. Likewise, wood can be polyurethaned with a matt finish.

Some building codes require a waterproof floor and baseboard. Walls behind the tub and shower should be water-repellant; the wall above can simply be water-resistant.

REPORCELAINING FIXTURES: I love the character and charm of old bathroom fixtures and belive that even a fixture with a dull or pitted surface may be worth rescuing. "Reporcelaining" is actually a misnomer; professionals spray the fixture, under pressure, with an acrylic or epoxy polyurethane coating. The new glazing will not adhere as well as the original porcelain, nor will it stand up to heavy abrasive cleansers. But the effect is shiny and clean, and with proper care, a reporcelaining will last indefinitely. A five-year warranty is usually given.

If your house is undergoing drastic

renovation and fixtures are being moved, your refinisher will probably suggest that the pipes be disengaged, the fittings removed, and the fixtures be hauled from your house and taken to the plant. If your renovation is less extensive, moving the fixtures will not be practical and the work will be done on-site. Workers carefully cover and mask all other elements in the room to protect them from the chemicals, and then don goggles, respirators, and rubber gloves.

In either case, the fixtures are shot-blasted with chemical cleaners to remove scale and stains. Nicks and scratches are filled, the surfaces are wet-sanded, washed, and dried. Either acid etching, in which a bond is created between the old and new glazes with a marine resin, or chemical bonding are used before the final finish is sprayed on. Once the fixture is reporcelained, it is buffed and polished. The coating remains toxic until fully cured, about three days.

Of course it is much better to locate antique fixtures that are in excellent condition. One can find these at salvage companies and at demolition sites. Hard-to-find hardware can be fabricated if necessary or located in similar places.

LEFT: **Judy Krammer of Fairfield hand-painted the walls with cabbage roses in a soft pink tint. They appear to be strewn over the walls.**

RIGHT: **The old tank toilet is not the original fixture, but it is the one Ruth Adams remembers from childhood. The pipes were replaced and hidden in the walls.**

THE SOUTHEAST BEDROOM

I decided to decorate this bedroom myself, painting the walls a soft, mellow gray, and the woodwork a pale beige using just half the formula for Martin Senour Williamsburg Biscuit. The ceiling was painted using only a quarter formula of the same biscuit. The floors were finished the same way as the downstairs pine floors, with coats of soft-luster polyurethane topped with a coat of buffed butcher's wax.

Because this bedroom faces the street, the windows were covered with old-fashioned wooden venetian blinds, custom-painted the same color as the woodwork. The cotton tapes were tinted by soaking them for several hours in strong Earl Grey tea, and then shipped to Wisconsin to the blind maker to be used on the blinds.

The mahogany bed is a 19th-century four-poster bedstead that I found at a tag sale in Westport. All four posts are beautifully carved. The canopy top is covered in a fine white cotton, the shaped valances are made of a scalamandré silk damask interlined with flannel and lined in cotton sateen. Some of my old 19th-century and turn-of-the-

LEFT: **For this house I developed several new paint colors, the gray and biscuit for the bedroom; Hunt Club Teal, a blue-green used on the shutters and doors of the exterior; and warm ochers and blues for the kitchen.**

century bed linens, collected over the years from antiques stores, tag sales, and auctions, are used as the bedclothes. The room also has period gilded mirrors, a semi-antique Heriz Oriental carpet, and two large armchairs that are very comfortable for reading.

LEFT: The mantel in this bedroom was substantially altered from the very plain one that was original to the house. The old brick facing was left, but the shelf and pilasters were built up with more millwork. The picture over the mantel is a 19th-century pastel in a fine gilt and gesso frame. The sconces are English brass, as is the fender and the pair of 19th-century andirons. The brass trivet is useful for keeping a pot of tea warm next to the fire.

The mantel garniture: a pair of old Parisian porcelain pierced baskets with an S monogram and an old Japanese Imari carp bowl, small pot, and dishes, all discovered at the same tag sale where I found the bed.

RIGHT: The small cherry wood tilt-top table with its delicate pedestal is an example of fine American craftsmanship. The chairs, covered in Italian striped damask with soft down cushions, are probably Centennial and could have been used in more public rooms, but because they are oversized I was attracted to them as comfortable bedroom chairs. The pretty pillows are recycled needlepoint seat covers from a set of old dining room chairs I bought from a consignment shop.

THE MASTER BATH

The house was not large enough or appropriate for its architecture to create a large master bath, but many contemporary families want such a room. This bath was the closest approximation to the modern ideal I could achieve. If space had permitted, I would have installed a large footed tub, a bidet, and a steam shower, all desirable items in a master bath. It would also have been nice to have room for a Stairmaster and some hand weights.

In keeping with the elegant treatment of the master bedroom, the newly created bathroom was decorated in a fashion unlike the others in the house. Marble walls, marble floor, and a spacious shower tiled entirely in marble set this room apart from the others; yet because the fixtures that were chosen looked old-fashioned, the room is not an anomaly.

Vermont white marble tile with gray veins was used in 4-inch squares. The walls were painted a warm shade of gray that works well with the stone. It was very difficult to find a shade of paint that worked in a pleasing, harmonious way with the marble. Most marble and stone looks cold, and warmth can be achieved by using paint toned with warm colorants or by using warmly toned wallpaper, fabric covering, or decorative finishing touches. I used chrome hardware in this room, preferring it to the harder-to-maintain brass.

Installing Tile

Ceramic tile is one of the most ancient decorative building surfaces—and one of the most practical for areas that must withstand moisture. The most popular size is 4¼ inches square, but there are many sizes and shapes, among them the small-square mosaic tile that we used in the upstairs hall bathroom.

Not all tile is ceramic. Because I love the luxurious look of a marble bath, I had Charles Perelli install marble tiles in the master bath: 6-inch squares on the walls and 6-by-12-inch rectangles, set in a brick pattern, on the floor.

Ceramic floor tile is thicker and stronger than wall tile; all marble tile is typically ⅜ inch thick. The procedure for setting tiles on floors and walls is essen-

RIGHT: **Cesare is the maker of this sink, which is very similar in size and shape to those made for the Continental market in the 19th century. Such sinks are still being imported by antiques dealers and cost many times the price of this new version. Dornbracht hardware, extremely well built and long lasting, is both good-looking and appropriate to the period. We used it in all the bathrooms, primarily with the chrome finish.**

The toothbrush holder is the nicest I have ever found—it is made by Czech and Speake, the English manufacturers of bathroom hardware and fixtures. The towels are Martex "rubdown" in pure white. The custom monogram is very understated in beige thread. The old linen hand towels on the sink are tag sale purchases.

tially the same, except that a floor requires special preparation. First, the subfloor should be checked to make sure it is stable and can carry the weight of the tile. Generally, plywood is laid down to create a firm base. Sometimes the tile is applied directly to the plywood with thinset or adhesive. For a more rugged installation, the plywood is topped with a layer of 30-pound felt adhered with an asphalt compound, followed by a mortar bed made with cement, sand, and water reinforced with embedded metal wire. (Some tile setters will use a cement board like Duroc or Wonderboard, which is reinforced with fiberglass mesh instead of mortar.)

Especially in a house as old as this one, the walls tend to be off plumb and

LEFT: **Charles Perelli cuts one of the 6-inch-square marble tiles to fit around a pipe in the master bath shower. Because the raw materials are so very expensive (marble now costs between $10 and $30 a square foot, uninstalled; $34 to $56 and up, installed), it is best to find the most expert tile installer you can. We interviewed several and visited previous projects of each before we chose Charlie. Marble work requires precision, lots of cutting, and careful application. A circular saw, fitted with a stone-cutting blade, and affixed to a special water-cooling bath is used to cut the marble to size. Spaces between the tiles must be exact; Charlie used toothpicks or matches as spacers. These tiles were installed with a very thin grout line, and uneven spacing would have been very obvious.**

the floors off square. The way a tile setter adjusts to these irregularities is essentially an aesthetic judgment, not a technical one. One approach is to make the dominant wall—typically the one you see as you enter the room—as perfect as possible, either by correcting the wall or by trimming the tiles or adjusting the spaces between them. Another approach is to mark the middle of the longest wall with a chalk line, bisect it at the exact center, then lay the tile from the center outward; if the wall is off, the installer will cut the last tile with a wet saw.

In either case, the tile setter begins by spreading the adhesive—thinset, epoxy mortar, ordinary mortar, or premixed mastic—with a trowel that has one smooth edge and one edge with two square notches. Working in sections, the installer smooths mortar over the wall, then rakes it, holding the trowel at a 45-degree angle, to create ridges in the damp adhesive. When a tile is pressed in, the edges help spread the adhesive evenly across its bottom.

To cut a tile to fit around a pipe, the setter uses tile nippers, which snip off chips until the cut is precise. To cut a hole through tile, he uses a carbide-tip hole-saw blade in a power drill, keeping the tile wet so the heat of friction will not crack it.

Many ceramic wall tiles come with two tabs called spaces or lugs; these separate the tiles by exactly the width of grout joint. Plastic spacers are sometimes used with tiles that have no lugs.

Travelers to Europe and the Far East may have noticed that antique tiles were typically laid with less space between them. If you like the European look, you can ask your tile man to reduce the space, though of course this requires tiles without lugs.

To finish off the edges, the setter uses trim tile; concave or cove trim turns inside corners, while the convex bullnose turns outside corners and rounds off the last course of a half wall of tile or the edge of a counter.

Once the adhesive has set, the installer

spreads grout across the surface of the tile, working it into the joints with a trowel called a grout float. After about ten minutes, the excess is wiped off with a clean damp sponge. Finally, silicone caulk is squeezed into the joint between the floor or the fixture.

ABOVE LEFT: The gilded mirror and the blue glass on the porcelain sink add a sense of intimacy to the room. The window frame was left bare, but because the room faces the street, a window covering was imperative; a wooden Venetian blind painted white was the perfect choice.

ABOVE: This is a good view of the shower and marble wall in the master bath. We chose to use a shower curtain instead of a glass door.

LEFT: The hand shower in the master bath is chrome-plated brass made by Dornbracht, a German manufaturer of extremely fine hardware for the bath and kitchen. A hand shower is great for bathing as well as cleaning the shower stall itself.

Lighting Fixtures

Lighting must be decided upon early in renovation. Ideally, the work on wiring is done while the walls are still open. Since I wanted the decorators for each room to choose their own, I couldn't install all the lighting while our walls were being repaired. I did pull the wiring to the most logical spots for wall sconces or ceiling fixtures so the decorators could install their pieces and make their connections as easily as possible.

Recessed lighting fixtures were used only sparingly in the old house.

I really did not want modern lighting, but made concessions in areas such as the laundry room, where sewing and ironing chores were to be done.

LEFT: In the 19th century, wonderful glass lanterns were made in Holland, India, Ceylon, and elsewhere for the colonial trade. These hanging lamps consisted of a bottom bell and a smoke glass and were suspended from the ceiling by means of three fine chains converging into one larger chain. Originally lit by candles or oil, they are now beautifully fitted with electric candelabra lights and are wonderful for illuminating hallways, stairways, and small rooms with high ceilings. Aquamarine examples like the one in the back hall are rather rare. Dark green, like the one shown here, blue, red, amber, or clear with etched, plain, or pressed glass are more common.

Old Hardware

Some old houses still have one style of hardware throughout the rooms. This old house had an amazing hodgepodge, and after the restoration/renovation, an even greater variety. To restore the Adams house to its original grace, I wanted to save as much of its wonderful period hardware as I could. The first thing we did when we took over the house was remove all the salvageable hardware for refinishing. Each piece was tagged so we could put it back in its correct location, then stripped of its accumulated paint and dirt and buffed and polished.

Then came a search for matching period hardware. I always prefer using old hardware if I can find it. George and I scoured the attic and basement to see if anything had been stored there. Then we inspected the hardware at Turkey Hill; since it was built at the same time as the Adams house, it served as a guide to what I needed to find. (You can also consult your local historical society or check your library for architecture books featuring houses of the same era as yours.) One resource guide, which includes listings of manufacturers for hardware reproductions, is the *Old House Journal*. There are many places to buy replacements for broken or lost items of hardware: catalogs, hardware stores, antiques dealers specializing in such items, and architectural and salvage shops. It's a good idea to take snapshots of original pieces with you so you can match them.

OVERLEAF: George and I did a lot of the cleaning of the hardware ourselves.

Paint-encrusted steel was dipped in paint remover and scrubbed with steel wool. Brass was polished and lacquered. (In some places, such as near the seaside, it is better to leave brass unlacquered.)

Switch covers were replaced or overpainted with wall paint or decorative stippling or ragging to make them inconspicuous.

A picture molding hook was polished and discovered to be brass.

Porcelain or glass knobs were cleaned of old paint and replaced if chipped.

A door key was faux painted on one of the walls as a symbol of the antiquity of the place.

All the keyhole escutcheons were cleaned of paint and polished or freshly painted. And all the box locks were given a new coat of black paint.

LANDSCAPING

THE PROPERTY

It has not been my habit to retain a landscape architect when redoing a property. Middlefield certainly had no plan: the little cottage sat in a rocky lawn, no driveway was necessary, nor was a garden design. Turkey Hill had no plan either: we planted the gardens on whim; that it turned out well was due to luck as much as anything else. When I bought the Adams house, I was still not inclined to hire a landscape architect. I knew I wanted the paths, edgings of walks, and driveway to be made of old materials—old cobblestones, brick, heavy bluestone pavers, and native crushed gravel. I knew also that I wanted an herb garden, and a gaze-bo near the stream as a focal point from the east parlor window. ■ Then I met landscape architect Tom Balsley and he persuaded me to consider a real plan for the old house. He drew a few sketches of the property and made suggestions for the location of the driveway, paths, and pools, both natural and man-made. His ideas were so intelligent and made such good common sense that I asked him to work up a formal plan. Some of this plan we implemented right away: the placement of the outdoor terrace, the pathways, the retaining wall garden, and some of the other walls. Other ideas of his have been put on hold but will hopefully

LEFT: **The house, renovated, decorated, and partially landscaped, left me free to do the chores I really love: raking up the giant tulip tree's leaves, planting bulbs, pruning bushes.**

RIGHT: **Old iron urns are decorative and useful as garden ornaments. They can be planted to bloom all season long.**

be integrated into the property in time: a swimming pool, a newly located driveway, new paths to the front of the house, property line demarcation, and proper screening with the use of shrubbery, evergreen borders, and fencing.

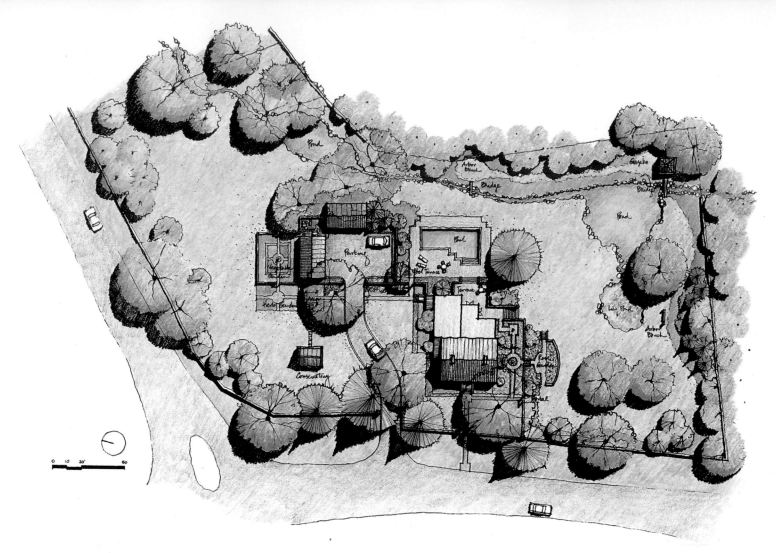

ABOVE: Tom Balsley's site plan. I would have liked very much to implement Tom's design at the new old house, but because I am not keeping it for my own use, I did not think the financial commitment to transforming the property into this wonderful architect's dream would be sensible from an investor's point of view. Nevertheless, the plan itself is an excellent selling feature.

Clearly, Tom's plan makes very good use of the property. The old large trees by the roadside would be supplemented with additional plantings of evergreens and other dense foliage plants to create a screen for the house from the road.

The orientation of the driveway would be altered just enough to rid the house of yet another straight line. The curve of the drive away from the house would provide new lawn areas in front of the kitchen door and help separate the parking and garage area from the house.

A screening of trees and shrubs would be planted around the parking area, blocking the driveway and garage fronts from view.

The swimming pool, a very important feature for many homeowners in this locale, makes the most of the new terrace that was built behind the house, increasing the outdoor entertaining areas.

The original two ponds at the northwest corner of the property would be dredged and the brook would be made a trifle wider, terminating in two smaller ponds situated in the lowest portion of the property.

The new walled garden to the east of the house was completed, but the stairway to the rose garden below has not yet been installed. This would be a very beautiful feature and would certainly create a "focal point" garden, something that a landscape architect strives for.

A formally designed vegetable garden and a cutting garden would be created to the west of the garage.

WORKING WITH A LANDSCAPE ARCHITECT

Landscape architecture is a profession devoted to applying the principles of design to our natural environment while at the same time taking into account the client's wishes and needs. The result is a master plan consistent with the lifestyle of the client.

The landscape architect first prepares a site analysis based on the personality of the property including views, topography, trees, plantings, drainage, rocks, and buildings. The space is then designed according to the function of each area and the relationships between them.

The best way to decide what kind of garden you want is to visit historic gardens and look at other gardens in your neighborhood. Making a tour locally also enables you to get a sense for the kinds of plantings that grow well in your specific locale. Choosing plantings that are clearly suited to your soil and climate conditions helps to ensure a successful worry-free garden. Also consider what appeals to you, what you've always wanted for your property. Perhaps it is an expanse of lawn, perhaps hedges for screening, or flowering trees, plants that attract birds, a pool or pond, a vegetable garden, an herb garden, or illumination on special plantings. Once you have a clear idea of what you want, you'll be better able to talk to your landscape architect and, together, develop a plan.

The best way to find a good landscape architect is by talking to the owners of gardens you admire. For local listings,

ABOVE: **A view from one of the parlor windows looking out on the newly created terrace garden and one of the espaliered McIntosh apple trees. The American boxwood is fast growing and disease resistant.**

look in the Yellow Pages; nurserymen can help, too. Professional landscape architects are also listed with the American Society of Landscape Architects in Washington, D.C.

It is best to interview several candidates before making a decision, inviting each to the property and discussing with them how you feel about the grounds, what you would like to accomplish, and what it is likely to cost in terms of your budget. The landscape architect you choose will then translate what you have

agreed upon into a site analysis diagram with specific plot drawings that detail plantings and construction. Landscape architects often make a master plan that is executed over several years, enabling you to spread out your financial commitment and also modify the plan as plantings develop. You will be charged a flat fee that includes the drawings as well as initial evaluation.

At this point, the landscape architect can be retained to supervise the entire job, or you can take the plans and go directly to a nurseryman who will execute the work outlined in the blueprints.

If you hire the landscape architect as supervisor, you will need a contract with him stating that he will apply for any necessary permits and that he will be responsible for subcontracting the craftsmen for building and planting. Since prices vary for plants and planting, he will obtain bids for your approval. The contract should include cleanup and plant replacement from the nursery during the first year in the event that plants die of natural causes.

Some architects charge by the day, but it is preferable to set a flat fee for the entire job. One-third of the payment is paid up front, another third halfway through the job, and the balance on satisfactory completion.

If you elect to work with a nurseryman, you will pay for the plantings and the labor, which is usually billed at an hourly rate. If you decide not to hire professional help, it is a good idea to rough out a plan of your property yourself so that you can think about garden plans as a whole.

CREATING A TERRACE GARDEN

To the east of the house, the ground dropped quite steeply from the parlor and library windows. There was nothing to look at except for a tangle of undergrowth and a few scraggly trees. It was Tom Balsley's idea to build up the earth and create a big stone retaining wall, allowing us to have a garden next to the house. The lawn below the wall was then regraded to slope down more gently.

The stones for the wall were found primarily on the property; they are large and in keeping with the rustic character of the other walls on the grounds. After the wall was finished and the terrace filled with good topsoil and compost, two flower borders were planted, intersected by a stone paved grass walk. Next to the house, holly was planted and a

border of daffodils for spring bloom. Once the daffodils died back, impatiens were planted, thriving for the rest of the growing season in the partial shade of the tulip tree and the house.

To the right of the path, grape hyacinths, American boxwood, and lavender tulips were planted. Five espaliered McIntosh apple trees, still supported by wooden frames, back the border. A giant hemlock, one of the few really nice trees on the property, stands majestically centered at the end of the path.

When creating a new garden such as this one, remember to fill it with the best soil you can find; the soil is the real basis, the foundation, of any garden. All the compost and manure and topsoil for this garden came from Bulpit's Brookside Nursery in Darien. Free of stone and weed seeds, this soil gives all plants and shrubs a better than average chance of survival and success.

OPPOSITE: Susan and Scott Robinson of Easton, Connecticut, designed the layout for this charming garden. The espaliered apple trees were grown by Henry Leuthardt on Long Island. I have been buying trees from him for a long time.

ABOVE LEFT: Work has begun on the building of the retaining wall to the east of the house. I had wanted this wall to look like existing stone walls on the property, all built without mortar.

ABOVE CENTER: A small, portable cement mixer used on-site helps a lot when building a terrace or repairing chimneys and foundations. Small amounts of cement can be custom-mixed for a particular job and are ready when needed without relying on a commercial mixing truck.

ABOVE RIGHT: Primitive pulleys were constructed by the masons for lifting rocks to create the east terrace garden visible from the parlor and library windows.

PRESERVING TREES AND SHRUBS

Although many people do not realize it, one of the great attractions of an old house is that it often has established plantings and big old trees. Trees lend an air of permanence and history to a house and give it a sheltered feeling. The Adams house was no exception. A marvelous large tulip tree (reputedly the largest in Connecticut) stood in the front yard, as well as a swamp maple, several hemlock and spruce, and large willows.

Unfortunately, almost all the trees on the property were suffering from neglect; dead branches on the swamp maple were hanging over the house and needed to be removed. A cluster of spruce was planted so close to the house that no light ever came inside. The property, so overgrown that it was reverting back to its natural state, cried for attention.

The first thing I did was consult with Charlie Hyatt of Evergreen Enterprises, tree surgeons in Connecticut. He pointed out all the serious problems, such as the severe scale in the hemlocks and the absolute need to prune the willows before they became too heavy and fell over and the magnificent tulip tree to give air to the main lateral branches. He agreed with me that it was a good idea to remove the scraggly and crooked spruces. He also contracted to remove and chip all the ash saplings around the house and all the barberry and other shrubbery that obscured the windows and lent an air of desperate loneliness to the house.

VICTOR'S METHOD OF
CLEARING AND GRADING

1. Cut down sizable, unwanted trees for firewood; split and stack them as close as possible to where wood is ultimately used.
2. Bulldoze remaining brush and small trees, pulling up roots of all trees. Take care not to disturb any that are to be saved.
3. Scrape topsoil from open areas (especially low-lying areas with thick deposits) into large piles to be saved for spreading after all grading and reshaping is complete.
4. Dig deep holes in the scraped areas; bury organic waste—stumps, branches, brush—being careful to crush as completely as possible with the machine.
5. Complete all grading, stonewall construction, and trenching. Replace topsoil in an even, thick layer all over property. Where gardens are planned, aerate subsoil, enriching it with whatever is necessary, and top with lots of compost and topsoil.

LEFT: Only the best of the trees on the property were saved. The others were cut down, or bulldozed and removed; all the roots were dug out. Two friends of Renaldo Abreu, Jadir and Luciano, helped cut the dead and downed trees with their chain saws. Those good for firewood were cut to correct length and split by a professional splitter. A wood pile was erected at the far eastern portion of the property and neatly stacked for future use.

RIGHT: Covered with brambles and vines, the 1½-acre property looked small and confining at first. Once the chaotic growth was removed, the entire piece of land took on a totally new appearance. It appeared spacious and open, and a vista or two seemed absolutely within the realm of possibility.

The soil, fallow for years, needed a bit of perking up; it was limed, fertilized, and even enriched with some of the moist compost found in the lower areas of the property, washed there by years of rain. Once the earth was smoothed and the edges of the wall surrounding the property cleared of brush, the soil was aerated, raked, and seeded. Within a few days, there was a healthy growth of lawn. Here is a view of the eastern side of the house while the retaining wall for the new terrace garden was being built.

ACCENTING WITH EVERGREENS

Because they blend in beautifully with their surroundings and retain foliage year-round, evergreens are extremely effective when used for boundary demarcation, screening, hedges, or edging. Your selection should be based on their growing habits as well as shape when mature.

Shrubs and Hedges

AZALEA (*Rhododendron*), a flowering compact evergreeen shrub, grows to 4 feet and is hardy in the north. It demands partial sun and lime-free soil with plenty of peat. Small round leaves alternate with many small snowy-white to fuchsia flowers that bloom in mid-spring.

BARBERRY (*Berberis*) grows to 6 feet in 6 years. The evergreen variety is not hardy in northern climates. It requires well-drained soil and tolerates light shade. The dense, spiked, arching yellow wood is covered with deep-green oblong leaves. Flower clusters are yellow to white.

RIGHT: I really enjoy doing as much of the planting as possible. Digging holes is good exercise as well as fun, and as long as the shrubs or plants are not too heavy for me I can plant all day long. These boxwood were great to plant; the soil prepared with compost was rich, friable, and free of rocks. Newly made beds like these are wonderful for bulbs (they can be planted deeply and easily) and for trees that need large holes to accommodate the roots.

BOXWOOD (*Buxus*) grows from 3 to 15 feet; the dwarf variety, *B. sempervirens* 'Suffruticosa' is excellent for edging. I planted these around the house. They should be pruned once a year to retain their roundish shape. Boxwood can be grown in well-drained soil in partial shade or full sun. Thin, oblong leaves are dark green and shiny; some are variegated.

COTONEASTER (*Cotoneaster*) is a semi-evergreen shrub that grows to 15 feet. It loves sun and fertile soil. The willow-like leaves appear on trailing branches, but it is often clipped espalier-style and supported on a wall or trellis. Its white springtime flowers are followed by clusters of bright orange berries in midsummer that may last through winter.

HEATH (*Erica*) is a delicate-looking shrub or small tree that grows from 1 to 3 feet high; a few varieties are hardy in the north. It loves lime-free acidic soil and prefers sun. The needle-like leaves spiral around the branches; clusters of nodding flowers, ranging from rose to white, bloom from midsummer to fall.

HEATHER (*Calluna*) grows from 8 to 20 inches and is hardy in the north. It requires slightly sandy, lime-free soil and partial shade. Leaves may be brilliant green, bronze, or yellow. Flowers range from rose to pink; some kinds are white.

HOLLY (*Ilex*), with its shiny dark-green leaves edged with sharp points, grows to 12 feet. It loves acid soil in partial shade; females produce red berries in winter. Holly bushes are often pruned short to create an impenetrable barrier.

PRIVET (*Ligustrum ovalifolium*), a semi-evergreen shrub, grows from 6 to 10 feet. 'Nanum' is the dwarf variety. It tolerates ordinary garden soil in both shade and sun. Oval leaves are deep green and glossy; varieties are edged in white or yellow; some are marbled.

RHODODENDRON (*Rhododendron*) reaches 10 feet and is hardy in the north. The long, oblong green leaves coil under in the cold. This shrub demands lime-free soil mixed with peat and loves shade. Large blooms appear in late spring in white, yellow, lilac, rose, and deep red.

SPOTTED LAUREL (*Aucuba*), popular in the Victorian era, grows 6 to 10 feet. This shade-loving shrub tolerates drought, but prefers moist, well-drained soil. The round large leaves combine several colors: green, yellow, orange, and maroon.

YEW (*Taxus*) can be a shrub or tree that grows as high as 15 feet. It tolerates shade in rather poor soil but prefers well-drained soil and room to thicken. Its dark-green linear leaves are poisonous. Yew, often pruned into shapes, bears bright crimson berries in the fall.

Large Trees

FIR (*Abies*) grows to 50 feet, though some cultivars reach twice that. They do well in a sunny location, planted in well-drained soil. Firs are pyramidal in form and grow flat, firm 1-inch needles. Their erect cones typically measure 5 inches, though some are as long as 10.

HEMLOCK (*Tsuga*) can grow to 100 feet if given plenty of space and lots of sun. It will not tolerate chalky soil. It is rather round in appearance with short, delicate needles and cones a mere 1-inch long.

JUNIPER (*Juniperus*) normally grows to 10 feet, although some reach 30 feet. The topiary Junipers that I planted near the front door have an 8-foot spreading habit, which I prune to keep under control. They tolerate dry conditions but do best in well-drained soil with full sun. Most varieties have sharp overlapping needles; some bear blue berries.

PINE (*Pinus*), pyramidal in shape with rounded tops, achieves heights of 10 to 40 feet if not crowded. Pine trees love well-drained soil and full sun. Thin, long medium-green needles grow in clusters; cones are egg-shaped or conical and measure from 2 to 10 inches.

SPRUCE (*Picea*) spires to heights of 100 feet. This narrow, pyramid-shaped tree needs full sun in well-drained soil. Branches sweep upward and bear sharp, bluish needles with 6-inch cones.

Plants are purchased either bare-root, burlap bound, wrapped in plastic webbing, or in containers. When they arrive, place them in a sheltered and shaded location. Submerge all bare-root plants immediately, just below the trunk, in a bucket of water. When it's time to plant, I take off the burlap, though it can be left on; it disintegrates over time and roots will grow through as they spread. Plastic webbing must be discarded.

The best time to plant is early spring as soon as the soil is workable and the plants are still dormant. Fall planting is risky; plants may be caught by an unexpected frost before roots have had a chance to take hold. Prepare the soil one week before you plant.

Dig a hole deeper and wider than the root mass. Remove all subsoil, darker in color than the topsoil, to a tarp spread alongside the hole. Supplement the topsoil with 50 percent compost and sprinkle 2 ounces of commercial fertilizer rated 10-20-20 over the mixture for each plant. Work the subsoil with a fork to aerate it. The day before you plant, completely soak the hole to ensure proper drainage; no plant likes to sit in water.

When planting, spread the roots in the hole and add enough of the topsoil-compost mixture to cover them. Walk around the tree to make sure it doesn't lean. Firmly but carefully press the topsoil around the roots with your foot. Add soil to ground level and pack it well.

Tall trees must be staked for one year to ensure that the trunk grows straight. If planting bare-root or burlap-bound trees, gently sink a pole at least 3 inches into the subsoil before replacing the topsoil. Tie with cotton strips at intervals along the trunk. Container-grown specimens need to be staked beyond their root mass.

Pruning is unnecessary during the first year, but broken or crossed branches should be removed. Once a week until fall, each plant needs to be saturated with water. It will help to add a layer of mulch over the root zone to ensure moisture retention. After the first year, use liquid fertilizer regularly in spring and fall, and water on a biweekly schedule.

RIGHT: Another view of the terrace garden to the east of the house. Large pavers of bluestone, set in the grass, form the center path. Grape hyacinth was planted in front of boxwood with tall lavender tulips and espaliered apple trees beyond.

Planting an Evergreen Border

I wanted a straight line of small boxwood along the right-hand side of the driveway. Taking lessons from my favorite nurseries (Marder's in Bridgehampton, Long Island, and Geiger's in Westport, Connecticut), I carefully planted these well-grown specimens according to their directions.

1. A rubber hammer is used to drive the wooden stakes into the ground. These are available in hardware or gardening supply stores.

2. To create a straight edge, use a strong string tied between two secure stakes. Nylon twine, an excellent string for this purpose, must be drawn tightly so that there is an accurate straight edge to follow in spading up the earth.

3. Use a straight-edged spade to cut through the sod to a depth of at least 4 inches, if possible. Remove the grass, shaking off the excess soil. I use the sod, if it is

thick, for patching holes in the lawn. If it is ragged, I throw it into the compost as green manure. My English rubber gardening shoes are excellent for this kind of heavy-duty work. The soles are thick and ribbed, allowing for a great deal of pressure while digging with spades and shovels.

4. I wanted the boxwood to be evenly apart, almost touching, and exact spacing was important. I used a tape measure for accuracy, leaving the string in place until the hole digging was complete.

5. Use a long-handled pointed spade to dig the holes. Pile the soil to the side of the hole or, if space is limited, onto a canvas or plastic drop cloth near the hole. Don't pile the soil on the lawn or right on the driveway—cleanup will be long and tedious. A bit of peat moss is added to each hole to lighten the soil and help moisture retention.

6. Peat moss is most economically purchased in 6-cubic-foot plastic bags. Dry, it can be moved around easily; wet, it becomes sodden and leaden, impossible to transport without a cart or wheelbarrow.

7. Use a hand cultivator to mix the peat into the soil at the bottom of the hole.

8. Remove the plant from its container, taking care not to disturb the root ball. I make an effort not to lose any of the soil adhering to the plant as I place it carefully in the prepared hole. If the shrub has been wrapped in plastic netting, carefully remove the covering before placing the plant in the hole.

9. Add enough water to fill the hole, allowing it to drain almost completely before filling in around the roots with the original soil. Add more soil than the hole requires, mounding it up around the base.

10. My gardening shoes are also great for pressing the earth around the base of the plant to fill any air holes around the root ball.

Water new plantings regularly during the first month, allowing the plants to establish themselves in their new location. During especially dry weather, always water regularly to promote growth and good health.

BUILDING A FLAGSTONE TERRACE

There are three essentials to keep in mind when building any patio or terrace: a stable base, a proper foundation, and good drainage to control water runoff. If you live, as I do, where winter temperatures drop below freezing, drainage is especially important, since ice can cause a great deal of damage. A terrace designed with a slight pitch, as little as a quarter of an inch per foot, will make drainage possible.

To create a stable base, George staked out the area and excavated to just below

LEFT: The spacious terrace that was constructed at the rear of the house improved the home immensely. Previously there was absolutely no place to rest or read outdoors. This terrace solved the problem. Its floor was topped with a geometric but irregular pattern of bluestone; a balustrade of white wood was constructed around the perimeter with square posts and square balusters. This terrace was large enough to accommodate a dining table, some reclining chairs, and an outdoor gas grill. With access to the kitchen through the sunroom it became a convenient place to cook and entertain. The puffy metal spring chairs, called Deauville chairs, were designed in France long ago and are now being made in reproduction. The glass-topped metal table is large enough for eight. The color of the metal is something I call cupboard blue, a combination of dark green, teal, and blue.

the frostline, about 40 inches deep. Footings were poured, as they were for the house foundation, and hollow concrete building blocks were hauled in to build a perimeter wall. George was able to obtain native stones from a nearby building site to cement to the outer surface of this wall, creating a facade. To keep the facade from falling away from the concrete blocks, building ties made of 1-by-8-inch galvanized steel with a serrated edge were buried in the mortar joints. These ties were inserted at random, like X's and O's in a tic-tac-toe pattern. Then fill was placed inside the perimeter wall.

Normally, rock or stone tamped down manually would be used for fill, but as it happens, my terrace rests on refuse. Victor Perkowski maneuvered a bucket loader around the building site to pick up waste and scrap material and dump it into the void: stones, pieces of masonry, chunks of concrete, iron pipes, even mattress springs. It's an excellent idea to find a way to use the heavy debris that accrues during construction as long as you are careful not to use any organic material. It must be solid, compactable, and contain no elements that might pollute the groundwater supply. If you are

ABOVE LEFT: Foundation walls of cement block have been laid. It is very important to build walls level, plumb, and straight. A surveyor's transit may be needed. If walls are tall, it may be necessary to use metal rods as reinforcement inside the cement block. As the walls were constructed and the mortar dried, Victor backfilled the space with small rocks and other inorganic waste from the building site. Glass, metal, and old concrete make good fill that does not decompose and compress.

ABOVE: A view of the cement block work for the east wall of the terrace, with some of the decorative stone facade work begun. This wall leads into the basement.

uncertain what such pollutants might be, check with your building department or a regional office of the Environmental Protection Agency.

After fill was added, the base had to be compressed—for solidity and to remove voids and air pockets. Water was sprayed on, and the base was backfilled, then allowed to stand idle for a couple of weeks to dry out and compress completely. George installed a system of

drainage pipes so that the water from the roof would travel under the terrace and into the rear yard.

The foundation for the terrace surface was a bed of mortar 4 inches thick that was poured over the base and pitched gently away from the house. After the mortar had hardened, we laid out the flagstones I had chosen. When the pattern looked exactly right, each stone was lifted and about 2 inches of dry-mix mortar was put down. This moist, but not wet, adhesive is stronger and dries faster than the poured variety. Next, George leveled the stones by tamping them with a rubber mallet. A length of 2-by-4 was used to check that the surface was level (a carpenter's level would work as well) and also that it was correctly pitched away from the building.

It took a day or two of hardening before the flagstones could be grouted with more dry-mix mortar. After it was allowed to sit untouched for about a month, the surface was cleaned with muriatic acid and coated with a silicone or masonry sealer. George did this to keep moisture from penetrating and causing the flagstones to move or crack. Sealer should be reapplied every two years to maintain this protection.

Steps leading up to the terrace were done using the same techniques as were used for the terrace itself. Footings were poured, fill was placed inside a concrete perimeter faced with stone, and flagstones were used for treads. George made sure the risers were all the same height and that each pitched forward slightly to carry off rainwater.

USING BRICK: To my way of thinking, a

flagstone terrace suited the style of the house, but slate or brick would have also worked well. Brick can be laid in a variety of ways and comes in many colors.

Instead of using grout, joints between pavers are filled with sand or a mix of sand and dry cement. Brick can also be laid without mortar, creating more of an "old world" feeling. Mortarless brick must be laid on a level site prepared on a base of compressed gravel or sand.

Used, old brick provides a particularly desirable texture and tone. Choose whatever appeals to you, but make sure the brick you buy is hard-burned, thus less likely to soften or crumble over time.

USING CONCRETE: Concrete, finished rough or smooth, and colored, either before or after pouring, can also be used for a terrace. Special effects can be achieved by tamping down pebbles, seashells, or exposed aggregate on the surface while still wet.

USING WOOD: A wood deck, more appropriate to a contemporary-style house than to this one, is a similar feat of construction that begins with concrete footings. Construction-grade redwood or any wood that is pressure-treated can be used, its size dependent on the deck's height, the area it will cover, and the load you expect it to carry. The actual deck surface should be 4- or 6-inch-wide planks of clear wood. According to George, "clear" means that if knots exist, they are a quarter inch in size or smaller, which will not compromise the strength of the wood. When your deck is finished and before it is used, coats of life-extending preservative should be brushed on and allowed to dry.

ABOVE: The stone used for the facing work came from a construction site nearby, as did most of the stone in the retaining walls. When building such a terrace or foundation and walls, it is important to locate stone that closely matches existing stonework. Stones vary greatly in appearance and new masonry can look very out of place if it does not blend in.

ABOVE RIGHT: The terrace with stonework complete. The facing stone matches the existing foundation. The stairs and terrace top are covered with slab bluestone in random sizes. Metal 4-by-4 posts were inserted into the top row of masonary block and used as anchors for wooden balustrades, assuring sturdy construction. A wood or metal fence and railing will define the terrace and create the feeling of an outdoor room.

BELOW: The finished terrace as seen from the north, looking into the sunroom. The new window dictated by fire regulations is seen at the right on the second floor.

BUILDING A STONE WALL

The old stone walls of New England, built by our forebears from the rocks pried out of their fields give a pleasing definition to property lines and roadsides. The stone walls of the Adams house, clearly over 150 years old, one running along the west side of the house, another along the southern border, had fallen almost completely to ruin and I wanted to restore them. There were plenty of rocks available from the excavation to use for this purpose as well as to face the cinderblock supporting the terrace. Stonework is an art; stone walls appear simple to build but require a good spatial sense and brute strength.

Stone walls are assembled one rock at a time, banked inward at a slight angle. Dry stone walls, requiring the most artistry, are built without mortar, the weight and size of the rocks securing the wall naturally, a perfect equilibrium achieved by the mason. One incredibly intricate technique known as a "lace wall" calls for large holes to be left between the rocks.

Mortar walls, though less aesthetic, are more substantial since the rocks are bonded together with a mortar mixed from cement, lime, and sand. The thicker the mortar, the more reliable the construction. Mortar walls are erected on a "footing," or foundation, twice as wide as the wall and buried below the frostline. Once the trench for the footing is dug, a layer of gravel is shoveled in and leveled, and concrete is poured in on top to just below ground level. Stones are then built up on this base. Mortar walls may be erected in the same manner as dry stone walls with the mortar troweled into the joints as the stones are set. Another method is to set the stones into layers of mortar, and then cement the joints. Once excess mortar is removed, the joints are smoothed.

LEFT: Work near the pond had to be done by hand—boulders were moved with crowbars, and the stone walls were built with raw manpower and sheer willpower. Trees were cut down, stumps dug out, and the pond bottom dragged with chains to help remove debris.

RIGHT: Renaldo and his friend moved great rocks to line the brook that was created every spring by runoff from the ponds down through the property behind the house. Iris and other water-loving plants were placed along the banks of this wet area.

BELOW: There is a lovely double pond behind the Adams house. Renaldo decided to clear the area around the pond with his brother and another friend, lining the brook with rocks. There were many boulders to be moved, and because it was so close to the edge of the water, Victor could not get his machines close enough to be of any help.

BUILDING FENCES

Fences are invaluable in establishing an architectural definition to the borders of a property and to areas within it. A sizable border fence will also afford privacy, muffle street noise, and protect plants from gusty winds.

ZONING AND PERMITS: Zoning restrictions sometimes prohibit or limit a curbside structure. The most common of these disallows a street-facing fence of over 6 feet; for some communities, the limitation is as low as 3 feet. A boundary fence requires a building permit; walls

RIGHT: The beautiful wooden fence and arched gateway was designed by Jim Bleuer of Casa Verde Gardens in Southport. The woodworking was executed to his specifications by Walpole Woodworkers of Ridgefield, a wonderful company that specializes in fencings and gates (they have made large and small ones for my Turkey Hill house, and I have always been very pleased with their craftsmanship). The crispy, bright white nature of this fencing added an extraordinary sense of order and simplicity to the yard opposite the kitchen door. Large bluestone pavers were used for the walk echoing the walkways I installed to the kitchen and terrace doors.

The gardens were very nicely planned, consisting of a cruciform design with a center round planted with a specimen Korean topiary lilac that bloomed during the showhouse tour. *Clematis montana* was planted on the arched gateway.

within the property do not. When applying for a permit, you must present a current survey map of the property, incorporating all buried town services that cross the property line from the street to the house. Surveys are filed at the town registry of deeds.

When you are planning a border fence, be sure to alert your neighbors to your intentions before you begin construction. The appearance of an unexpected fence often provokes strong reactions. Because you will want to be sure your fence does not infringe on your neighbor's land, you may want to have your lawyer draw up an agreement that both of you sign based on your survey map. Specify whether or not you need to gain access to your neighbor's property, either for construction or for maintenance. If the fence is to be shared, outline mutual responsibilities; if it is temporary or removable, removal procedures should be in writing.

DESIGN: A fence should enhance the house and its surroundings and be appropriate to the period and architecture of the house. A rule of thumb: a larger house can take a taller, wider fence; a cottage looks better with a low-lying one. Federal houses such as Turkey Hill are often picket-fenced; a Victorian house, by contrast, looks wonderful with wrought iron.

POST-AND-RAIL CONSTRUCTION: Whatever their design, wood fences are assembled with posts and horizontal boards called rails. Posts typically measure 4 or 6 inches square; they may also be round. Posts can be enhanced with decorative caps protruding slightly beyond the post,

or with round balls or finials. Rails come in several widths: 2 by 2, 2 by 3, 2 by 4, and 2 by 6. The best boards to use are slightly beveled to allow water runoff.

Unlike the select kiln-dried lumber specified for interior framing, common air-dried and less expensive lumber is used for outdoor structures such as fences. Because of its durability and natural resistance to moisture and pests, especially termites, redwood is popular and does not require any special treatment, except for the portion of posts buried in the soil. Another moisture-resistant wood, common to the Northeast, is white cedar, which can be sawed easily and does not warp. If left untreated, it weathers to a soft gray.

Other wood stock, including fir, spruce, or pine, must be weatherproofed or pressure-treated to guard against moisture, decay, and pests, and also sealed as an additional protection against rot.

ABOVE: **One of the four corners of the picket-fenced perennial garden on the west side of the driveway. These gardens, designed by Jim Bleuer, were planned so that plants would bloom consecutively all season. Spring was heralded by dicentra, foxglove, pansies, and artemisia. Campanula, hollyhocks, lilies, dianthus, and delphinium were planted for successive bloom. The late-summer garden came into flower with asters, scabiosa, daylilies, tansy, and coreopsis.**

RIGHT: **Alongside Jim Bleuer's garden fence, I planted hundreds of van Engelun's white Imperator tulips. They began blooming in early May, and because the bulbs were so healthy and the beds so well prepared, the flowers, almost 30 inches tall, lasted for more than three weeks, an extremely long blooming time for tulips of any kind. Three years later, although not as tall or as strong, these same bulbs are still putting forth a rather good show.**

The sealer should be thinned with denatured alcohol to avoid cracking, and several coats should be applied. Shellac is to be avoided, as it turns wood yellow or orange. Wood can be primed and stained or painted with an oil-based paint, which repels moisture. Stain and paint can be sprayed or brushed, but avoid windy days when soil and debris can stick to the wet surface. The best nails are galvanized, as they resist rust.

Fences are built in sections called bays, a bay being the unit from one post to the next. A gate may be set into one of the bays or between them. Bays can be custom-built or ready-made. Ready-mades come in a selection of heights and lengths that can be altered to fit a design and the terrain.

Whether using ready-made bays or nailing in the uprights by hand, all posts should be in place three days before assembly to ensure a solid base. Post holes are dug and are usually filled with wet concrete to create firm footings for the posts.

Fences based on the post-and-rail design include:

PICKET: The basic post-and-rail is overlaid with vertical slats, or pickets, which often come to a gentle point on top. Points may also be cut into complex shapes, a service that is often available at the lumberyard. Pickets may be uniform in height or cut to form an indulation within the bay. Victorian picket fences can be very elaborate with parts topped with intricate caps and finials.

FEATHER BOARD: Vertical boards are installed so that they overlap each other.

STOCKADE: Sold in ready-made sections, vertical, thin, slightly rounded boards are joined by tightly woven galvanized wire.

LATTICE: To form each bay, wood strips are crisscrossed diagonally into a frame. Lattice 1 by 4, 1 by 6, 1 by 8, and 1 by 10 are available.

WOVEN: Rails nailed horizontally to the posts form a frame through which slender, pliable vertical slats are woven. This kind of fence is available in ready-made sections.

RIGHT: The driveway was lined with granite cobblestones, each of which was set in concrete to prohibit heaving during cold weather. The surface of the driveway is ⅜-inch native crushed stone, specially processed to remove the sharp edges. (Raw gravel is impossible to walk on barefooted, and it also cuts the heels of one's shoes.) The crushed stone is spread over a well-prepared base: 8 inches of gravel compressed by a large roller, then topped with the ⅜-inch stone applied 2 inches thick. Crushed stone can also be applied over a base of asphalt, which prevents weeds, but I find that it creates a hotter surface in the summer, making the large expanse of driveway uncomfortable. On the right are the holly bushes waiting to be planted along the stone foundation.

Laying a Stone Path

A path was needed to provide access from the driveway to the kitchen door. I decided to build it myself with the help of Renaldo. First we defined the perimeters of the walk with strong cord, then leveled off the area.

1. Renaldo used a maddock to break up the hard ground and loosen any stones. With a hard rake, I broke up the clumps of earth and smoothed the soil to make the subsurface of the walk. We wanted the surface to be level with the surrounding ground yet slightly sloped away from the building; about 3 inches of topsoil was removed.

2. Using a pad tamper (a common stone mason's tool that comes in 8-by-8-inch or 12-by-12-inch sizes), the subsurface is pounded hard. When this step is completed, the base will be ready to top with stone dust, a heavy, finely ground black stone that makes a perfect bed for a brick, stone, or aggregate path.

3. During the entire process, it is important to use a long level to check that the path is even, both side to side as well as front to back.

4. A local crushed stone supplier, L. H. Gault, delivered 6 cubic yards of stone dust to the driveway, an amount sufficient for the path, the herb garden brick walks, and the path leading to the terrace. I transported the stone dust in a mason's wheelbarrow—this type is very sturdy. The load is easily dumped from the barrow exactly where you want it.

5. I raked the stone dust with a hard rake until it was level and smooth, using about 2 inches as a base for the bluestone. If the subsoil had been less firm, I would have done two base coats—one of crushed stone, 3 inches thick, with a topping of 2 inches of the same stone dust. I used a pad tamper to compress the stone dust into a solid bed.

6. I pulled a straight-edge board (almost as wide as the path itself) for a final leveling and smoothing. All of this work can be done with little or no help, but depending on the finished surface you may need an extra pair of hands to move the materials.

7. The level confirms that the subsurface is ready for the stone placement.

8. We used large bluestone slabs, 4 feet wide and from 2 to 3 feet long. These are extremely heavy, so Renaldo and Renato helped me lay them on the prepared path. I've told Renato to always wear gloves when handling stone—fingertips are easily crushed—but he doesn't always remember.

9. Each stone is approximately 1¼ inches thick, but thickness does vary; it takes a bit of fitting to make the stones level. Pushing, digging out a bit of stone dust, even jumping on the stone are techniques we used to make the stones lie flat.

10. I did not want any large spaces between the stones, so we fitted them as tightly as we possibly could. Using the back side of a rake, Renaldo pushes the stone to square it off in the space allotted. It is easier to move the stone by pushing than to lift and place again.

11. I used a piece of wood to tamp the stone dust into the seams.

12. Each stone is checked again; they must be level front to back and side to side. Fresh earth is used to fill the spaces along the edges so that the adjoining soil is level with the path itself.

For messy work, I always wear protective clothing: my English rubber gardening shoes, loose-fitting, very comfortable khaki pants, cotton socks a couple of sizes too large so that they don't slide down into the rubber shoes, and a loose-fitting shirt. Of course I always try to wear gloves, especially when raking or digging, to help prevent calluses.

BUILDING THE GAZEBO

Walpole Woodworkers provided the materials and built the gazebo according to a plan drawn by Melanie Taylor, a very talented architect-designer from the New Haven, Connecticut, firm of Orr & Taylor. This whimsical ornament graces the lawn and provides a distant focal point for the rooms on the eastern side of the house. The rustic log columns, eight in all, reflect a casual relaxed style.

The gazebo, with its beautifully constructed and finished wood details, lattice panels, and gates, is very much in keeping with the character of the main house. The lattice is swagged between the cedar columns like lace curtains and is painted the same Hunt Club Teal as the house doors and shutters.

Finely crafted woodwork and long-lasting materials are the Walpole Woodworkers' trademarks. This gazebo made of cedar and redwood will weather well.

LEFT: With the column posts in place, and roof frieze installed, the gazebo takes on a real shape. A lattice door opens onto the gurgling brook. The rough-sawn floor of redwood will weather gray like the bark-covered posts.

RIGHT: The east parlor offers a romantic view of the finished gazebo near the property border. The peaked roof, constructed of painted blue 2-by-6-inch wood boards, is "thatched" with bark-covered twigs. Although not totally rainproof, it does offer some protection from the elements.

PLANTING A HERB GARDEN

Having an abundance of herbs available for teas, cooking, and simply for the pleasure of their fragrance is a great luxury and one easily come by if you have even a bit of land. All they require is well-drained soil, sun, and some screening to buffer the wind.

DESIGNING THE HERB GARDEN: Historically, herb gardens were surrounded by framing to shelter the plants from wind and to make a clear demarcation from other areas of the garden. But today, not all herb gardens are framed and many are now planted in borders. Maggie Daly, who planted my fan-shaped herb garden, did not find it necessary to surround it, as the property boundary is amply framed by sheltering trees. Still, the framing idea is very attractive. Evergreen hedges are a classic framing solution, as are gray-green herbs like lavender, santolina, or artemisia, which contrast beautifully with interior plants of a darker green. A low stone or brick wall surrounding the plot can also be used and can double for seating or displaying planted urns.

A herb garden is usually laid out in sections, framed within a square, rectangle, circle, or half-circle. Individual beds within the overall plan are usually also laid out in geometric shapes—squares, rectangles, wedges, circles, or ovals, the last two sometimes intersecting each other. Individual beds can be devoted to specific herbs or they may combine several kinds.

Some gardeners prefer to plant in raised beds. These are beautiful and practical, too, because they provide good drainage. Weatherproofed boards, bricks, or stones (I used bluestone at Turkey Hill) can be installed to edge the beds and protect against erosion.

A herb garden is both defined by and tied together by borders and paths. Paths provide access to the garden when it's time to plant, trim, weed, and harvest. Paths may be made of gravel (which should be underlined with black plastic to prevent weeds), brick, or stone such as cobblestone or flagstone. These paths can be edged with brick, stone, or sealed 1-by-3s sunk into the ground. Paths can also be planted with grass or even with herbs such as chamomile (*Chamaemelum nobile*) or thyme (*Thymus praecox,* 'Coccineus'), and creeping pennyroyal

RIGHT: **Maggie Daly of Fairfield masterminded the fan-shaped herb garden that was planted at the back of the house. All old houses, and I think all new ones, should have some form of herb garden. The use of fresh herbs in cooking greatly enhances any dish one makes, and the fun of growing herbs—once planted, they usually thrive—should encourage everyone to have these fragrant and useful plants. This shapely garden creates a focal point for the backyard and provides a lovely place to sit and an area in which to display a pair of antique urns and a superior twig cast-iron bench. Each of the rays of the garden is planted with a single herb. The chart on the following page indicates the details and also lists other herbs that are useful for a garden of this kind.**

(Mentha Pulegium). Once established, herb paths yield a savory fragrance when grazed by foot traffic. The herbs, if planted 6 inches apart, will fill in by mid-summer and can be walked on soon after. Their dense matting can be kept under control with bold trims in early and late summer, as can a grass path.

If you have a site plan, review it to see where on your property the herb garden would be most ornamental and most useful. A herb garden near the kitchen is ideal. If you don't have a site plan, draw a rough sketch of your grounds. Then take measurements of the specific area you have chosen for your herb garden and transcribe them to grid paper equating 1 foot to ½ inch. Make photocopies of your plot so that you can experiment with a variety of ideas. Once you've made the initial design, divide it into sections in a larger scale—1 foot to 2 inches on the grid paper—to give an idea of where each plant should be placed and how much room it will require to fill out.

SOIL PREPARATION: To get a good sense of the proportions, stake out the beds and pathways before digging the garden. This also enables you to observe both light and shade over the course of a day and make sure you've planned the garden in a suitable spot. If possible, cultivate the soil in the fall for spring planting. Remove all sod, including the long running roots. Work the ground with a tiller or fork; remove all topsoil to a tarpaulin. Break up subsoil, lighter in color than topsoil, with a fork. Aeration in this manner contributes to the well-drained environment that all herbs demand. Next, mix one-quarter sand, one-quarter manure, and one-half compost with a granular fertilizer rated 5-10-10 (the amount of fertilizer is determined by how large your mixture is). Thoroughly blend along with your topsoil and replace. If your soil is compact, you will need greater amounts of sand. A good growing medium has a texture that is dark and crumbly with a neutral to slightly acid pH level (pH 6.3–7). Take a soil test to verify your pH. Deep soak the ground before planting.

Larger amounts of the growing medium with topsoil are needed for raised beds. After the ground is cultivated, establish your edging. Within this edging, layer 2 to 3 inches of crushed gravel before mounding the growing compound. Deep soak with water to make sure it freely drains; if not, work in more sand. The day before planting, thoroughly soak all the beds.

Once planted, herbs need to be top-dressed in the spring, fertilized with a 10-20-20 commercial granular fertilizer in the spring and fall, and covered with hay to prevent frostbite in winter.

HERB PLACEMENT: Plan your perennials first. They are permanent and require the most room. Leaf shape and color will set these plants apart, rendering an often-times all-green herb garden into an individual creation. In planning the final design, height is key. Heights vary enormously (see chart). Angelica, goldenrod, and lovage rise above 5 feet, whereas thyme, sweet marjoram, and oregano grow no more than 14 inches. Short plants work well in front of tall specimens for border plantings, and around taller herbs in island arrangements. Pro-liferation is another consideration. Lemon balm and borage crowd other herbs; spearmint and germander have lateral roots that send up new plants where they may not be wanted. To confine them, plant them alone in individual beds. Be sure to leave room for your annuals; though they live for only one season and are not set out until frost is well passed, they add color and bloom, and you need not plant them in the same place year after year. Caraway, borage, dill, and fennel, considered annuals, will self-seed new plants throughout the garden the following year. They can be controlled by pinching off their flower heads before they produce seeds.

Laying a Brick Path

Brick is a material that instantly confers warmth and charm to a garden. And laying a brick path is a simple process, one you may choose to do yourself.

Bricks are packed in "cubes" comprising 544 bricks. Colors include ocher, beige, burnt orange, and slate gray; surfaces may be rough or smooth. The standard brick is 3¼ by 7½ by 2 inches thick. Square or octagonal bricks can sometimes be found, however, and old brick is also available in many supply yards. Though it may require scraping and cleaning with muriatic acid, old brick creates a beautiful effect.

In preparing the ground, it is important that it be graded slightly to slope away from buildings, and then leveled with a 2-inch layer of sand to provide drainage. Where traffic is heavy, a bed of mortar delivers a sound foundation. Begin by turning the soil over, rake it flat, then level it using a drum roller if available. Three inches of coarse gravel is then spread and pounded with a flat metal tamper. If you choose to use mortar, cover the gravel using a mixture of one quarter cement and three quarters sand. Working in sections, spread a layer of wet mortar—cement, lime, and sand—with a trowel, and place bricks on top. Use a section of wood for consistent spacing, or simply lay bricks as close together as possible. (This provides a more European and old-fashioned look.)

The space can be edged in 1-by-4-inch or 2-by-4-inch weatherproofed wood that is pegged below ground level. Bricks can also be set next to one another end up and tops level with the paving, or set at an angle, a method I used in the Turkey Hill gardens.

To prevent plant growth between bricks, point with mortar. Dry mix one-third cement with two-thirds sand. Pour this into the joints, brush off all surface dust, pack joints with a bit of wood you used for spacing, and trickle water over

the entire area until it is thoroughly soaked. Keep traffic away.

Bricks are an amazingly versatile material. They can be laid in several patterns: running bond, where one brick is laid so that it lines up with the center of the brick next to it; herringbone, where bricks are laid in a repeating V pattern; or they can be laid to create curved paths or circular patterns.

We used a simple running bond pattern for the fan-shaped herb garden by the back steps.

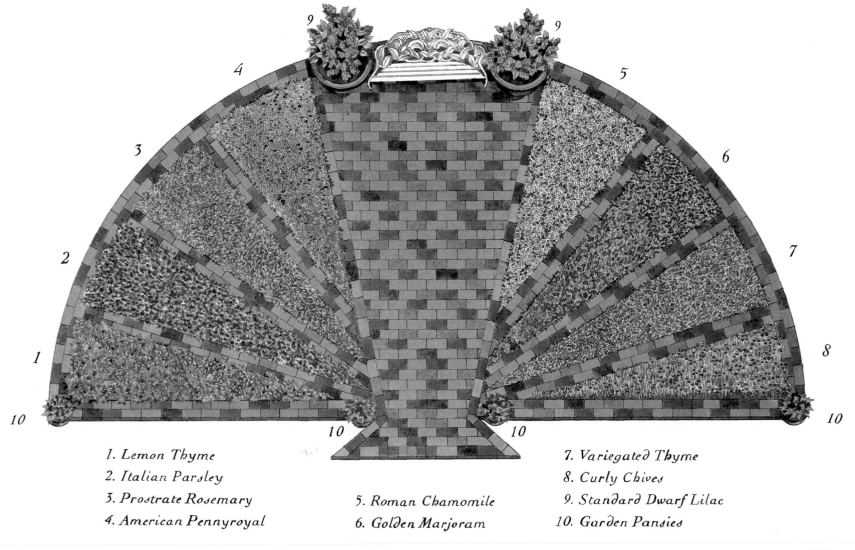

1. Lemon Thyme
2. Italian Parsley
3. Prostrate Rosemary
4. American Pennyroyal
5. Roman Chamomile
6. Golden Marjoram
7. Variegated Thyme
8. Curly Chives
9. Standard Dwarf Lilac
10. Garden Pansies

A Few Herbs to Grow

Herbs found in Adams house herb garden.

ANGELICA (*Archangelica*) Height: 5 to 8 feet. Large, toothed green leaves. Needs partial shade.

*BASIL (*Ocimum Basilicum*) Height: 1 to 2 feet. Oval, toothed, 2- to 3-inch leaves that are purple, yellow, or green. Needs full sun.

CARAWAY (*Carum Carvi*) Height: 2 feet. The upper section of the plant is feather-like. Needs full sun. Seeds and leaves may be used in salads. Cooked seeds turn bitter; add 15 minutes before serving.

*CHAMOMILE (ROMAN) (*Chamaemelum nobile*) Height: 2 to 4 inches. Fern-like leaves with a feathery texture. Needs full sun/partial shade. Makes a nice border; good in potpourri.

CHERVIL (*Anthriscus Cerefolium*) Height: 1 foot. Feathery, soft green, fern-like leaves. Needs full sun. Good with fish or in salad.

*CHIVES (CURLY) (*Allium senescens* var. *glaucum*) Height: 1 foot, with about 5 to 8 green spikes. Smooth and onion-like bulb. Needs full sun.

CORIANDER (*Coriandrum sativum*) Height: 1 to 3 feet. Round, toothed leaves. Needs full sun. A staple in Mexican food and Chinese dishes.

DILL (*Anethum graveolens*) Height: 3 feet. Width: 2 feet. Bluish-green leaves with a fine, feather-like texture. Needs full sun. Naturally repels cabbage looper, cabbage worms, and tomato hornworm.

FENNEL (*Foeniculum vulgare*) Height: 4 feet. Width: 1 to 2 feet. Deep green or bronze feather-like leaves. Needs full sun. Repels slugs.

GERMANDER (*Teucrium Chamaedrys*) Height: 2 feet. Width: 2 feet. Bright, dark green leaves with serrated edges. Needs full sun/partial shade. Nice dried for wreaths.

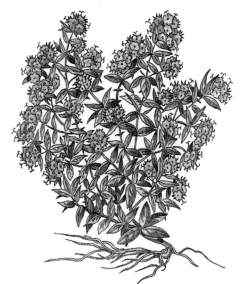

Roman Chamomile

Golden Marjoram

American Pennyroyal

Variegated Thyme

LAVENDER (*Lavendula angustifolia*) Height: 2 feet. Slender, gray-green, 2-inch leaves repel insects. Needs full sun. Good in jellies, vinegar, potpourri.

LEMON BALM (*Melissa officinalis*) Height: 2 feet. Width: 2 feet. Round 1- to 3-inch toothed leaves with a lemon scent. Needs full sun/partial shade. Throwing a few leaves in an open fire keeps bugs away. Tasty in tea, marmalades, or stuffed inside a whole fish.

*LEMON THYME (*Thymus* x *citriodorus*) Height: 4 to 12 inches. Small bush. Glossy, dark green leaves with a lemon scent. Needs full sun/partial shade. Use in tea.

LOVAGE (*Levisticum officinale*) Height: 5 feet. Width: 3 feet. Dark green, glossy leaves. Needs full sun/partial shade. Good for low-salt diets.

*MARJORAM (GOLDEN) (*Origanum*) Height: 2 to 2½ feet.

MINT (*Mentha*) Height: 1 to 2 feet. Pointed, oval, bright green leaves. Needs full sun.

OREGANO (*Origanum* spp.) Height: 1 to 2 feet. Oval, medium green, 2-inch leaves with toothed edges. Needs full sun.

*PARSLEY (ITALIAN) (*Petroselinum crispum*) Height: 28 inches. Compound, smooth, tooth-edged leaves with 3 leaflets. Needs full sun/partial shade.

*PENNYROYAL (AMERICAN) (*Hedeoma pulegioides*) Height: 4 to 16 inches, with ½- to 1-inch elongated leaves. Likes full sun. Works well as an insect repellant.

*ROSEMARY (PROSTRATE) (*Rosmarinus officinalis* 'Prostratus') Height: 1 foot; stalks 2 to 4 feet. Leathery grayish-green or dark green leaves about ⅓-inch wide. Needs full sun.

SAGE (*Salvia officinalis*) Height: 1 to 1½ feet. Long, oval, bumpy leaves. Needs full sun. Good with fish and chicken.

*THYME (VARIEGATED) (*Thymus* 'Silver Queen') Height: 10 inches. Linear, ¾-inch, white-edged leaves. Needs full sun/partial shade. Nice accent plant.

Italian Parsley

Curly Chives

Prostrate Rosemary

Lemon Thyme

Working with a Real Estate Professional

When you are ready to buy a house, you will probably deal with a real estate professional who is paid a percentage of the sale price to represent the seller. A good real estate professional will disclose to you all pertinent information about the property, both good and bad, and help you to complete all of the details involved in financing the house.

There are several categories of real estate professionals:

REAL ESTATE AGENT: A person licensed by a state real estate commission to list and sell property. To get the license, the agent must have taken accredited courses and passed state-approved examinations in real estate law and terminology, financing, business practices and ethics, and marketing. Most of them work in an agency managed by a real estate broker.

REAL ESTATE BROKER: An agent who has taken additional courses and passed additional tests to qualify for a higher degree of licensure. Many states require by law that agency heads be real estate brokers.

REALTOR: An agent affiliated with the National Association of Real Estate Boards.

REAL ESTATE LAWYER: A lawyer who

specializes in the legal transfer of property is always involved in the closing and sometimes in the sale itself.

Even before you visit the house, you should discuss a number of issues with the real estate professional:

THE LAND: The size of the lot, either in square feet or in acres, and its configuration and slope are usually spelled out on a plot map. Ask about the condition of any outbuildings and access to the property, including the amount of street or road frontage and who is responsible for maintaining the road. Is there wiring for telephone and electricity, and is there a municipal sewer service or an on-site septic system?

THE HOUSE: The agent should be able to give you an information sheet detailing the age and square footage of the house, number and types of rooms, condition of the kitchen and bathrooms, property taxes, and annual heating costs. If the building is historically important, there may be a special information sheet with details. Ask about the general condition of the house and its systems (foundation, roof, plumbing, and so on) and whether any appliances are included.

RESTRICTIONS: If the house is historic, are there rules governing its renovation? Are there zoning restrictions against operating a business from the house? Is there a second mortgage or any liens against the property?

THE PRICE: What is the selling price? Is it negotiable?

FINANCING: What is the down payment? Are the sellers willing to finance the sale themselves?

If you are still interested in the house after considering this information, the agent will arrange a tour, usually at a time when the seller is not present so you can talk freely to the agent.

Obtaining a Mortgage

Most people finance their homes by obtaining a mortgage. A mortgage consists of several components: the principal (or cost of the house); real estate taxes; home owner's insurance; the interest on the loan; and "points," the fee paid up front to the lending institution (1 point equals 1 percent of the amount of the loan). Sometimes it may be worth paying an extra point or two to get a lower interest rate.

Your immediate financial situation and your plans for the future will determine which kind of mortgage is the most appropriate.

FIXED-RATE LOANS

1. The traditional way to finance the purchase of a house, the conventional or standard loan has an interest rate that is set when the loan is granted and remains consistent for the life of the loan, usually 30 years. Shorter fixed-rate mortgages—15 years is the most popular—mean higher monthly payments but less interest over the life of the loan. Be sure to shop around, as the rates can vary widely.

2. A balloon, or term, mortgage is a short-term fixed-rate loan, usually for three to five years. It is commonly used in commercial real estate ventures and may be advantageous for home buyers who know they will move within the life of the loan. Relatively small monthly payments are followed by a large one at the end, the balloon. Often the monthly payments cover only the interest, and the last installment, the principal.

3. A biweekly payment loan is structured like a conventional mortgage but requires 26 payments a year instead of 12, reducing its term and thus its cost.

FLEXIBLE-RATE LOANS

1. An adjustable-rate mortgage, or ARM, is exactly what its name implies. The opening rate—often called a "teaser" rate—is generally lower than the rate for a fixed-rate mortgage. After the first year the interest is adjusted to reflect the prevailing prime rate, which is what banks charge their best customers to borrow money. ARMs are most attractive to short-term buyers who expect to move within five years. A reasonable ARM has two key provisions: a limit on the number of annual increases and a cap on the interest rate.

2. A negative amortization/deferred interest loan has lower monthly payments that do not cover all the interest; the balance is due at the end of the loan.

3. A graduated payment mortgage is structured so that interest payments increase for a specific length of time, then level off for the term of the loan. A typical GPM starts at 25 percent below the prevailing interest rate and rises about 7.5 percent a year for the first five years. This flexibility is appealing for borrowers who expect their incomes to increase over the life of the loan.

4. The two-step mortgage (also called "super seven" or "premier") provides for a below-market interest rate for the first seven to ten years, after which the rate is adjusted to reflect the current state of the financial market.

THE APPLICATION PROCESS: Most mortgage loans are made by mortgage companies, which either extend loans directly or act as middlemen between borrowers and third-party lenders; by commercial banks, which often require that you maintain an account at the bank to get a loan; or by savings and loan institutions. Given the state of the savings and loan industry, it is wise to check on the stability of any S&L you are considering. Credit unions and some life insurance companies also write mortgages.

Lenders reviewing mortgage applications consider three items:

INCOME: Each institution has its own formula. Generally, monthly carrying charges must not exceed 28 percent of the borrower's gross monthly income. All monthly obligations (house note, car payments, revolving charge accounts) have historically been limited to 36 percent of gross monthly income.

CREDIT HISTORY: The lender will contact a local credit-reporting agency for a report on what credit accounts you have and how promptly you pay. You can obtain a copy of your credit report from the agency; ask the lender for the name and address.

ASSETS: Includes stocks and bonds, real estate, automobiles, and savings.

To apply for a mortgage, you must have signed a sales contract for the house. You then meet with a mortgage loan officer, fill out the application for the type of loan you want, and pay a processing fee that ranges from $50 to $300.

Then you wait while the lender investigates your credit history and references, verifies your income with your employer, and assesses the property to determine if it is worth what you have agreed to pay for it. A problem in any of these areas is sufficient reason for the lender to deny you the loan. It usually takes 30 to 60 days for the information to be gathered and sent to the lending institution's review board.

This delay is sometimes awkward for people selling one house to buy another. The solution is a bridge loan (also called gap financing) from the financial institution that is financing the purchase of the new house. Once the sale of the old house is completed, the bridge loan is paid off. Most bridge loans last no more than six months.

Once the loan is approved, a closing date is set for the official transfer of ownership of the property.

Budgeting a Renovation

When you are buying an old house, devising a realistic preliminary budget for renovation is essential. As soon as you have a renovation plan, ask your architect to give you a rough estimate of the cost of labor and materials. If the figure is too high, decide what is most important to you and revise your plans accordingly.

Once the project is ready for bidding, give each potential contractor a copy of the plans, specifications, work list, and list of materials. Set a deadline for submitting bids, perhaps two to three weeks.

Review the bids with your architect or designer. Usually they will recommend accepting the lowest bid, but occasionally an exceptionally low bid may reflect an error or misunderstanding on the part of the contractor that will create problems later.

If all the bids are beyond your budget, consult with your architect about cutting costs, then ask potential contractors to revise their bids.

The easiest way to cut costs is to specify less expensive materials; use stock windows and doors rather than custom-made ones and standard plumbing fixtures rather than top-of-the-line hardware. Other ways to save:

1. Don't make changes after you have begun renovating. Think everything through at the start. Making changes on paper costs little; making changes once work has begun can be costly. This is the single most important thing you can do to keep costs under control.

2. Keep the plan simple. Avoid complicated heating and cooling systems, which are expensive not only to install but also to maintain.

3. Build in the off-season. In most parts of the country, construction is done between the months of April and October. Scheduling renovation for the winter may result in lower cost—and better workmanship, since the crew is not as rushed.

4. Insulate well. Insulation is not expensive; energy savings will pay back the investment many times over.

Financing a Renovation

Five factors determine the best financing strategy: the cost of the project, the amount of cash you have on hand, your equity in the house, the cost of borrowing, and the amount of money you feel comfortable borrowing.

GOVERNMENT LOANS: There are two types of loans that are available through the Federal Housing Administration.

1. FHA Title 1. This program offers two options: a personal loan or a new mortgage. Interest rates and the length of the loan vary according to the borrower's financial strength and the size of the loan; generally the rate is 12 percent for 5 to 15 years.

A personal loan is available for projects costing less than $5,000; because the loan is not secured by property, the interest is not deductible.

A new mortgage can secure an FHA loan of $5,000 to $17,500. The debt is a lien against the property, so the interest is tax-deductible. This loan is subordinate to all others, making it possible to qualify even if you have already borrowed against the house.

2. The FHA 203(k) program provides second mortgages for up to $124,875, minus the amount of the first mortgage and the cost of renovations. The down payment is 5 percent of the loan.

HOME IMPROVEMENT AND PERSONAL LOANS: These are useful if you have little money and little equity in the house, but the interest rates are higher than those for other types of loans because they are not secured by property. Interest charges are not deductible.

MORTGAGE REFINANCING: Refinancing can be attractive when interest rates fall. Many lenders will refinance existing mortgages for 75 percent of the current value of the house. If your accrued equity equals more than 25 percent of current value, remortgaging may be an excellent way both to lower interest charges and to spread the cost of renovations over the life of the mortgage, usually 15 or 20 years. Interest payments are deductible. You must close on the refinanced loan, however, which can cost as much as 5 percent of the loan.

HOME EQUITY LOAN: Your house serves as the security for a loan of 70 to 75 percent of its current value, minus the amount still owed on the first mortgage. The interest is slightly higher than the prevailing rate, but closing costs are usually low; some lenders charge nothing. Interest payments are deductible.

These loans take two forms:

1. A second mortgage is a lump sum loan made at a fixed rate, usually 2 percent above prime, for a specified period of time, typically 15 or 30 years.

2. A line of credit provides a specific sum of money against which you can draw, either by check or credit card. You pay interest on the money you withdraw. The initial interest rate is often low, around 6 percent, but can raise to 25 percent.

A Note About Asbestos

Asbestos was once favored by many contractors as the most effective insulation material. Used in construction as early as the turn of this century, it was most prevalent in the 30s, 40s, and 50s. In practically every house built between the early 1900s and 1955, asbestos had been installed around pipes, pipe joints, and boilers. Sometimes the house itself was sprayed with asbestos as a fire retardant.

However, in the last 50 years, the dangers of asbestos to human health have been recognized. By the mid-1970s, the Environmental Protection Agency revised its assessment of asbestos dangers and positively linked the barely visible fibers to lung disease and cancer. As a result, asbestos is no longer used in the construction industry.

Previously installed asbestos is not a danger if it is permanently encased, as in asbestos-cement siding, and left undisturbed. It does become a hazard when airborne. For this reason, asbestos insulation around pipes or ducts is the most dangerous of all forms since it becomes soft and friable with age and small particles can be released into the air.

If you are uncertain whether or not asbestos has been used around the piping and duct insulation or anywhere else in the house in which you are living or the house you intend to buy, a licensed asbestos-removal firm can test suspect locations for you. A test usually costs less than $100.

Other locations inside the house where asbestos might be present are:

CEILING TILES: About 10 percent of the ceiling tiles remaining in older houses contains asbestos. Until 1977, asbestos was used in all acoustical ceilings, but as long as the tiles remain intact, there is no danger.

FLOOR TILES: Over 70 percent of all residential-grade, resilient floor tile more than ten years old is vinyl asbestos. The mastic used as adhesive may also contain asbestos. Left as is, the tile virtually never triggers an emergency. During a renovation, it is safest to leave the tile alone and use it as a base for new flooring. If the tiles are removed, sanding the subfloor will undoubtedly release residual asbestos particles into the air.

WIRING: Old cloth-wrapped wiring may have a layer of asbestos beneath the cloth. Although the danger is not great, the electrician should take special care when removing and replacing the wire.

PLASTER: If plaster is between 20 and 90 years old, it may encase asbestos fibers and so it should not be sanded or roughed up. The same is true of joint compound and wallboard in which asbestos was used.

Asbestos should always be removed and discarded by a licensed and EPA-certified asbestos-removal firm. The cost of removal varies. In the Connecticut area, labor runs about $3 per square foot, and the disposal into a government-approved dump costs in the $1,000 range for half a dump-truck load.

In each of the cases outlined above, the asbestos-removal firm takes precautions to protect the homeowner and the interior of the house. First the workmen isolate the area containing the asbestos with temporary framing covered with sheets of plastic. Then they don disposable coveralls, hats, and boots. Wearing goggles and respirators, the crew uses a vacuum to produce a negative pressure in the isolated space; the vacuum gently draws out all the asbestos-laden material, including any airborne fibers, and collects them in a special container for disposal. After the job is completed, each worker enters a three-compartment temporary shelter supplied by the removal firm to discard the disposable clothing, shower, and dress in clean clothes.

Resources

The following sources supplied fabrics, wall coverings, carpets, and furnishings for the Adams house, many of which are available at retail or through decorators ("to the trade").

IN THE WEST PARLOR

The top wallpaper border: "Black Gold Greek Key" (#CB80). **The lower border:** "Olympiad" in black and green (#C30). Both to the trade at Clarence House. For showrooms (212) 752-2890. **Swag trimming:** to the trade at André Bon. For showrooms (212) 355-4012. **Marble garden figure:** Michael Trapp, Cornwall Bridge, CT, (203) 672-6098. **Hudson River School painting:** Eagle's Lair Antiques, Norwalk, CT, (203) 846-1159. **Wrought-iron and marble corner table, Federal side chairs, and mahogany screen:** Lisa Krieger, P.O. Box 221, Green Farms, CT, (203) 259-8571 **Mantel:** fabricated by Early New England Rooms, Inc., 37 McGuire Road, South Windsor, CT, (203) 282-0236

IN THE EAST PARLOR

Curtain and upholstery fabric: "Lafayette" (#7500), 54 inches wide, cotton; to the trade and retail at Pierre Deux, 870 Madison Ave., NY, NY. For other stores (800) 874-3773. **Carpet:** Chinese grass matting; to the trade at Stark Carpets, 979 Third Ave., NY, NY. For showrooms (212) 752-9000. **Sheraton sofa, Connecticut candlestand, and Newport drop-front desk:** Morgan MacWhinnie, 520 North Sea Road, Southampton, NY, (516) 283-3366.

IN THE OFFICE STUDY

Carpet: "Seagrass Natural" (#36); to the trade at Fraser Gold Carpet Co., NY, NY, (212) 751-3455. **Fabric on chair seat:** "Jungle," 48½ inches wide, linen and cotton; to the trade and retail at Bennison Fabrics, Ltd., 76 Greene Street, NY, NY, (212) 941-1212. **Fabric on ottoman:** "Monochrome Beige Roses," on beige linen and cotton, at Bennison. **Scroll-arm button-back armchair and ottoman:** retail and to the trade at George Smith Sofas and Chairs, 73 Spring Street, NY, NY, (212) 226-4747.

IN THE LIBRARY

Carpet: Chinese needlepoint; to the trade at Stark Carpets, 979 Third Ave., NY, NY. For showrooms (212) 752-9000. **Victorian slipper chair:** to the trade at Hines & Co. For showrooms (212) 685-8590. **Leopard print on the slipper chair:** "Bonaparte" (#160081F), viscose and cotton; to the trade at Quadrille Fabrics & Wallpapers. For showrooms (212) 753-2995. **Tapestry pillow:** "Ile de France" (#32621-2842), 51 inches wide, in rubus and vert; to the trade at Clarence House. For showrooms (212) 752-2890. **Sofa and sofa fabric:** to the trade at Brunschwig & Fils. For showrooms (212) 838-7878. **Club chair silk damask:** to the trade at Cowtan & Tout. For showrooms (212) 753-4488.

IN THE SUNROOM

Table skirt fabric: "Chestnut Leaves" (#105), 52 inches wide, in color 1; to the trade at Rose Cumming. Showrooms, (212) 758-0844. **Chair Fabric:** "Douglas" (#32563-4), 59 inches wide, cotton, in vert; to the trade at Clarence House. For showrooms (212) 752-2890.

IN THE UPSTAIRS HALL BATHROOM

Curtain fabric: "Meryle," 48 inches wide, linen, cotton, and nylon; to the trade at Payne. For showrooms (212) 725-0330. **Needlepoint rug:** Sonia Chapell, 1047 Madison Ave., NY, NY, (212) 744-7872. **Table:** The Stock Market, Southport, CT, (203) 259-1189. **Antique boxes and accessories:** Sallea Antiques, New Canaan, CT, (203) 972-1050

IN THE HALL BEDROOM

Dust ruffle and curtain fabric: "Hampton," to the trade at Cowtan & Tout. For showrooms (212) 753-4488. **Furniture and accessories:** Rosemary Casey Interiors, Inc., 17 Comstock Court, Ridgefield, CT, (203) 432-5195.

Bibliography

Benjamin, Asher, *American Builder's Companion*, Dover Publications, 1969.

Berg, Donald J., ed., *How to Build in the Country,* Ten Speed Press, 1986.

Chaney, Dale, and Miller, Jeff, *House Inspection: A Buyer's Guide*, Contemporary Books, 1986.

Chrisman, Katherine, *Dreaming in the Dust: Restoring an Old House*, Houghton Mifflin, 1986.

Early American Society, The, eds., *The Early Homes of New England*, Arno Press, 1977.

Evers, Christopher, *The Old House Doctor*, The Overlook Press, 1986.

Fletcher, Banister, *History of Architecture*, Charles Scribner & Sons, 1961.

Greene, Fayal, *Anatomy of a House: A Picture Dictionary of Architectural & Design Elements*, Doubleday, 1991.

Handlin, David, *American Architecture: A Critical History*, Thames and Hudson, 1985.

Harrison, Henry S., and Leonard, Margery B., *Home Buying: The Complete Illustrated Guide,* National Association of Realtors, 1980.

Herdmann, Carl, *Be Your Own House Contractor: How to Save 25% Without Lifting a Hammer*, Garden Way, 1981.

Howard, Hugh, *How Old Is This House: A Skeleton Key to Dating & Identifying Three Centuries of American Houses*, The Noonday Press/Farrar, Straus & Giroux, 1989.

Howells, John Mead, *Lost Examples of Colonial Architecture,* Dover Publications, 1963.

Innes, Jocasta, *Exterior Details*, Simon and Schuster, 1990.

Kelly, J. Frederick, A.I.A., *Early Domestic Architecture*, Dover Publications, 1963.

Kidder, Tracy, *House*, Houghton Mifflin, 1985.

Kirk, John T., *Impecunious House Restorer*, Alfred A. Knopf, 1984.

Kitchen, Judith L., *Caring for Your Old House,* Preservation Press, 1991.

Krotz, Joanna L., *Renovation Style*, Villard Books, 1986.

Langdon, Philip, *American Houses*, Stewart, Tabori and Chang, 1987.

Levine, Mark; Pollan, Stephen; and Pollan, Michael, *The Field Guide to Home Buying in America: A Home Buyer's Companion from House Hunting to Moving Day*, Fireside/Simon and Schuster, 1988.

Litchefield, Michael, *Renovation: A Complete Guide*, Prentice-Hall, 1991.

McAlester, Virginia and Lee, *A Field Guide to American Houses*, Alfred A. Knopf, 1984.

Orme, Alan D., *Reviving Old Houses*, Storey Communications, 1989.

Owen, David, *The Walls Around Us,* Villard Books, 1991.

Ramsey, Charles G., and Sleeper, Harold R., *Architectural Graphic Standards*, John Wiley, 1988.

Roskind, Robert, *Building Your Own House*, Ten Speed Publishers, 1984.

Rybczynski, Witold, *Home: A Short History of an Idea*, Viking Penguin, 1986.

Rybczynski, Witold, *The Most Beautiful House in the World*, Penguin Books, 1989.

Scutella, Richard, and Heberle, Dave, *How to Plan, Contract and Build Your Own House*, Ten Speed Publishers, 1991.

Sherwood, Gerald E., *How to Select and Renovate an Older House*, Dover Publications, 1976.

Stageberg, James, and Toth, Susan Allen, *A House of One's Own: An Architect's Guide to Designing the House of Your Dreams,* Clarkson Potter, 1991.

Stanforth, Deirdre, with photographs by Louis Reems, *Restored America*, Praeger Publishers, 1975.

Vila, Bob, *Bob Vila's Guide to Buying Your Dream House*, Little, Brown & Co., 1990.

Vila, Bob, with Davison, Jane, *This Old House: Restoring, Rehabilitating and Renovating*, Little, Brown & Co., 1980.

Index

air-conditioning, 44, 87, 100,
105, 106
anteroom, 195, 197
appliances, kitchen, 35, 89, 143,
145, 146, 147–48, 150–51,
153, 155
architects:
fees of, 33
working with, 32–39, 40
architectural historians, 32, 33,
49
architecture:
Federal, 15, 18, 77, 178, 226
retaining integrity of, 18, 32,
49, 87, 145
artists, 174, 195, 218–19; see also
interior designers; painters
asbestos, 283
attics, 19, 20, 73, 88, 108, 140,
141, 219

baseboards, marbleizing of, 206
basements, 19, 28, 50, 51, 60,
65, 103, 155
bathrooms, 18, 87, 123, 125,
211, 234
renovation of, 50, 51, 88, 89,
140, 141, 228–29
beams, see post-and-beam
construction
bedrooms, 22, 50, 51, 88, 89,
123, 140, 141, 222, 231–32
blueboard, 87, 88, 90, 109,
117–18, 122
borders:
painting of, 214
planting of, 256–57
bricks:
in foundations, 58
paths of, 276–77
for siding, 81
for terraces, 260–61

building codes, 44, 58, 73, 78,
87, 100–101, 102–3, 107,
108–9, 123, 228
building permits, 33, 42, 44,
264, 266

cabinetmakers, 211
cabinets, kitchen, 157–63
carpenters, 42, 60, 78, 87, 88,
93, 97, 118, 140, 141
ceilings, 18, 35, 50–51, 88, 90,
97, 117–18, 170, 211
cement, 65, 88, 89, 260
chimneys, 18, 27, 31, 50, 51, 53,
66–69, 88, 105, 140, 145
clapboard, 53, 74, 78–81, 141
cleanup, 42, 50, 82, 141, 247
of hazardous materials, 114
kitchen space for, 146, 153
clothing, protective, 65, 74, 90,
108, 114, 229, 256, 257, 271
color palette, 77, 140, 150, 153,
162, 163, 171, 182, 184, 195,
200, 203, 211, 219, 222, 226,
231
contractors:
fees for, 42, 171, 247
general, 32, 40, 42
see also journal pages; specific
contractors
contracts, 171
house inspection prior to, 16,
18–20, 22, 27–28
items covered by, 40, 42, 247
copper leaf, 220
countertops, kitchen, 143, 146,
147, 155, 157

damage, water, 18, 27, 50, 131;
see also infestation
dampers, 68
decoration, of interiors,
169–241

decorators, see interior designers
demolition, 90–93, 145, 146
diagrams, see plans and diagrams
digging, see excavation
dining rooms, 140, 141, 186–92,
195
documentation:
of insurance coverage, 42
permits, see permits
photographs as, 25, 51, 89,
140
doors, 35, 74, 87, 95, 141, 170,
173, 186, 195, 203
framing of, 51, 97
installation of, 140
location of, 35, 50
moisture around, 80
renovation of, 51, 88, 89, 134
down spouts and gutters, 25, 27,
53, 73
drainage, drains, 27, 89, 259,
260
driveways, 25, 50, 51, 245, 246,
268
drywall, 117–18
Dumpsters, 42, 50, 82

electrical systems:
circuits in, 98, 100–101
codes for, 100–101
inspections of, 19, 27, 28, 98
outlets for, 35, 98–100, 101,
123
wiring of, 50, 87, 98–101, 109,
140, 141, 239
electricians, 33, 50, 51, 88, 98,
109, 118, 140, 141
evergreens, 252, 254–55,
256–57
excavation, 42, 50, 54, 56–57,
58, 65, 82, 103, 259–60

decorators, see interior designers
exteriors:
inspection of, 25–31
restoration of, 49–82
exterminators, 89, 93, 140

faux finishes, see trompe l'oeil
Federal-style architecture, 15,
18, 77, 178, 226
fees:
of architects, 33
of contractors, 42, 171, 247
of decorators, 42
for permits, 44
fences:
building of, 264–68
lumber for, 266
neighbors and, 266
types of, 268
fill, 260
fireplaces, 27, 50, 66, 68, 89,
106, 141, 143, 145–46, 184,
186, 198, 200, 203, 205, 232
fire safety codes, 44, 52, 78, 101,
134, 261
fixtures:
bathroom, 87, 88, 211, 226,
228–29, 237
lighting, 22, 239
flagstones, 260
flashing, 27, 53, 58, 69, 73, 80,
140
floor plans, 35, 36–39, 149
floors, 20, 87, 88, 93
coverings for, 22, 89, 173,
184, 186, 195, 197, 198,
205–6, 211, 216, 222, 226,
228, 234
excavation for, 65
finishes of, 126–28, 164–65,
200, 216, 231
repairs to, 18, 50, 51, 140, 141
trompe l'oeil painting on, 195,
197, 205–6

WORK SHEET FOR THE ADAMS HOUSE

BASEMENT: Treat w/ woodlife. GUTTERS: Bert Dumas, 286-4033, estimate scheduled for 10/21–copper gutters to be used, chimneys reflashed. PAINTING: Need estimates for interior and exterior work; exterior includes careful power sanding–interior should include repair of old plaster walls. Work excludes prep for windows, which is to be done by person working on the window restoration. (1) Langston Construction Co., 384-1796, est. 10/16 10:30. (2) CFD, 374-5051. DRIVEWAY: Rip out old blacktop and replace with loose stones. MASONRY: Need estimate for: back patio and foundation repair in kitchen area, new foundation for sun porch, repair of chimneys. V. Ianonni, 838-0798. D&J Masonry, 261-6002. ELECTRICITY: Bring in electric and phone lines underground–upgrade service to 200-amp–rewire entire house. Conn. electric–Steve Davidson. Ray Brown, est. sched. for 10/21–came, needs plan. HEATING: Install new heating system in entire house. Kaufman Fuel Arnie's, 368-3022, est. sched. for 10/16, 9:30. Harry Hulse, 268-8282, will come when we have plans. SEWER: Hook up house to town sewer lines. V. Perkowski–schedule to be done week of 10/19. NEW OIL TANK: Remove old tank and put in Dumpster 10/15–per Gault 10/12. New 550 tank $1026.53 includes hookup. Will pump out old oil–call 10/16 & have done. Bill came on